THE BENEVOLENCE
OF MANNERS

THE BENEVOLENCE OF MANNERS

OF

MANNERS

Recapturing the Lost Art of

Gracious Victorian Living

(*previously published as Simple Social Graces*)

L I N D A S. L I C H T E R

ReganBooks
An Imprint of HarperPerennial
A Division of HarperCollinsPublishers

A hardcover edition of this book was published in 1998 by ReganBooks, an imprint of HarperCollins Publishers under the title *Simple Social Graces*.

THE BENEVOLENCE OF MANNERS. Copyright © 1998 by Linda Lichter. All rights reserved. Printed in the United States of America. No part of this book may be used or reproduced in any manner whatsoever without written permission except in the case of brief quotations embodied in critical articles and reviews. For information address HarperCollins Publishers, Inc., 10 East 53rd Street, New York, NY 10022.

HarperCollins books may be purchased for educational, business, or sales promotional use. For information please write: Special Markets Department, HarperCollins Publishers, Inc., 10 East 53rd Street, New York, NY 10022.

First ReganBooks/Harper Perennial edition published 1999.

Designed by Laura Lindgren

The Library of Congress has catalogued the hardcover edition as follows:

Lichter, Linda S.
    Simple social graces : recapturing the joys of Victorian life / Linda Lichter.
    — 1st ed.
      p. cm.
    Includes bibliographical references (p. 319) and index.
    ISBN 0-06-039170-7
    1. Etiquette—United States—History—19th century. 2. Etiquette—United States—History—20th century. 3. United States—Social life and customs. 4. United States—Civilization. I. Title.
    BJ1852.L52   1997
    303.3'72'097309034—dc21   97-33162

ISBN 0-06-098745-6 (pbk.)

99 00 01 02 03 ❖/RRD 10 9 8 7 6 5 4 3 2 1

CONTENTS

ILLUSTRATIONS

INTRODUCTION

America is hurting. We are rich in goods but poor in spirit. Public life is splintered, crude, and violent. Too many private lives are a shambles of broken relationships, broken homes, and stressed-out, time-squeezed families. We search frantically for quick fixes to fill a deep internal void that we struggle to describe. The answer lies neither in sixties-style government programs nor fifties nostalgia, and certainly not in accumulating more high-tech toys. To continue buying the constantly recycled versions of these solutions is to invest in damaged goods. Our best hope for finding a more rewarding way of life as individuals and as a country is to reclaim our long lost Victorian sensibilities and what Edith Wharton called "the art of civilized living."

We devour the remnants of Victoriana in magazines and period movies because they evoke far more than wistful images of safe, civilized streets, good manners, and stable families. We also hunger for an era when people lived with dignity, instead of just dying with it. We crave the beauty, grace, charm, and passionate romance of the past. What gave this era its mystical aura, that loveliness of life so sorely lacking now? It wasn't simply a question of the proper way to use a fish fork. Consult Emily Post for that; we have bigger fish to fry. Hillary Clinton hinted at the answer in a 1993 *New York Times* interview. After reading the correspondence of ordinary people from the nineteenth century, she observed:

> The whole cycle of life and its meaning is tied into their daily life. And you know, by the nature of how we spend our time today, we have walled ourselves off from that. I mean, we get up in the morning and we go to work and our children don't know what our work is, because they don't see us plowing a field or making a quilt. We go off and push papers and then come home and try to explain it. Our relatives age and die often in places far away from our

homes. We've compartmentalized so much of our lives that trying to find even the time to think about how all of it fits together has become harder and harder.

Harder and harder, yes, but not impossible. Life once had the cohesion and intricate detail of a tapestry. Understanding this is essential if we are to reweave all the broken links that will make us whole again. In the words of William Blake, we can learn "to see the world in a grain of sand / And a heaven in a wild flower / Hold infinity in the palm of your hand / And eternity in an hour."

This different way of seeing, this Victorian second sight, will take us through the intimate nooks and crannies of historic rituals, objects, and buildings that represented more than mere materials or the quaint customs we ridicule—or envy. These objects and rituals expressed a broad spiritual environment that ennobled all of life and its comforting kinship to the afterlife. In this book, you'll rediscover grand ideals, but you'll also learn how the Victorians controlled coarseness, rudeness, crime, and hateful speech with a shared code of conscience and daily conduct—a contrast to our endless nightmare of litigation and legislation.

Our century has slammed this code as elitist and divisive. Wrong on both counts. I will show why common courtesy, like a common currency, was vital to establishing a strong sense of community and preventing chaos in the ethnically diverse Victorian world. Ironically, our politically correct prescription not only fragments the nation, it is elitist—the alleged Victorian sin. PC practices and politics are the exclusive province of certain victimized groups, whereas the commonness of courtesy makes it all-inclusive. Civility was once considered everyone's civil right.

Imagine a time when courtesy was the rule, not the exception, and men were manly without being macho. A word of warning to modern women accustomed to exploitation and abuse: You may be shocked to learn that masculinity used to be defined by how well, not how badly, men treated the opposite sex in and out of bed. This book will show women the immense social, political, and personal power they have lost, and how they might reclaim it. The book also challenges the historical misconceptions that have steered us wrong, right into misery. Just one example: The Victorians weren't high-buttoned prudes but supreme sensualists who pursued the art of great love, not just a great lay. True passion was their religion. In contrast to our fast-food sex, which fills the body—maybe—but not the soul, Victorian sex was subtle yet consuming, a banquet to be savored course by course. No one left the table hungry when men and women made love instead of war. We've been looking for love in all the wrong places. This book will help to chart a new direction.

The same road map will guide us to the Victorian home, whose affordable beauty, bounty, and binding ties knocks the stuffing out of all the Cleaver family values. Learn from the past how to create a home where the threads of family are woven together in a tapestry that doesn't unravel.

Bill Clinton won reelection in 1996 by promising to build a bridge to the next century. But we will surely repeat and magnify the tragedies of this one unless we build a bridge to the last. We won't wear hoop skirts again or abandon motor-powered transportation. Above all, we won't revert to denying women and minorities full legal and economic rights. As the architectural and landscape designer Calvert Vaux wrote in 1864, "The past should always be looked on as a servant, not a master."

The bridge I picture is a two-way road where the best of the present and the past will meet. We have already begun to build these roads with popular concepts like cracking down on "trivial" quality-of-life crimes in order to prevent more serious crimes. Slowly but surely, Victorian common sense is becoming our wisdom.

You won't find my bridge on the political maps of prominent liberals or conservatives. As a sociologist, I have grown tired of hearing the right and left battle over the great social issues of our day, oblivious to the fact that many of these very problems were addressed, and successfully so, by the Victorians. Liberals are allergic to history, unless it belongs to specific victimized groups. Conservatives are no better. The columnist Jonathan Yardley observed, "Conservatism as it now exists in these United States is no longer a force for the preservation of the best in the past's legacy but a force for the diminution and elimination of barriers erected by government against the uncontrolled exercise of individual and institutional avarice."[1]

Conservatives just won't leave the Beaver Cleaver ideal behind because their stunted view of the good life began in Levittown, died in Woodstock, and survives only in TV reruns, where history spans less than a half century. Their solutions to our vast social problems and our aching need for personal fulfillment are as modern and ineffective as those prescribed by liberals. Both are chips off the old block of an anti-Victorian century that shaped them and the mess we're in.

So why should we turn our battered faith and our rhetoric-weary ears to the Victorians' distinctive message? Why journey to a past that, for all its glories, had manure in the streets, allowed robber barons to plunder, and discriminated against women and minorities? Why risk traveling yet another promised route to salvation when so many have led us astray? Because for all our travels, this is a road we moderns have not yet taken. Because our own proliferating experts, who always know so much about so little, have failed us. Because Victorian sensibilities worked, and nothing else has worked as well since then. Because Victorian notions of how to live life achieved far more than crime control, civility, and stable families: They perfumed daily experience, and in turn nourished the soul with beauty, grace, and the bounty of layered meanings that found grandeur in fine details while living by grand designs. This holistic vision, this different way of seeing, is our legacy, but we have been robbed of it. We must learn to reassemble all the pieces of this quilt—morals, manners, crime, clothes, aesthetics—that have unraveled since the 1920s. To the Victorians the minutiae of life were never minute.

So let us return to the premodern era and see what treasures we so casually and carelessly tossed out at the beginning of the modern era. Americans pride themselves on being open to new ideas. It is time we tried some old ones.

PART I

HOW FAR WE HAVEN'T COME

I

The Age of Impudence

Virginia Woolf once said that human character changed in 1910. If so, it took another decade and a cataclysmic war before the radical ideas and lifestyles of Bloomsbury and Greenwich Village affected ordinary people. Critics who confuse history with memory may blame our current epidemic of self-indulgence and incivility on a Reaganesque "decade of greed" or the "me decade" or the Woodstock generation. In fact, its origins lie in the seemingly innocent times of flappers, jalopies, and raccoon coats.

In the 1920s "Victorian" became a dirty word, as the postwar generation set about dismantling their parents' ideals like children attacking a tower of building blocks. As Frederick Lewis Allen recalled in *Only Yesterday*, his 1931 memoir of the 1920s, "It was better to be modern—everybody wanted to be modern—and sophisticated, and smart, to smash the conventions, and to be devastatingly frank. And with a cocktail glass in one's hand, it was easy at least to be frank." In our own day, "Victorian" has become a synonym for sexual repression (but read on!). To those smart young things downing gin fizzes in smoky speakeasies, "Victorian" was still an entire worldview.

"A CULTURE OF CHARACTER"

What was the worldview that they rebelled against so insistently, and why should we bother to remember it (much less recover it) today? In contrast to the chaotic muddle we now call values, Victorian values were so consistent, and so consistently taught, that they formed what historian Warren I. Susman called a whole "culture of character." This culture was so powerful and pervasive that it did not need to be legislated or litigated; it was internalized.

Clarence Day, who immortalized the age in his 1935 memoir *Life with Father*, said the rules his parents taught him weren't written down in any single book. "It was a code, a tradition. It was to be upright and fearless and honorable . . . and in general always do the right thing in every department of life. . . . In my boyhood, I never had a doubt that the beliefs they taught me were true. The difficulty was to live up to them." Yet Day was not alone or helpless in his struggle. In his youth during the 1880s, he recalled, people talked without irony about "true nobility and noble deeds. The atmosphere that my generation grew up with was thick with nobility."

In our Beavis-and-Butthead culture, it takes a leap of faith to realize that nobility of character was once a widely accepted ideal for young people. When Bill Clinton recently proclaimed a "Character Counts Week," it was a pathetic reminder of how little character does count these days. For this lost nurturing atmosphere cannot be recaptured by presidential declarations, at a time when our role models are celebrated deviants like basketball star Dennis Rodman, who titled his bestselling memoir *Bad As I Wanna Be*. Before we can even attempt to recreate the Victorians' environment of virtue, we need to remember what it was all about.

SELF-RESTRAINT AND SACRIFICE

What were the nuts and bolts of the remarkable code that sustained the lawfulness and civility we associate with the Victorian era? It had a broad and inclusive religious foundation that was a far cry from Bible-thumping moralism. It stressed hard work, frugality, sobriety, honesty, civic responsibility, sexual decency, good deeds, self-restraint, and self-sacrifice.

To our own generation, equating love with sacrifice and self-restraint is difficult to understand, much less accept. Isn't love a vehicle of individual happiness? If you randomly stopped people on the street and asked them to assess their lives, most would ask themselves, "Am I happy?" But a Victorian would ask himself, "Am I a good person?" In the seamless web of Victorian connections, self-fulfillment required social virtue. Conversely, the fate of the community depended on a view of happiness that transcended a personal wish list of experiences and acquisitions. As Sara Josepha Hale, the influential female editor of *Godey's Lady's Book,* America's leading magazine for women, put it in her 1868 book *Manners; or Happy Homes and Good Society All the Year Round,* "In 'the pursuit of happiness,' the first right step is to seek that which is good to do, not merely for one's self, but for others: ultimately we reach the public good."

The hallmark of Victorian character—self-restraint—was more than a means to test your mettle. It was a key deterrent to crime. The rise of modern industry and big cities, and a consequent weakening of family ties, boosted crime in the first decades of the nineteenth century. Yet in the second half of the century, crime declined rapidly, as a result of what social scientists James Q. Wilson and Richard J. Herrnstein, writing in *Crime and Human Nature,* call "intense efforts to inculcate an ethic of self-control." In contrast, they note that crime rates "rose faster in the twentieth century than can be explained by higher birth rates, owing to a shift from that ethic to one emphasizing self-expression."

More than a hundred years before we needed Ph.D.s to legitimize this insight, Henry James, Sr., warned in a letter printed by the *New York Tribune* that if man is "free not only in respect to outward compulsion, but free also in respect to inward constraint . . . he is essentially devoid of obligation either to his fellow man or to himself; in a word, his own sole law."[1] "His own sole law"—is there a better definition of criminality?

AIMING FOR PERFECTION

This painful lesson was central to Victorian aspirations for the human spirit and social prosperity. Whereas we have had to pay a heavy price for indulging our "healthy" natural instincts, most Victorians believed with Elizabeth Blackwell that our "natural" state of instinctive desires "is really a state of rudimentary life, which does not display the real nature of man, but only its imperfect condition." As history's most ardent moral self-improvers, the Victorians thought humanity could and should strive toward perfection. They would have been puzzled by the current quest for self-esteem; they sought to create a self that would be worthy of esteem.

In place of this vision of striving upward, we began "defining deviancy down," as Senator Daniel Patrick Moynihan put it.[2] By lowering our social sights, we made it possible to normalize unprecedented levels of antisocial behavior, ranging from petty boorishness to vicious violence. In so doing we lost a philosophy that made crime and incivility the universally condemned exception, not the rule. Even worse, we lost the Victorian "cosmic sense" that underlay this philosophy—the optimistic faith in grand designs and eternal truths that linked every aspect of our lives to something larger than life.

Current-day conservatives may think the "grand plan" drowned in the mud at Woodstock. Actually, it met its end in the 1920s, when a lot more than hair was bobbed. Dumbed-down versions of the works of thinkers like Freud, Nietzsche, and Einstein began to popularize the since then widespread notion that values are relative and rules of morality are made to be broken. Here was the tragic beginning of the moral mobocracy that left everyone free to make and break their own rules. These days, according to a recent poll, two out of three Americans reject the notion of irrefutable moral truths.

The Victorians always knew what we have only recently discovered: When the tides of history wash away our old sand castles of ethics, we simply build new ones to suit our needs. The "bridge generation" of the Roaring Twenties whose members experienced the transition to our brave new world learned this lesson too late. As one bewildered contemporary, quoted by the historian Arthur M. Schlesinger in *Learning How to Behave,* mused in 1926, "It is a new age, new thinking, new ideals. Does it mean no ideals?" The answer was a cocksure, scorched-earth yes!

Even Edith Wharton, famed for deftly skewering the foibles of the old social order, came to regret the loss of its rules and rituals. In her memoir *A Backward Glance* (1933), she lamented how the Great War had swept away this world and rendered its codes unintelligible:

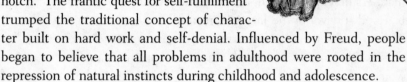

"The unalterable rules of conduct became
. . . as quaintly arbitrary as the domestic rites
of the Pharaohs."

In the hoochy-koochy age, morale
replaced morality. One of the leading psychologists of the day, G. Stanley Hall, called
it a time when "animal spirits" were at "top
notch." The frantic quest for self-fulfillment
trumped the traditional concept of charac-
ter built on hard work and self-denial. Influenced by Freud, people
began to believe that all problems in adulthood were rooted in the
repression of natural instincts during childhood and adolescence.

THE LOSS OF GRACE

But breaking the bonds of restraint went far beyond a new fascination
with fulfillment. Advice and child-rearing manuals printed during this
era shifted their emphasis from developing character to improving
one's personality. Words like "decency," "truth," "unselfishness," "justice"—the vocabulary of Clarence Day's "atmosphere of nobility"—
were ridiculed. The new lingo shifted the focus from social virtues to
surface gloss. People were told by advertisers, the movie industry, and
cosmetic manufacturers to become fascinating, magnetic, stunning,
and attractive. In sum, the world became one's mirror.

The new ethic of self-expression rode a wave of generational
rebellion that has yet to crest. In the 1920s the etiquette authority
Emily Post declared that each generation was entitled to make its
own rules. Many bashers of Victorian mores denounced their elders'
"stilted formalities" and "worn-out hypocrises." Similar sentiments are
still preached by current historians. Milton Rugoff, in his 1971 book,
Prudery and Passion, portrayed the Victorians' notion of character as
"intolerant and unrealistic" as well as insufferably pretentious,
because "it truly overreached itself in the virtues and ideals it set up."
John F. and Robin M. Haller, in their book *The Physician and Sexuality in Victorian America,* called the Victorians "burdened, as no generation before them, with the weight of their own image. . . . They
struggled to gain the highest planes of achievement . . . for their highest duty lay not to themselves, but to future generations." Translation:

How dare they aspire to goals that nowadays might waylay modern pilgrims on their pursuit of self-fulfillment?

Is it any wonder that the mentality of the 1920s, in the words of the historian Paula Fass, "sits solidly at the base of our culture?" Many of us would feel right at home in an era when, as Frederick Lewis Allen claimed in *Only Yesterday*, even the "best classes displayed their worst, and trashing was the order of the day." When morals collapsed, manners quickly followed, as the Victorians knew they would. Allen, a battered survivor of the Jazz Age, recalled that guests couldn't be bothered to speak to them on arrival or departure; that "gatecrashers" at dances became an accepted practice; that thousands of men and women made a point of not getting to dinner within half an hour of the appointed time lest they seem insufficiently blasé.

Sound familiar? Similar complaints about the guests from hell are routinely lodged these days in Miss Manners's and Ann Landers's columns. But we are too far removed from the golden age of civility to notice any but the most egregious offenses. Writing about the twenties in his 1950 book *New Cosmopolis*, James Hunecker lamented not only the spread of alcohol, gambling, sexual frankness, and general bad manners but also gum chewing and sloppy appearance. To the Victorian mind even such venial sins were important, because they "debase the currency of life."

This might seem like ridiculous nitpicking; we all know how fussy those Victorians could be. Yet it highlights a loss more poignant than the etiquette or morals that went bankrupt along with social currency. Before her death in 1937, Edith Wharton pined for the beauty of what she called the the age of innocence, also the title of one of her most famous novels. According to her memoir, she found the new age to be "a world in which so many sources of peace and joy are already dried up that the few remaining have a more piercing sweetness." Gone was that intangible, almost mystical, loveliness of life that still holds the power to enthrall us when we glimpse it in old artworks and photographs or recreated on a movie screen.

HEDONISM, CONSUMERISM, AND GREED

Wealth of a different kind—our kind—was supposed to adorn the world when all the Victorian gilding was stripped away. The twenties spawned the age of mass-produced goods and the megamall, the all-you-can-eat mentality that measured happiness and achievement in dollars, not good deeds. The spread of movies, radios, autos, home appliances, and seductive installment plans turned savers into spenders and created the modern consumer.

Meanwhile, newly aggressive advertising tactics urged people to gratify their whims by emptying their wallets. They had yet to be told to shop till they dropped, but they would surely have embraced that slogan, along with the current television ad for a discount mall that promises, "You can buy happiness; just don't pay retail for it." The end result, concluded the sociologists Robert S. and Helen M. Lynd in their classic 1929 study *Middletown*, "was that people seemed to be running for dear life in the business of making the money . . . to keep pace with the even more rapid growth of their subjective wants."

The results were obvious even if the implications were not. In their study, the Lynds compared everyday life in the 1890s and 1920s in a typical midwestern city—they called it Middletown. They found that increased consumerism and commercialized leisure had brought a decline in manners, morals, parental control, and community participation. These early social scientists were more concerned with explaining the present than predicting the future. But they were peering through the crack of a doorway that their grandchildren would fling wide open.

Even as the nineteenth century produced robber barons, corrupt industrial monopolies, and unprecedented prosperity, the Victorian ideal of character made it possible to protect the soul from becoming a cold cash machine. But the buying binge of the twenties had no place for the Victorian adage that reckless spending was a form of false pride. The Victorians saw this as a "deadly" sin long before the crash of '29. Believing, as the suffragist Mary Livermore wrote in her autobiography, that "the highest civilization is not material only, but mental, moral, and spiritual," they rightly feared that upsetting this delicate balance meant the triumph of personal greed. In the end, such a triumph would, in the words of Elizabeth Blackwell in 1852, "reduce every phenomenon to the limits of the senses." The mushrooming choice of market goods could never transcend those limits. Today the array of goods has become more dizzying, but no more fulfilling.

The spiritual vacuum created by such hedonism undermined both civility and the moral foundation that sustained it. When Katherine Lee Bates wrote "America the Beautiful" in 1893, she was inspired by the spacious skies and fruited plains that she viewed from Pikes Peak in a moment of epiphany. But her lyrics also expressed an inner vision of her country's spiritual wealth: "America! America!/ May God thy gold refine/ Till all success be nobleness/ And ev'ry gain divine." These sentiments resounded with her listeners three decades before Calvin Coolidge proclaimed the business of America to be business.

When was the last time you heard anyone sing this verse? Even modern conservatives who rail about "traditional values" have been strangely silent on the immorality of greed, of which the Victorians were quite aware. We have grown to expect campaign speeches that promise rising standards of living, with no mention of frugality or the demoralizing toll of rising debt. To the heirs of Reagan, self-restraint applies to crime and extramarital sex, but not to personal spending. But to the Victorians, who religiously connected all the dots to see the big picture, breaking one bound meant breaking all others.

The forces unleashed in the 1920s are in full gallop today. By constantly pushing the envelope of civility, advertising's apostles of narcissism have driven us over the edge. The calculated outrages of Calvin Klein and his ilk are only the most visible symptoms of Madison Avenue's promiscuous willingness to turn the impulses of teenage rebellion and childish self-indulgence to the ends of retail profit. We should wear Nikes because "we're all hedonists and we want to feel good. That's what makes us human." A Nintendo TV spot best sums up this tawdry mixture of infantile narcissism and adolescent nihilism: A boy spits at the camera as an announcer exhorts young video-game customers to "hock a loogie at life."

At the Container Store, I once received a shopping bag with the written instruction CONTAIN YOURSELF. Even as it made me smile, this gentle pun reminded me how farcical Victorian virtues appear to the modern sensibility. No one will ever make a perfume ad defining love as self-sacrifice. In its ceaseless efforts to add value to products by associating them with primitive desires and juvenile fantasies, corporate America devalues all that was once precious in life. Nobility of character and the aristocracy of virtue are no match for the democracy of consumption and the equality of desire.

To the Victorians, the celebration of limitless desire was not just wrong, it was literally childish. Without self-control—the hallmark of

Strollers on the Coney Island boardwalk on a summer day in 1897 show a sensibility about public dress and decorum that is in stark contrast to the modern era.

mature adulthood—they believed that morality, civility, and community would crumble. You can hear it in another rarely sung verse of Katherine Lee Bates's anthem: "America! America!/God mend thine ev'ry flaw,/Confirm thy soul in self control/Thy liberty in law." By turning this notion on its head, the Jazz Age laid the groundwork for the mental diapers that still bind us today. "Self," wrote the Victorian poet Henry Van Dyke in *The Prison and the Angel*, "is the only prison that can ever bind the soul." If we are ever to reclaim our souls, we must first recognize how far we have fallen.

2

Buy Now, Pay Later

Shared ideals of character and civility formed the bedrock of Victorian community. In our own day, these standards of personal development and social behavior have been almost totally inverted. Society's moral arbiters, the pop psychologists, exhort us to satisfy childish impulses rather than transcend them. In trifles and essentials, we seek the right to indulge our desires and to be indulged by others when they backfire. Meanwhile, we are tenuously bound together by our shared dysfunctions, addictions, and A-to-Z support groups. What the Victorians called virtue—doing for others—has been replaced by the virtue of victimhood, or what's been done to us. And we flaunt it like a badge of honor, while the word "honor" is now as dated as the notion of character it defines.

I'M DYSFUNCTIONAL, YOU'RE DYSFUNCTIONAL

We support an army of lecturers and authors, who are always on the lookout for new dysfunctions to cure. Now that nearly half the population either attend support sessions themselves or have friends or family members who do so, a 1995 *New York Times Magazine* article reported that Hallmark has introduced a lucrative line of "recovery cards" offering encouragement for sticking to a diet or a course of therapy.[1] Company officials say that the line is selling "far beyond expectations." The circle of support keeps stretching, but as in the game of "ring around the rosy," all we can do is tread the same narrow turf until we all fall down.

The TV talk show has become a national confessional of addictions and dysfunctions, where we can find forgiveness before the closing credits. Everyone is blamed but "poor little me." We have become a culture of victims.

PAINLESS LIVING

The modern game of shifting blame was once a favorite of liberals, but all sides have learned to play. For example, in her well-reviewed 1994 memoir *Motherhood Deferred*, the journalist Ann Taylor Fleming faulted feminism for her decision to postpone childbearing beyond her fertile years. Both the careerist feminism Fleming criticized and her high-tech, high-priced procreative efforts stressed the primacy of self-gratification. She needed to bear a child to feel personally fulfilled. Despite the marvels of science and Fleming's professional success, however, she learned too late that in the glittering bazaar of lifestyle choices, nothing is free.

Even though fulfillment so often proves elusive, the prospect of a painless fix is firmly embedded in the modern psyche. Our boundless sense of entitlement is evident in national opinion polls showing that we want to reduce our bloated "nanny" government, but not if it requires trimming the specific programs that benefit us personally. (Let him who is without sin cast the first stone at welfare mothers.)

We expect all our wounds to be tended, even those we consciously inflict on ourselves. Despite well-publicized warnings about soaring rates of skin cancer, we keep bronzing in tanning salons and baking on beaches. This dangerous and disfiguring practice began in the 1920s, when the prized pale complexions Victorian women guarded with parasols and veils became passé. "People wonder why I take the risk," one hardcore twenty-something sunbather recently told a reporter for *The Washington Post*. "But I figure if I need plastic surgery when I'm forty, I'll just go out and get it." When questioned about the possibility of cancer, she replied, "It's off in the future. By then they'll have a cure."[2]

Of course, no age is immune to selfish or self-destructive behavior. The late nineteenth century produced its own share of rascals and rogues, including some whose notoriety has survived to the present day. What makes the current crop of whiners and dysfunction junkies any worse than the charlatans and robber barons of the Gilded Age? Quite simply, the answer is that Victorian miscreants skirted and sometimes flouted the rules, but they didn't try to rewrite them. Even the greatest Victorian villains understood that the moral fiber of a civilized society would fray and break if there were not dire consequences for flouting society's rules.

Consider the case of Jim Fisk. As his biographer W. A. Swanber noted, in an age that revered humility and discretion, Fisk was a flamboyant self-promoter—the Donald Trump of his day. Along with his partner, the reviled Jay Gould, he nearly cornered the country's gold supply in 1869. Their failed attempt did succeed in bankrupting half the brokerage houses on Wall Street. The married Fisk was equally notorious for flaunting his affairs with actresses, dancers, and other "loose women."

Not only was Fisk socially shunned and roundly condemned by prominent preachers and politicians, his sins hit him squarely in the wallet. Many men refused to do business with him because he was not a "gentleman." Fisk expected this and accepted it as a cost of doing business his way. He never thought to question society's right to ostracize him, much less to turn his flamboyant style to his advantage. He broke the rules in good faith and didn't expect any credit for his bad behavior.

Can we imagine the philandering Donald Trump paying such a price for his high-profile affair with Marla Maples? (Of course she had a successor and was later dumped herself by yet another look-alike blonde.) On the contrary, he was rewarded with more publicity, which conventional wisdom claims is never bad. A front-page story in *The New York Times* featured the city's mayor kissing mistress Maples when Trump and she eventually applied for a marriage license. Politicians and celebrities attended the wedding, and the minister who presided claimed no authority to pass any moral judgment on the happy couple since "I'm in a very different place today than I was when I was a young minister."[3]

The difference between the 1860s and the 1990s is that public vice once carried a price, and those who played expected to pay. Jim

Fisk certainly did. According to Swanber, before Fisk met what society termed his fitting end—the lover of a former paramour shot him—he bowed to the power of the moral code he had consciously breached:

> There isn't any hope for Jim Fisk. I'm a gone goose. . . . I am too fond of this world. If I've got to choose between the other world and this, I take this. Some people are born to be good, other people are born to be bad. I was born to be bad. As to the World, the Flesh, and the Devil, I'm on good terms with all three. If God Almighty is going to damn us men because we love the women, then let him go ahead and do it. I'm having a good time now, and if I've got to pay for it hereafter, why I suppose there's no more fair shakes; and I'll take what's coming to me.

Today, every talk-show therapist worth his sheepskin would tell Jim Fisk or anyone else who thought vice carried a price: "Don't worry; be happy." We have spent a century learning to take things easy. Of course, it is easier to take it easy if you don't have to worry about the hereafter. The Victorians were well aware of this connection. As Catharine Beecher wrote in her 1841 *Treatise on Domestic Economy*, the Victorians saw democracy as the "practical Christianity" of "trained and disciplined good temper that produced a general elevation in the character of the people [and] the highest form of interaction between men and their beliefs . . . in all public and private life."

SIN NO MORE

Nowadays we order our religion over easy, like eggs. Not that God is dead; He has just mellowed out. We could see His change of heart in the recent movie version of *The Scarlet Letter*, which ends with its lovers freely riding off into the sunset. Perhaps the Hollywood talents that bowdlerized Hawthorne's message about sin and guilt presumed a modern audience would squirm at watching the cowardly Arthur Dimmesdale confess his guilt before dying, revealing a red stigmata on his chest. Or perhaps they found it difficult to deal with Hester Prynne's redemption through suffering for her sins. After all, as the modernized Hester asks in the film, "Who is to say what is a sin in God's eyes?"

The Victorians were no Puritans, but their social code was powerfully reinforced by activating the same sense of shame that was sewn into Hester's scarlet letter. Nor had this approach to punishment gone entirely out of style in the early part of this century. After the San Francisco earthquake of 1906, children who vandalized shops and homes were publicly shamed with placards that announced their crimes. (Adult looters were shot on sight.) Ultimately, the power of shaming rested on the public's acceptance that human conceptions of right and wrong were rooted in divinely ordered judgments of good and evil.

We wouldn't expect the notions of shame and sin to flourish in a world where New Age healers define "spirit" as getting in touch with who you are. But touchy-feely spirituality is no longer confined to fringe groups that walk on hot coals and run with wolves. In the spirit of the age, mainstream religious groups are busily adapting their messages to fit the tailor-made morality of self-affirmation.

Traditional churches are fast losing ground while new feel-good megachurches that cater to "customers" are thriving. Some makeshift churches, seeking space as well as convenience, even rent space in malls. The most successful model for this approach, Willow Creek near Chicago, is the best-attended church in America.

The diligent research staffs responsible for these amenities and activities proudly affirm that they were inspired by Disney World themes. Churches should be "fun" and "user-friendly," declared a

with-it pastor, and "customers" heartily agreed. One resumed attending church after a long absence because "it's like going to the movies." He found this brand of religion "easy," adding, "I like things easy." So theater seats have replaced pews. Crosses are banned so they won't "alienate" those who are still just "investigating Christianity." In fact, actual theaters are being used for church services in a suburb of Washington, D.C. "I advertise [that] we have the most comfortable seats in town," brags the unapologetic pastor, George Beavens.

Ladder of Fortune

The like-minded executive director of the Mount Vernon (Virginia) Baptist Association, Bob Perry, explains the appeal of such settings: "Baby boomers and baby busters are just not into the thing of getting the whole family up on Sunday morning and getting dolled up.

They roll out of bed and put on jeans and a T-shirt and go to church. We have a number of churches appealing to that trend." Freed of the once obligatory "Sunday best," many people now wear their worst.

According to a March 1995 ABC News report, "In the Name of God," national surveys say most of us think "something in society is morally amiss." But pollster Daniel Yankelovich warns that people are put off by anything "preachy and abstract."[4] No problem. "Most churches you go to are boring," complained a progressive pastor in an April 20, 1995, article in *The New York Times*. "It's like you're captured behind the stained glass. . . . Our sermon moves. There's no dead time." Gone are the days when people flocked to hear the long eloquent homilies of renowned Victorian clerics like William Ellery Channing and Henry Ward Beecher, and major newspapers routinely printed their texts. Now sound-bite sermons cater to our shrinking attention spans.

In keeping with this relaxed approach, the King James Bible is being ousted for simpler editions stripped of the inspiring lyrical language the Victorians treasured. No *thee*'s, *thou*'s, *verily*'s, or sense of the sacred elevate the common lingo that makes poetry sound like a weather report. In the au courant *Everyday Bible*, God no longer says to Adam and Eve, "Behold, I have given you every herb bearing seed." Now He sounds like an annoyed Valley girl: "Look, I have given you all the plants that have grain for seeds." In the Twenty-third Psalm, the Lord is no longer the shepherd who "restoreth my soul." Instead, "He gives me new strength." What does He strengthen—your gluteus maximus?

An ad for one of the new breed of Good Books promises "God's Word in your words." If that's what we want to hear, we can always talk to ourselves. Perhaps the assumption behind these nursery school Bibles is that we can't tell the difference anymore. As for self-sacrifice— the essence of Christianity and, not coincidentally, Victorian civility— fewer than half of those surveyed call it a positive moral virtue.

While it may feel as comfortable as a Barca-Lounger, our modern amusement-park approach to religion demands a tradeoff. In this cushy chair there is only room for one—no challenges to grow beyond the chair, no moral tests to strengthen spiritual muscles, no links to community, to higher goals, or to the God, Who would hardly be godly if His Word were really reducible to our words. But in a culture where living, not just loving, means never having to say you're sorry, the very concept of sin is itself a sin against humanity, because it lowers our self-esteem.

THE FALSE RELIGION OF SELF-ESTEEM

The self-esteem movement is a natural expression of our ongoing effort to sanctify self-indulgence in place of that old-time Victorian religion of self-restraint. The gospel of self-indulgence was recently related by a new disciple, in whose writing the link is especially clear. In *Revolution from Within: A Book of Self-Esteem,* Gloria Steinem argues that our paramount problem is having our "preferences repressed" by a racist and sexist society, which fosters obedience to its "external authority" by undermining confidence in our "internal wisdom." Ms. Steinem blames deficient individual ego for crime, violence, drug/alcohol/spousal/child abuse, dropping out of school, and welfare dependency.

Unfortunately, we have yet to taste the proof in this pudding, despite the efforts of countless authors, lecturers, consultants, and the National Council on Self-Esteem. The University of California sociologist Neil Smelser says that after reviewing thousands of studies, scholars have failed to document claims that high self-esteem is a consistent predictor of higher grades or of which kids will experience substance abuse, child abuse, or teen pregnancy.[5] Experts not only failed to document a link between violent behavior and low self-esteem, they found that violence-prone individuals have unrealistically high opinions of themselves. They become hostile when their inflated egos are challenged. Rather than trying to reduce violence with "I am special" prison chants, Roy Baumeister, a Case Western Reserve University researcher, suggests, "Perhaps it would be better to try instilling modesty and humility."[6]

Our insistence that self-esteem is a cure-all is fostered by pop culture venues that feed our hunger for spiritual self-transcendence with "self-esteem makeovers," and gurus who offer easy trade-in terms on exchanging old selves for new ones. Before the final credits rolled, one renovated guest on Phil Donahue's talk show in July 1995 giddily explained that she finally understood why her live-in boyfriend habitually beat her, and why she took it: "He had low self-esteem, I had low self-esteem, and his beating me lowered my self-esteem more."

ME FIRST

Ironically, many feminists who complain about narcissistic, juvenile men (the "Peter Pan Syndrome") preach their own version—that women can have it all. It has become a cliché that marriage, like work or hobbies, is just one means of self-fulfillment. To the Victorians, the mutual spousal obligations of this institution were so deep that they could "only be discharged through eternity," as Henry C. Wright put it in *Marriage and Parentage*. But surveys show that only a minority of American adults in our disposable age still include "being married" in their definition of family values. Should this particular lifestyle become constraining or displeasing, you take your toys and leave.

Moreover, according to a recent report by the Rockford Institute, "Marriage in America," most adults now *reject* the antiquated idea that the family—the first school of civility—should stay intact for the children's sake. Unfortunately, experts have begun to marshal hard evidence documenting what the Victorians regarded as common sense: the devastating social and personal impact of equal-opportunity self-indulgence. As documented extensively by Barbara DeFoe Whitehead, children suffer, financially and otherwise, when moms or dads get tired of playing adults.[7] And so, after decades of insisting that kids would adjust to divorce, researchers now recant with a boatload of wreckage from broken homes. And there isn't a whiff of self-esteem in this equation.

The Victorians would say that a culture of self-indulgence in which parents don't take responsibility for teaching character and civility eventually takes its toll on children's development of self-restraint and a social conscience. And so the cycle is repeated, as adults expect little of themselves and even less of their children. These basement standards, which are no bargain, have done more than change the relations between parents and their children. They have changed the very relationship between childhood and adulthood.

3

Alone in the Toy Store

Young children are naturally, sometimes charmingly, uncivilized. . . . Selfish and he-donistic, they are strangers to self-restraint. Aggressive and rebellious, they expect un-conditional love. They make countless demands, whine endlessly when they're not satisfied, and blame everyone but them-selves when something goes wrong. They require constant reassurance but rarely need ego boosting. "Whom do you love more than anyone in the world?" I heard a cousin ask her four-year-old daughter. "Me!" the little girl gleefully replied.

There would be no cause for concern if I had just described an average child who, with age and training, would develop the trinity of a social conscience—civility, duty, and self-control. But Victorian standards of character development have been so inverted that today's parents are expected to satisfy childish impulses and desires, rather than to help their children grow out of them. The results have been as bad for kids, for parents, and for the larger society as the Vic-torians feared.

RAISING (UP) CHILDREN

Victorian standards of child-rearing demanded much of parents and children alike, because learning how to use the building blocks of civility was never optional, even in the nursery. When these parents spoke of *raising* children, they meant it literally. As Dr. E. H. Ruddock wrote in *Vitology*, his 1899 encyclopedia of home and health, the goal was to "lead the child gradually from its natural egoism to a reasonable altruism." No corners could be cut in civilizing the selfishness out of the next generation, because every youngster had to be carefully formed "physically, mentally, and morally." This was a fullfledged "parental duty," not a lifestyle choice with loopholes, and its success meant more than personal satisfaction. Raising a moral and mannerly child was "the highest guarantee of the stability of the whole fabric of the state." In this sense, even the smallest child was part of a big picture.

Although well-mannered children doubtless made their parents' lives easier, manners were taught for the children's benefit. However, the Victorians saw manners as far more than a surface gloss that would win friends and influence people. In his 1911 essay "The Decay of Manners," Thomas Nelson Page wrote, "'Manners maketh the man' holds a deeper philosophy. . . . This matter of manners goes much nearer to the heart of life." If that heart skipped too many beats, he warned, we would have "the most intolerable class that any society has ever been called on to carry."

We are carrying this burden now, from shopping malls bulging with children who don't want to grow up to prisons bulging with children who never got the chance. For, as Page predicted, "Having been . . . led to imagine that their own desires can be gratified at any cost, they not unnaturally . . . feel at liberty to pursue their desires at whatever cost either to themselves or to others."

The current crop of parents is not the first to shy away from exercising the duties that Catharine Beecher found so essential to social stability. Researchers such as the Lynds, the authors of *Middletown*, trace this trend back to the 1920s, when modern parents began to behave like "pals." By the 1950s, the ideal family was expected to have what Susan Kellogg in her 1988 book *Domestic Revolutions* called a "carefree, child-centered outlook with relaxed methods of child discipline." This enlightened attitude is popularly identified with Dr. Benjamin Spock, who, according to Kellogg, described his own mother as "very tyrannical, very moralistic, very opinionated," yet "very dedicated to her children." Apparently, she was also very Victorian in her approach to the "inner child." Dr. Spock recalled that he and his siblings "didn't realize that she instilled such a sense of guilt in us that it showed all over when we came in having done something naughty."

Now that we are more concerned with consciousness raising than conscience raising, Mrs. Spock's moralistic approach might be considered psychologically abusive. Indeed, the whole notion of child raising has given way to "parenting." The new term is revealing: The focus is on transforming ourselves into parents, rather than transforming our children into mature adults. And who is the best judge of this effort? Who else but the child to whom we are trying to "relate"? Hence the complaint of one elementary school counselor that parents constantly seek their children's approval of their decisions. This gives new meaning to the phrase "children raising children."

PASSIVE PARENTS, PERMISSIVE PARENTS

Part of the problem is that many parents don't want to have to be the bad guy, the disciplinarian, preferring to be their children's friend. Even so, the kid down the block often seems to have more authority over the children than the parents do, because parents have abdicated their responsibilities. It's not that Mom and Dad don't love their offspring. Most parents who stay together tell pollsters they want to spend more time with their kids. Yet kid time has decreased dramatically over the last generation. The growth of dual-income families is an obvious culprit, but this fails to explain why an astonishing amount of the waking hours today's go-go family members actually spend together is devoted to watching TV. Lest we think this is the contemporary equivalent of gathering round the campfire to roast marshmallows and share ghost stories, researchers say we relate most directly to the set, not to each other. And even as the size of the average household decreases, TVs proliferate like mold. A growing number of American homes have three or more sets, so we can watch whatever we choose—alone.

According to surveys, parents spend less time talking to their own kids than they do calling telephone operators for information or chatting with gas station attendants (who are not easy to find). Because family time is sliced thin as diet bread, experts tell us parents are reluctant to use it "hassling" their kids to learn discipline. This is the intersection of indulgence and neglect, as "home alone" means free to roam in every sense. In a 1993 Metropolitan Washington Council of Government study of drinking habits, nearly three out of four teens admitted they had gone home visibly drunk, yet only one in five parents said they noticed. When questioned about her own son, one mom admitted to *The Washington Post*, "In the end it all comes down to . . . the realization that I'm very powerless over this person's choices."

Victorian children were expected to help with the housework from an early age.
Through chores, youngsters learned the details of running a home or farm.

Such a casual assertion of parental powerlessness would have amazed the Victorians. We have experienced a sea change in outlook, which has drastically reshaped what we take to be reasonable or commonsensical responses to everyday problems that parents have always faced. Consider how an advice column called "Family Almanac" responded to the mother of an eight-year-old girl who threw incorrigible temper tantrums and constantly berated her obedient younger sister: "Take the older child out to a proper ladies' lunch at the department store . . . without once reminding her to mind her manners. Talk with her instead as you would talk to a friend, asking her how she has been, and what she thinks about the latest book she's reading, and also confide in her."[1]

The columnist goes on to advise that the parent confess to the child that she is concerned about problems at home, which will cause the girl to reassure the parent: "Your daughter will probably tell you quite seriously that you shouldn't fuss so much, but she will ponder the problem later and try to be better, as long as you haven't blamed her for the problem." Granting the child this "respect" will compel her to behave, and "you'll find her much easier to handle."

Put aside the difficulty of finding that "proper ladies' lunch" in an era when the very idea of being a "proper lady" has become controversial. The premise here is that an unruly child isn't going to behave until she gets some respect. But what is the value of respect that isn't earned but is dispensed like party favors? To the Victorians, respect was granted not as an incentive to behave properly but as a reward for having done so. By giving our children something for nothing, we get what we ask for in return. And so today's parents worry about earning their children's respect, rather than vice versa. Looking back on his youth, the prominent Victorian cleric Henry Ward Beecher recalled being so inspired (not cowed) by his father "that when he said anything to me . . . it was like the speaking of God."[2] We shouldn't be surprised if our kids are more likely to hear the voice of Rodney Dangerfield.

MONEY TALKS

Unable to command their children's respect, parents increasingly try to buy it. The total discretionary funds controlled by America's kids exceed the annual budgets of most Third World nations. This country's yearly expenditure on toys, not including video games, has sky-rocketed to $24 billion, according to Pennsylvania State University history professor Gary Cross. As he noted in a *New York Times* article titled "Too Many Toys," that represents a 260 percent increase since 1980, at a time when middle- and working-class incomes have stagnated.³ Experts ascribe the increase to dual-income couples and guilt-ridden divorced parents who spend money on their kids instead of spending time with them.

The apotheosis of this buying binge and the habits it teaches can be glimpsed in a toy for girls called "Melanie's Mall." It contains a mini-Barbie-like doll, her shopping bags, and boutiques where she can charge to her heart's content with her own gold credit card.

To find the intersection of material indulgence and spiritual neglect, take a trip to any upscale shopping mall. Ask the security guards about the runaway parents who leave their toddlers to wander alone in toy stores, while they go off to shop undisturbed. When they return, they comfort the anxious child by buying him or her new toys. Parental desertion became so rampant at a Discovery Zone in the Washington, D.C., area that the manager had to hold parents hostage by requiring them to leave their shoes at the front desk.

This behavior is not just a product of sheer affluence. The late nineteenth century witnessed what was then the greatest explosion of material wealth in history. This fueled a vast expansion of the middle classes and the comforts they enjoyed. But the Victorians believed that perpetually playing Santa Claus, even if you had the means to do so, meant being a bad parent and a bad citizen. As Dr. E. H. Ruddock wrote in *Vitology*, "Such indulgence is apt to lead to pride of person, of position, and of purse, . . . and expose those so educated in false kindness, to the ever present risk of being stranded upon the shoals of utter helplessness by the first unexpected tempest of adversity." Not to mention turning parents into absentee checkbooks for their kids.

Clarence Day, Sr., the eponymous Victorian patriarch of *Life with Father*, was a successful stockbroker who owned a brownstone on Madison Avenue and a pew in the local Episcopal church. But even in this affluent household, Clarence Jr. and his brothers received new toys only at Christmas. Mr. Day was no Scrooge; this was a matter of morals rather than meanness. A popular rhyme of the era spelled out the modest and practical gifts children could expect: "Something to eat, something to read, something to play with, something they need." This presents quite a contrast to contemporary scenes of parents slugging it out in toy stores over the last Tickle Me Elmo or Beanie Baby, and reflects the Victorian ethos that parents show more concern for their children's good than for their goods.

KIDDIE CONSUMERS

Of course, Clarence Day's parents didn't have to compete with a popular culture obsessed with lowering the age of consumption. It was during the 1950s, a decade now idealized by conservatives, that charmingly innocent shows like *Howdy Doody* and *Walt Disney Presents* began pitching ads directly at children. As Stephanie Coontz writes in *The Way We Never Were,* this was a time when children were "pampered as never before," and everyone thought "you must eternally give to your children: otherwise you are not a loving parent." No left-wing sociological tract ever did so much damage to Victorian values. If you have any doubts, pull out those old Kodak moments of birthday parties and Christmas mornings. Loot was the name of the game.

It was in the 1950s that a TV cartoon brat first screamed, "I want my Maypo!" until Mom quickly fed him his favorite cereal. Forty years later, daily life imitates popular art. We have all stood in line behind some octopuslike child in a shopping-cart seat, as she strained to grab strategically placed toys while wailing at a pitch that could shatter nerves and glass. In my latest such encounter, the mother (who seemed to have far fewer arms than her child) finally distracted her little girl by coaxing her to sing a TV jingle—from a toy commercial. Understandably, Mom seemed too frazzled to recognize either the irony or the cultural hole she was stuck in.

THE BURDEN ON SCHOOLS AND TEACHERS

With help from Hollywood and Madison Avenue, kids keep upping the ante until parents throw up their hands. It should come as no surprise that teachers are being forced to step in where parents fear to tread, if only to avoid utter chaos when the orbits of these little angels intersect in a single classroom. School officials increasingly report that the babies of baby boomers know all about self-assertion and empowerment but lack a sense of basic decency and key social skills. So the schools must teach them the ABC's of how to raise their hand in class instead of calling out, how to say "Good morning" (rather than some less savory remark), even how to play with each other.

But learning that play has any rules, much less a code of sportsmanship, can be derailed by role-model parents whose own role models seem to be British football fans. An article in the February 23, 1995, *Washington Post* noted that in one wealthy Maryland county, so many parents attending various youth league games loudly ridiculed kids on opposing teams, cursed at coaches, and harassed officials that the recreation department mandated a "Spectators Code of Ethics." This measure barred children from participating in games unless their parents signed a pledge of allegiance to the "principles of decorum."

Sometimes parents even manage to undermine civility in the classroom. They file official complaints, or unofficial ones with their kids, when teachers dare to control chaotic classes by rebuking or ejecting troublemakers. Teaching any values while placating parents has become such a dance on banana peels that teachers are attending special programs and institutes recently established for that purpose. For example, Boston University's Center for the Advancement of Ethics and Character emphasizes teaching "the basics," such as honesty, hard work, decency, justice, caring, and friendship. Who can argue with those? No one, which is why one member of the institute, Kevin Ryan, has said that teachers should "save other issues for later on down the road."[4]

Left unclear is where that road leads or what happens when you hit a pothole. Here's a big one—a values manual for middle-schoolers with the inspiring title *Help! My Teacher Hates Me: How to Survive Poor Grades, a Friend Who Cheats off You, Oral Reports and More.* The book's author, Meg Schneider, states that cheating is wrong but then gives several reasons why people cheat. Instead of explaining why these don't excuse the deed, she cops a plea of relativism: "Can't there be exceptions? In some instances isn't cheating, well, necessary? Perhaps the best answer to [this] question is that there may not be a clear-cut answer. . . . Sometimes people simply have to make their own tough choices."[5]

How can this Swiss cheese diet nourish a child's conscience? According to the author, conceptions of right and wrong are not "clear-cut." So she can only present the menu, then leave the kids to select their favorite dish. At best, you recommend the chef's special, according to Ms. Schneider: "You can't give a kid a moral. You have to help that kid come to the moral on his or her own." This amounts to telling nascent travelers to draw a world map, then crossing your fingers that they don't get lost.

This kind of juggling act was unknown when the public school movement spread during the late nineteenth century. In 1912, the retired president of Harvard, Charles W. Eliot, summarized its gospel, which used to be the gospel truth for most Americans: "Since the safe conduct of democratic society . . . depends on an unprecedented development of mutual good-will, manifested kindliness, and hearty cooperation, the function of common schools in teaching manners and morals is plainly one of the most important parts of public education, and the main reliance of democratic optimism."[6]

Because manners have always been nourished by the oxygen of morals, Victorian educators tried to teach children to forge the connections between them. When teachers wrote simple plays in which students acted out the proper way to respectfully address their elders, they intended to civilize the child, the classroom, and the streets simultaneously. Such lessons were not intended to substitute for those learned at home, unless home was a Dickensian slum plagued with crime and physical neglect. Otherwise, schools built on home base.

In 1899 E. H. Ruddock, a popular writer on civics and child-rearing, could assert confidently, "It may be assumed that all parents . . . will take care that the character of youth is founded in honesty, industry, sobriety, integrity, fidelity, economy, perseverance, and self-reliant determination, which are the weapons in the armory of character by which success is wrested from all conditions of life." This is something we may no longer assume, to put it mildly.

WHEN CHILDREN RULE THE ROOST

In a sure sign that the spread of overindulgence has reached critical mass, Oprah Winfrey recently devoted a show to it. In one segment a parade of frustrated parents moaned about the extortionary rates charged for household chores by those few kids who deigned to do them under any circumstances. The Victorians would be grabbing their smelling salts. They believed children of both sexes should master and perform every domestic chore, from mending clothes to repairing windows—without compensation. "A child as young as six," said Lydia Maria Child in her 1833 advice manual *The American Frugal Housewife*, "should be taught to consider every day lost in which some little thing has not been done to assist others."

Building character meant contributing to the common family maintenance, acquiring various survival skills for later life, and becoming self-sufficient. Victorian parents showed that they "cared" by giving their children a sense of morality, the tools of civility, and the Golden Rule, which made both possible. If you view the world through Victorian eyes, as a complex tapestry of threads, you'll see why material and even emotional overindulgence can damage more than your credit rating.

These threads cohered for me a few years ago, during a trip to the airport. Waiting next to me at the arrival gate was a woman and her squirming child of five or six. As the child's father deplaned, she shouted, "Daddy, what did you bring me?" The horror on this well-trained parent's face revealed that he had forgotten the expected gift. A promise of swift compensation failed to stop the caterwauls that quickly dimmed the ambient noise of jet engines and public-address announcements.

Finally, sighing with resignation, the woman carried her flailing bundle of hysterics toward the luggage carousel, along with a bag of toys and kid supplies that looked heavy enough to dislocate her shoulder. Dad carried himself and a slim, monogrammed briefcase. With his glassy, tuned-out stare, he was as self-absorbed as his offspring. Though the couple had yet to greet each other, the resentful woman finally tugged her husband into a public therapy session about their squalling daughter. This mutual blame game quickly extended to whose needs weren't being met in and out of the bedroom.

With both of these well-dressed thirty-somethings emoting and sporadically cursing almost as loudly as their little carbon copy, I saw the perverse harmony in that distinctly modern picture. They were truly creatures of their time, three would-be stars equally oblivious to the planets that were supposed to revolve around them. I lost sight of them in the baggage claim area, surviving my close encounter at the cost of a bruised rib. (Not surprisingly, they assumed that their feelings—tired, testy, and wanting to get home—justified wielding their elbows to carve out more personal space.)

"Big deal," an acquaintance remarked when I recounted this experience scene by scene. "Nobody died." Not there; not that day. But something precious that could not be tallied in a body count had died long ago. Even this lapsed Catholic began praying for its resurrection.

4

Portrait of a Lady

Victorian women, those constantly embroidering and crocheting seamstresses of history, are uniquely qualified to serve as our teachers. It was they, not their fathers or husbands, who embodied their culture's unified vision of etiquette, values, and morality. Their lives and works still contain the keys to those elevated codes of conduct and aspiration that were orphaned nearly a century ago and are so sorely needed today. To understand what they have to teach us, though, we must first understand how radically our notions of womanhood have changed.

The tragic tally of recent statistics on sexual abuse, rape, and domestic violence brutally demonstrates how the collapse of basic decency levies its greatest toll on women. Less obvious is the story of how modern feminists abetted this tragedy, and their sex's social suicide, by renouncing the broad moral mission of their predecessors, the trailblazing Victorian suffragists and reformers.

This is a tale of two roads—the high and the low. The first was proudly genteel, altruistic, optimistic, visionary, politically pointed yet spiritually driven, and unshakably empowered by the femininity it carried as the lamp of human progress. The second road was crude, negative, self-absorbed, soulless but religiously political, and so sexually insecure that it masculinized the world in the name of helping women, which sent us all down a dark cul-de-sac.

FEMINISM OLD AND NEW

This divorce between two centuries of feminists, and the two traditions of feminism they represent, can be glimpsed on Gloria Steinem's desk. Prominently displayed there is a framed letter written by Victoria Claflin Woodhull, one of history's most infamous and truly dysfunctional deviants. Woodhull hailed from a family of blackmailers, hucksters, charlatan spiritualists, and murderers worthy of an old dime novel. When not peddling quack lethal potions, the Claflin clan pursued its favorite hobby: constantly suing each other. They were such a social menace that the citizens of their Ohio hometown actually paid them to leave.

According to Johanna Johnston's 1967 biography of Woodhull, she was a shameless self-promoter and publicity hound who became a major advocate of the short-lived Free Love Movement in the 1870s. (On this score, there was nothing new at Woodstock in 1969 but the mud.) She packed them in on her lucrative lecture tours. In a speech in the 1870s, Woodhull declared, "I have an inalienable constitutional and natural right to love whom I may, to love [for] as long or as short a period as I can, to change that love every day if I please!" She proved true to her convictions of the moment by having a string of affairs with single and married men who were discarded when they ceased to further her career. Outdoing even Madonna, she juggled one lover while living with another who had abandoned his wife for her. Like all modern moral arsonists, this very un-Victorian Victoria never cared who got burned. "What does it matter whether the child or anyone knows who its father is?" she asked rhetorically. Nothing mattered but her rights and those of like-minded rebels to breed randomly and recklessly.

Victoria Woodhull's housekeeping arrangements were as elastic as her conscience; she simultaneously shared quarters with her children, her legal ex-husband, and his probably bigamous successor. Following a farcical but headline-grabbing run for president (at a time when women still couldn't vote), this proponent of adultery divorced her second husband for that very offense. Then she sailed for London with a pocketful of hush money paid by a prominent family trying to avert a scandal. England provided her with a soft landing. Previously a professed communist, the versatile Victoria changed her tune after she married a wealthy blueblood. She also denied having preached free love and claimed she had been misused and victimized by men.

Despite Woodhull's pro-suffrage views and acclaimed oratorical skills, Susan B. Anthony, Elizabeth Cady Stanton, and other principled suffrage leaders quickly distanced themselves from her when they discovered she was a trouble-prone hypocrite whose chief cause was herself. But modern feminists rush to sing her praises. For example, in her book *Fire with Fire,* Naomi Wolf applauds this self-gratifying "power feminist" for being "free thinking, pleasure loving, and assertive," instead of the more typical "morally superior" and "self-denying" Victorian reformer whose unpaid "good works" contributed to her sex's "suffocating condition." And Woodhull earned her place of honor on Gloria Steinem's desk, Steinem explained in *Moving Beyond Words,* for "liv[ing] out in public the principles of female emancipation and sexual freedom that were not only unusual in her day but illegal." Ms. Steinem sees an inspiring "strength" in this "rare woman who had escaped all training to be a lady."

Goodnight All You Ladies

Though in England the term "lady" was originally a title one had to be born to or acquire by marriage, in the democracy of America any woman could become a "lady" by virtue of her behavior. Alas, the term is now on the hit list. In a recent book on workplace diversity, *Workforce America*, management consultants Marilyn Loden and Judy Rosener decry the word's objectionable implications of white gloves, unflagging politeness, and general "gentility." At a time when such traits are regarded with suspicion, the word "lady" is disappearing from public discourse as rapidly as it is vanishing from the doors of public restrooms. I once witnessed an elegantly attired woman lodge a loud and inelegant complaint with a maitre d' about the sexist labels on his restaurant's facilities.

The most telling inversion of the old lexicon that honored women is that both genders use the universal term "you guys" in barrooms, boardrooms, classrooms, and on network news shows to address absolutely everyone. It seems God retired from the creation business after making Adam. For all their consciousness raising, when women talk to each other, the lingo of guyhood often subsumes their sisterhood. Even Victorian prostitutes would have balked at such a denial of the feminine identity.

In this century, men have patronized women as "gals" and "broads," or compared them to animals from "chicks" and "foxes" to the increasingly popular "bitches." Even women have sometimes called each other by these names, but there is a big difference between a "foxy lady" and a true lady. Any of these terms for women would have horrified the residents of an age that even frowned on the word "female" as insulting, since it describes both higher and lower forms of life.

<hr />

THE AGENDA OF NINETEENTH-CENTURY FEMINISTS

That despised label "lady" would keep most Victorian feminists off the desktops of their present-day successors. Victorian suffragists and reformers never toed a single party line, but they shared one quality that today's feminists hate more than hoop skirts. As Julia Ward Howe, who knew and worked with most of these women throughout her long career, wrote in *The Woman Suffrage Movement*, they all had "a great heart of religious conviction and a genuine spirit of self-sacrifice." Elizabeth Oakes Smith, a suffragist and cousin of Elizabeth Cady Stanton, wrote in her autobiography, "Duty was my motto everywhere."

The fight for female suffrage wasn't a mere lifestyle choice for Victorian women, nor was it motivated by sheer self-interest or a desire for redistribution of patriarchal power. The leaders of this hunt were after much bigger game than the ballot. Unlike modern-day feminists who have pushed a totally female-centered rights agenda in

Suffragettes such as these, shown in an 1899 photograph of The League of Political Education in New York City, had a far-reaching agenda and a moral authority current feminist activists lack.

the past quarter century, the Victorian-era reformers regarded the vote as a stepping stone to nothing less than "the better development of humanity," as Mary Livermore wrote in her 1889 autobiography *The Story of My Life*. Even when crusading for themselves and their sex, activists of old knew that unless everyone shared in the prize— including men—theirs would be a shallow victory. The suffragists did not promote so-called "women's issues," or demand the vote so that they could usher in politicians sympathetic to their special interests. According to *American Home Life 1880–1930*, the suffragist Julia Ward Howe believed that "[Voting] is a part of the duty which our sex owes to humanity. Religion, purity, peace, temperance are as much in place at the polls as at the altar or the fireside."

The reformer Consuelo Vanderbilt wrote in her autobiography that she found Paris gowns, glittering parties, and charitable dabbling left her as cold as her family's marble palace in Newport, so she abandoned "contemplations of a purely personal nature" for the deeper satisfaction of "higher idealism" and a "life lived for others." Jane Addams, suffragist, peace activist, municipal reformer and founder of the settlement house movement, put her money and herself to work among Chicago's immigrant poor. The robber baron Jay Gould's eldest daughter, Helen, continuously opened her home and her wallet to vast numbers of needy children, some of whom she adopted. Among middle- and upper-class Victorians, a Mother Teresa spirit was the venerated rule, not the exception.

This concept is alien to those feminists who define success as making partner so that male associates have to sleep with *you* to get ahead. NOW's founding manifesto of 1973 urged the liberated to shun traditional volunteer activities because they reinforced women's second-class status. What was once upper-class, even aristocratic, behavior had officially become déclassé. Small wonder that contemporary feminist scholars mock their nineteenth-century Samaritan sister as a masochist who "loved her crosses," as Ann Douglas wrote in *The Feminization of American Culture.* Not only was she "delusive, oppressed, and damaged," but her elevated spiritually driven aspirations were "fakery and crippling for all." Just studying these women is deemed a "painful" and "frightening" task, whose only reward appears to be academic tenure.

In her book *The Second Stage*, Betty Friedan analyzed some of the excesses of feminism's take-no-prisoners first stage. She half-heartedly conceded that it was wrong to denigrate "selfless service," because a "life lived for oneself does not truly satisfy men or women. There is a hunger in America today for larger purposes beyond the self." Once again, modern "wisdom" vindicates the Victorian common sense we had to relearn in the hardest possible way. Although national polls confirm how soul-starved we are, Friedan's revisionist view is not shared by "power feminists" who urge women to channel their energies and Ivy League brains into economic and politically self-interested pursuits. Are bimbos who measure their self-worth by their cup size any more limited than women who define themselves by the size of their résumés or bank accounts?

Bringing Womanly Virtues to the Public Sphere

Self-described "radical" feminists who want to scratch the entire capitalist system scorn the "womanly virtues" that were once a welcome antidote to the truly rough-and-tumble Victorian economy. Nurture, generosity, religion, and a sense of redemptive mission feminized nineteenth-century culture through the home, or private sphere, which was women's domain. These values were then applied to the "enlarged housekeeping" of the public sphere of society, which was considered men's domain. With a vast agenda that the Prohibition crusader Frances Willard termed "do everything" reform, Victorian women lost neither time nor their dignity by whining about inequality. Before they saw the inside of a voting booth or glimpsed a glass ceiling, they mobilized what Elizabeth Cady Stanton called "a great moral revolution" to improve public sanitation, education, prison conditions, and housing for the poor; build parks and playgrounds; and eliminate sweatshops and child labor, alcohol, prostitution, and pornography.

Even with this overflowing plate of ambitions, the Victorian ladies, as always, had higher goals. These supremely confident "do everything" women were spiritually charged up and hell bent on eliminating "the selfish and brutal elements which lead to war and bloodshed," as Julia Ward Howe put it (according to *American Home Life 1880–1930*). In this the Victorian reformers failed, but their vision will not fail to inspire those who hunger for more than victories they can take to the bank.

Selfish vs. Unselfish Feminist Agendas

Modern feminists have picked apart the agenda of their Victorian "sisters" as if carving up a chicken to select the tastiest parts. They advocate specific social programs that directly or indirectly benefit women, like child-care facilities that help working mothers. Larger issues with no direct payoff are ignored or given only lip service, and any curbs on sex are denounced as "censorious." After all, our culture is not sexually permissive enough. According to Naomi Wolf, writing in *Ms.* magazine, "There's too much sexual judgment going on."[1] To eliminate such judgmentalism, we have seen feminists advocate axing the word "normal" from sex-ed courses and threaten to sue schools that eject pregnant teens from cheerleading squads.

Victorian crusaders were not sexless schoolmarms who jealously foiled everyone's fun. Their social purity campaign transcended sex, just as sweatshops meant more to them than bad wages or working conditions, and raw sewage in the streets spread more than epidemics. In an age when everything had a moral dimension, these Dickensian-style horrors demoralized people, and were considered evils that rivaled illness or physical hardship. The Victorian reformers would have considered such denial of the moral dimension of these social problems and their effect on human souls the ultimate dereliction of their duty.

They delivered the full punch of this power in the late nineteenth century, when their voices, pens, and petitions defeated efforts by prominent male physicians and police officials to legalize prostitution in many towns and cities. These men proposed licensing prostitutes who were certified as "clean" so they and their clients would not spread venereal diseases. Susan B. Anthony, Elizabeth Cady Stanton, Frances Willard, Dr. Elizabeth Blackwell, and scores of other influential women opposed such laws on grounds that must mystify marketplace feminists who view "lifestyle choice" as the highest goal of a liberated woman's movement. The physician William Acton, in his 1857 book *Prostitution,* echoed the beliefs of the Victorian reformers when he wrote that reducing sex to a mere commercial venture "not only breeds distaste for virtuous society, but causes the mind to form a degraded estimate of the sex, until all women seem mere objects of desire and vehicles of indulgence . . . a toy, a plaything, an animated doll; a thing to wear like a glove, and fling away . . . instead of an immortal being, composed, like himself, of body, soul, and spirit."

This argument illustrates the way Victorian thinking wove together the threads of personal, social, and moral consequences. This kind of needlework was highly valued and effective woman's work, and no one did it better.

Woman were so instrumental in the Prohibition movement that it became known as "the woman's war." Alcoholism was a serious problem in the nineteenth century, especially in saloon-infested slums. Bar owners routinely set out "free" buffets to entice men to spend the paltry wages their families desperately needed on booze that was adulterated at best and poisonous at worst. It was common for men "polluted by drink" to physically and sexually abuse their wives and beat their children. The Society for the Prevention of Cruelty to Children was founded in 1875 to rescue many of these youngsters. One year earlier, praying, preaching, and chanting women shut down hundreds of saloons in the Midwest. The tireless efforts of a broad coalition of female reformers resulted in the passage of the Eighteenth Amendment, banning alcohol, in 1919, the year before women won the vote. By the time the law was repealed in 1933, the invincible "conservators of public and private morals" were extinct.

THE MORAL AUTHORITY
OF VICTORIAN REFORMERS

Today we have countless factions of politically active women, but none can claim the moral authority that women shared and wielded so effectively a century ago. The Victorians would view this as a devastating loss of female power that can never be recompensed by political and economic rights. The admirable work of Mothers Against Drunk Driving is based on one of our few shared moral values: that operating a vehicle while intoxicated is a gross imposition on the rights of fellow citizens. But for all its importance, drunk driving is a single self-contained issue, unconnected to a grand design for elevating the human race. I cannot imagine the president of M.A.D.D. or any woman from a "most admired" list publicly warning the nation's men, as Julia Ward Howe did (according to *American Home Life*), that they must "recognize in us not only a moral sentiment which they must respect but a moral determination to which they must conform."

Mrs. Howe could make this sweeping demand because her rock-solid self-esteem was not built on the quicksand of self-worship or the approval of men. Woman as the "nigger of the world," a term coined by Yoko Ono in the early 1970s, expresses a modern attitude, not a Victorian one. Victorian men did not denigrate women; on the contrary, they craved the approval and inspiration of the superior sex. No less celebrated an iconoclast than Mark Twain venerated woman as the "the civilizer of mankind." Comparing the sexes, Henry James called woman "a diviner self than his own." His father brought that notion down to earth when assessing his "slothful, self-willed, petty, obstinate, selfish" character against his wife's: "I should simply have gone to hell long ago if my wife had not saved me . . . by *unconsciously* being the pure, good, modest woman she is" (emphasis added).[2]

What modern male ego would freely confess such faults and credit a woman with his survival? Or admit, as A. J. Ingersoll, M.D., did in his 1889 book *In Health,* that he depends on his wife's "spiritual hand when he goes forth into the hurry of life [where] he may feel its grasp warm and strong to help him rise above the billows of vice and corruption which are everywhere, ready to drag a man down to moral death"? What modern male would attribute this country's "extraordinary prosperity" to "the superiority of their women," as de Tocqueville wrote in *Democracy in America?* Or concede, as Henry C. Wright did in *Marriage and Parentage*, that "men degenerate in every particular when left . . . without the refining and elevating influence of women"?

Women Did and Can Set the Standards

Occasionally a voice in the masculine wilderness speaks up for Victorian notions of social sanity. The renowned black newspaper columnist William Raspberry wrote in a 1993 column in *The Washington Post* that, as a group, "Young women in low-income neighborhoods have neglected—forgotten—their power to control male behavior. If they could learn again what 'everybody' used to know, they could break the violent young men to the domestic yoke."[3] (Why limit this reclamation of female power to the poor?) At the perilous risk of being called sexist, Raspberry dares to suggest that "unless we can re-induce young women to take on the task of civilizing young men, social chaos may well be both unavoidable and irreversible."

One hundred and ten years before this message was rare enough to be newsworthy, Frances Willard stated the obvious when she said, "It is rather by holding men to the same standards of morality [as women] that society shall rise to higher levels." as Richard Leeman pointed out in his book *"Do Everything" Reform*. Raspberry didn't lay odds on whether modern women would accept or achieve this daunting mission. Victorian men had no doubts. The English art critic and philosopher John Ruskin spoke for his age when he said, "What woman wills will be accomplished."

The source of this distinctive female force of will was nature and what it nurtured. Both sexes regarded motherhood with religious reverence. Because women could be mothers, they were the "better half of humanity," in Mary Livermore's phrase, the natural enemies of

A lady could expect a Victorian gentleman to assist all ladies in any way he could. This engraving from a Victorian-era etiquette book shows gentlemen the proper way to help a lady into a carriage.

injustice and the natural allies of the weak and helpless. The stamp of the mother of mankind was first and final. "The standard of manhood really derives from that of womanhood," wrote Julia Ward Howe in her 1881 book *Modern Society.* "The woman's influence comes before that of man and outlasts it."

Mothers to the World

This influence emanated equally from those who never bore children. Some of the most prominent Victorian reformers and suffragists were biologically childless and unmarried but proudly maternal. Miss Beecher, an ardent advocate of female education, acted as a surrogate mother to her students and helped raised her sister Harriet Beecher Stowe's seven children, enabling the author to write *Uncle Tom's Cabin.* Susan B. Anthony had many informally adopted nieces, and Dr. Elizabeth Blackwell officially adopted a daughter.

Modern feminists have long been split on the importance of the "maternal virtues" Victorian society ascribed to women. The psychologist Carol Gilligan is famous for her controversial argument that women value personal relationships and responsibilities, while men value autonomy and cold logic. Whatever the validity of her conclusions, Gilligan rightly argued that the male-defined standards of her profession branded "women's" traits as deficient in moral development. To the Victorians this sort of double standard would have seemed like heresy verging on lunacy.

VIVE LA DIFFÉRENCE

Rather than embracing *la différence*, modern feminists prefer to see gender as merely an artificial label. Yet there is a growing body of scientific research that documents another nineteenth-century precept: that male and female brains function differently. As Anne Moir pointed out in her 1991 book *Brain Sex*, sophisticated magnetic resonance technology now shows that the left and right brains of women constantly communicate, while men's barely speak to each other. Thus, women excel at language skills, intuition, and judging the subtle cues of emotions. Men, however, use more of their brains when solving math problems, which may explain their greater aptitude for math and for estimating spatial relationships. Women are more likely to recall specific landmarks, not distances. (But no one needs studies to tell us who stops to ask for directions, and which ego-driven mammal would rather drive aimlessly and endlessly than ask for help.)

Some conclusions emerging from this research have lit a short fuse in the gender wars. For example, male brains are more focused and less easily distracted while women have a harder time separating feelings from thoughts. Alarmed feminists who fear they will lose hard-won economic and political ground if science can demonstrate that women don't match men neuron for neuron have tried to suppress this research, although it shows promise in understanding and treating such "female" problems as higher rates of depression. And of course there is a flip side to such male "superiority"—which is female "superiority." If the typical male brain is more focused and logical than a woman's, the typical female brain has the converse advantages: the ability to perform more than one task at a time and consider emotional factors when making a decision.

But the real problem here is not the First Amendment, the pursuit of knowledge, or feminist paranoia—it is a modern tragedy and a travesty of women. The same culture that spreads the gospel of racial and ethnic diversity with an evangelist's fire has desanctified the distinctly female qualities the Victorians revered. This is far more threatening to men, women, and civilized life than a mountain of magnetic resonance pictures of physiological difference in male and female brains.

Long before science could photograph the brain in action, women celebrated their uniqueness and the complementary "strengths" of the sexes. In her book *The Laws of Life* (1852), Dr. Elizabeth Blackwell wrote, "Man is just as dependent on woman as woman is on man. Man by himself is powerless, so is woman; but united both are perfected." The educator and etiquette authority Eliza Duffey agreed, writing in her popular 1873 book *What Women Should Know* that the sexes were "halves of a perfect whole." She believed in a "male and female process of reasoning," though neither was "inferior nor superior."

Even courage had two faces. Writing in 1912 about female survivors of the *Titanic* disaster and the chivalrous men who drowned to save them, a reporter at the time, quoted in *The Titanic* by Wyn Craig Wade (1979), lauded "the courage of woman seeing her dear one standing on the sinking deck" and "the heroism of the woman who would rather see the dear one dead than dishonored."

The differences between men and women, believed the suffragist Mary Livermore, were complementary. Furthermore, she wrote in her autobiography, *The Story of My Life*, "The man is never intended to be measured by the woman, nor the woman to be measured by the man; for they are intended to be different, while, at the same time, one is as important to the whole as is the other."

Contemporary feminists can find few dichotomies more offensive than Livermore's assertion that man was "the head" and woman "the heart." But this heart was more than some frivolous chocolate valentine, and it certainly did not belong to the stereotypical swooning damsel. It was wisdom, strength, inspiration, life, home, and God. It epitomized the ennobling intangibles that were mother's milk to the Victorians.

THE MODERN MASCULINIZED WOMAN EMERGES

These treasured qualities of "the heart" were lost in the 1920s, as women began to masculinize themselves by drinking, smoking, cursing, and sexually experimenting. In so doing they took as their new models of behavior not just men but "ungentlemanly" men. It was during this period that dedicated social reformers like Jane Addams were displaced on lists of most admired women by movie queens like Mary Pickford. In the twentieth century, we began to admire public figures such as actresses for extremely superficial reasons. Now that we have come to revere image over substance, the enduring marriage of admiration and inspiration is divorced. We are all its damaged children.

When women disempowered themselves by leaping off the moral pedestal, no one and nothing took their place as the "civilizers of mankind" and the visionary agents of "higher growth." Organized religion was no match for the rough, raw, masculine values that conquered every corner of life like an invading army. The breadth of their victory forces modern women to adapt or pay dearly for behavior that was once rewarded.

In *Listening to Prozac*, the psychiatrist Peter Kramer notes that our culture denigrates "overly feminine" Victorian virtues like sensitivity and loyalty. Popular antidepressants don't just brighten moods; they allow women whose "personality styles are no longer socially favored or fashionable" to become more robust, risk-taking, competitive, combative—in short, more like men. Two of his patients, the fastidious Julia and the romantically reticent Sally, illustrate his point:

> Contemporary convention demands that women be more assertive (here meaning aggressive, outgoing, and flexible—not firm in defense of the right to be passive and perseverative), but . . . social circumstances tend to frustrate women who use too cautious a strategy. If Julia is to be happy in a two-career marriage, she will need to tolerate disorder. For Sally to avert depression, it is required that she ask men to dance—that she have a more extroverted temperament. A degree of introversion that might have been rewarded in a different social climate here leads only to deprivation, disappointment, and depression.

Compared to the Victorians, modern women do not have more freedom, just a different kind of freedom. They have a briefcase full of economic and legal rights, but they have lost the right to be women on Victorian terms and to be admired or rewarded for it. We should not be fooled into thinking that women can have it all when old choices have been swept away like discontinued merchandise. While none of us would want to trade places with those who couldn't vote or own property, gaining the right to crash men's-only clubs does not seem like a very good trade-off for giving up the right to be feminine. We never got to vote on the trashing of values that not only empowered women but made them the nation's moral arbiters.

Suzanne Gordon documented the cultural and personal fallout from this loss in her 1991 book *Prisoners of Men's Dreams*. These "prisoners" of male standards were professional women who had learned not to care about coworkers, friends, or family members. These women had adopted the compulsory detached and aggressive attitude of the male-oriented marketplace, which denigrates traditional nurturing feminine qualities. "Over and over again," Gordon writes, "whether they are single or married, with children or without, women

This engraving from Harper's Weekly, *November 5, 1887, is an example of the type of courtesy Victorian women experienced as a matter of course.*

say they can't find enough time for their close relationships, or even for civility—the small gestures of politeness or neighborliness that have always been nurtured primarily by women." Now these "success-ful" women lack the time "to support and sustain one another emo-tionally, as well as to do the work that kept communities together."

At the turn of the century, Jane Addams summarized this lost sentiment that inspired her labors, and those of many other female reformers: "Woman is responsible for the gentler side of life, which softens and blurs some of its harsher conditions" (as quoted in *Jane Addams: A Centennial Reader* by Emily Cooper Johnson). Similarly, in her 1889 memoir, *Glimpses of Fifty Years*, Frances Willard described a "cardinal doctrine of my creed" when she said "the woman['s] touch is to brighten every nook and corner of the earth."

FEMININE ROLE MODELS

Women like Willard and Addams would see the problems revealed by Gordon's research as involving much more than a time crunch. Women, especially prominent ones, must be civil before they can civ-ilize. But many of our role models have chucked the female standards of civility that were once a secular religion. Julia Ward Howe paid her sister suffragist Lucy Stone a high compliment when she said that Stone's actions were "always guided by her faultless feeling of propri-ety." In contrast, in a 1993 *Ms.* magazine roundtable article, Gloria Steinem called mannerly women "female impersonators."

Yet even in pursuing what belonged to men—like the right to vote—Victorian women continued to insist on being womanly. When Susan B. Anthony rented public halls for suffrage meetings, she insisted that the "mannish" appearance of the room be transformed with "ladylike" touches, such as flowers. Julia Ward Howe's daughter recounted the many long train rides to campaign for suffrage, on which Mrs. Howe and her fellow workers always brought all the accoutrements they needed to prepare the consummate civilized rit-ual: afternoon tea.

Nice as Vice
Modern feminists would still be chasing the ballot without the efforts of these ultraproper, flower-loving tea drinkers, who softened the

world's harsh edges. Yet they continue to heap contempt on Victorians who had the restrictive social training to be "ladies." Now women are told they can be anything but the dreaded L-word. Female college basketball teams have even begun removing "lady" from their nicknames, which traditionally distinguished them from their male counterparts. In *Fire with Fire*, Naomi Wolf counsels her would-be sisters to "cast off the lace nets of our niceness." The journalist Elizabeth Hilts, author of a book entitled *Getting in Touch with Your Inner Bitch*, believes that "toxic niceness"—putting other people's needs first—foils a woman's happiness. She found her happiness by getting de-toxed. Now a confirmed "bitch," she says, "I don't back down from what I believe in or apologize for saying what I think."

To the Victorians, behaving like a female dog was considered toxic to both personal happiness and social civility. But times change. Now this philosophy is emblazoned on T-shirts sporting the slogan, THAT'S MS. BITCH TO YOU. One mail-order catalog promises that buying this less-than-subtle fashion statement "ensures that you get your due respect! Let all misinformed males know that you have a title to uphold." Such bold demands may seem on the surface to be empowering. Instead, they are not only ineffective but serve to lower women to the status of a barking hound or yapping poodle, easily dismissed as an object of contempt.

Feminine Power

Victorian women embraced the distinctly feminine qualities that society deemed anything but frivolous. Being exemplars and ennoblers of public and private conduct was widely viewed as their choice, their God-given right, and an awesome responsibility that rivaled any man's. "As women are, so will the whole nation be," wrote Eliza Duffey in 1876. And so we slide toward the sewer via the masculine vulgarity of the gutter that has become commonplace. Leading us there are new feminist "role models": the unennobling likes of Madonna, the queen of in-your-face sexuality, and Roseanne, who considers obnoxiousness a badge of female power.

Current conventional wisdom once again allows us to condemn the growing coarseness that corrodes civility. But we tread on sexist landmines by suggesting that women who embrace the male weapons of aggressive rudeness and selfishness denigrate themselves and bring society to even lower levels of civility. Woe to anyone who believes, as Thomas Nelson Page wrote in his 1911 essay "On the Decay of Manners": "Women make both the manners and the morals of a people. Neither rises higher than the gauge which women set in a community. . . . Where a woman has bad manners, it always has in it an element of vulgarity which is more painful than it could be in a man. . . . The result will be a society hopelessly vulgarized . . . with no end but to sink in an ever deeper abyss of vulgarity."

Now that women have resigned themselves to acting like one of the boys, they have unknowingly brought men to record low levels of masculine coarseness. Sadly, the most hard-hit victims of the new male incivility are women themselves.

Men II Boyz

"Boys will be boys." With a shrug and that abhorred excuse, too many Americans dismiss a smorgasbord of abuses against girls and women. . . . A 1994 *New York Times* editorial denouncing young males in public swimming pools who surround girls to fondle them and rip off their bathing suits—called "whirlpooling" by some—quoted local citizens who resorted to that familiar if outrageous excuse for despicable male behavior: Boys will be boys. News reports show that citizens also cited the "boys" mantra to excuse the horrendous results of a 1992 nationwide study cosponsored by Wellesley College and the NOW Legal Defense and Education Fund. The study revealed that a staggering 89 percent of girls in elementary and secondary schools were subjected to demeaning sexual comments or gestures. Nearly as many said they had been touched or grabbed—a far and frantic cry from the days when "bad boys" dipped girls' pigtails in inkwells. If girls survive the gauntlet at school, they run into another one at work. Three out of five women executives have experienced sexual harassment in the workplace, according to a recent UCLA survey.[1]

MALE VIOLENCE IN AMERICA

Feminists widely believe that such boys have been around since the cavemen and that patriarchy is to blame for men's abominable behavior throughout history. As Gloria Steinem put it in her book *Revolution from Within*, "Patriarchy requires violence or the subliminal threat of violence in order to maintain itself." On PBS's prestigious *NewsHour*, the former Carter administration foreign policy official Patricia Derrian stated flatly that women have always been battered; the twentieth century just hid the abuse via a "gentlemen's agreement." Some gentlemen!

Feminists aren't shooting off their mouths when they rail about the physical and sexual abuse of modern women. According to the American Medical Association, two million women are battered each year. A scary 1994 survey by *Esquire* magazine found that a majority of college males would commit rape if they could get away with it. The Justice Department estimates that 160,000 rapes occurred in 1993. While others believe the actual number far surpasses this official figure, most experts agree that the "silent epidemic" of violence against women is drastically underreported to legal authorities.[2]

The problem is all too real. Yet those who attribute it to unchanging human nature or social relations do a disservice to our heritage. They blind us to the real reasons so many boys and men act like beasts, and to the best means to civilize them. The first major fallacy is that the true character of "boys" is to be cruel, selfish, and disrespectful. This is a myth that needs debunking.

The saying "Boys will be boys" originated in the 1849 novel *The Caxtons* by the once-popular English author Edward Bulwer-Lytton. In the book, a father says this in reference to his son's extravagance and gambling debts. The comment had no connection to sexual abuse or any form of violence against women, a connotation added in the twentieth century. While this etiological tidbit may seem trifling, it reminds us that the predatory image of "boys" is strictly a modern one. The Victorians could not revere women as they did and "wink away" crimes against them. On the contrary, such criminals felt the hard hand of justice in two courts—the community and the law.

Writing about rape in *Democracy in America* (1835), Alexis de Tocqueville said, "No other crime is judged with the same inexorable severity by public opinion . . . as Americans think nothing more precious than a woman's honor and nothing deserving more respect than her freedom; they think no punishment too severe for those who take both against her will." If patriarchy or the quest to maintain it causes rape, then the supremely sexist nineteenth century should have been a rapist's paradise. Instead, rape was his passage to prison or the gallows. Until the enlightened 1960s, rape was one of the few violent crimes besides murder that merited capital punishment, a tradition America adapted from English common law.

The Myth of Patriarchal Violence

The one-size-fits-all patriarchy theory is especially ill fitted to the present day. The rape rate in America is four times higher than Germany's,[3] thirteen times higher than England's, and twenty times higher than Japan's. These rates reflect the comparatively low levels of all violent crimes in these countries.[4] Cathy Young, whose findings on global patterns of rape and domestic abuse appear in her book *Gender Wars*, wrote:

> There are undoubtedly men who enjoy hurting women because they hate them. But in many countries far more male-dominated than ours (Japan or Israel), women run far lower risks of victimization. The "backlash" explanation— men use force to reclaim power when their traditional supremacy is eroded—doesn't hold. "Liberated" Sweden also has far less male-on-female violence. What all these societies have in common is dramatically lower rates of violence in general.

The Myth of Violent Victorian Men

The historian Elizabeth Pleck of the University of Michigan has studied wife beating in Victorian America. Her analysis of court decisions, state statutes, and other related documents revealed that no "gentlemen's agreement" protected wife beaters. Pleck also debunked the myth that a man could legally assault his spouse if he used a stick or whip no wider than his thumb.[5]

Pleck found that wife beating was illegal in most states by the 1870s. Even in states where specific laws did not address this crime, husbands were arrested on assault charges. Convictions brought heavy fines, imprisonment, or the poetic justice of a whipping. Far from encouraging violence, the sexism of Victorian men protected the "weaker sex." Men's physical advantage, which we still can't legislate away, brought a moral obligation to guard the "weak," not an entitlement to exploit them.

Aside from concrete legal sanctions, Pleck found that women were shielded by "vigorous and extensive" informal networks of friends, relations, and concerned community members. There was a strong "male prerogative to discipline other men." Thus, men in the community frequently flogged men who ignored their warnings or were merely suspected of beating their wives.

Then as now, most abusers were poor or working class. The severity of this problem in saloon-filled slums figured prominently in the Prohibition movement. Many female crusaders, including those who knew and aided victims by working in urban settlement houses and missions, described a causal chain that still holds firm. Drunken men often beat and raped their wives. (Contrary to contemporary stereotypes, middle- and upper-class Victorians believed nonconsensual marital sex was rape.) In every century, a cocktail of alcohol and men could be toxic to women.

Spousal battering was so unthinkable in civilized circles that marriage manuals and etiquette books had no need to mention it. Now public service ads must actually tell women that a man who loves you doesn't beat you. Men used to be stigmatized as brutes, bounders, or worse for what now seem like ridiculously trivial infractions against women. For example, if a male dinner guest failed to bow his head to the lady of the house when raising his first glass of wine at the table, he was deemed rude (the Victorian kiss of death) and would not receive another invitation. Other men—not lawsuits, sensitivity classes, or chanting demonstrations—put the fiercest punch in such stigmas. In the Victorian version of the "big chill," men ostracized the offender from social activities and their sacred clubs, or even refused to do business with him. Duels were fought over insults to ladies that today would not raise an eyebrow—his, or hers.

Just threatening to mistreat women could severely wound a man's career and reputation. The autocratic General Benjamin "Beast" Butler, who became military governor in New Orleans when it was captured by the Union army in 1862, aroused outrage when he issued an order that all women who showed disrespect for the Union flag or Union soldiers would be treated like prostitutes. President Lincoln promptly recalled him.

THE VICTORIAN MALE

To understand the depth of the Victorians' indignation over General Butler's attitude, we must understand the Victorian concept of manhood. The Victorians assumed that all males aspired to be heroic. The influential *Godey's Lady's Book* editor Sarah Josepha Hale claimed in 1873 that "the true hero worships God and honors women" (quoted in Ruth E. Finley's 1931 biography of Hale). Women were the core of the social religion that raised man to the civilized peak of his potential—the gentleman. Modern males rely on faddish movements, marches, and mountains of conflicting how-to books to define themselves. The Victorians had a single ideal of manhood, whose embodiment was the gentleman and whose essence lay in being masculine without being macho.

A Gentle Man

The gentleman, as Hale wrote in her 1868 book *Manners*, was first and foremost a "gentle man." She portrayed a gentleman's balanced character: He was "respectful but not groveling to his superiors, tender and considerate to inferiors, and helpful and protecting to the weak."

According to *Arthur Martine's Hand-book of Etiquette* (1866), a gentleman possessed "a high sense of honor—a determination never to take a mean advantage of others—an adherence to truth, delicacy, and politeness" toward all. As Mrs. Humphrey's 1897 *Manners for Men* put it, the Victorian male was "dependable in trifles as well as the large affairs of life." He was fearless but God-fearing, had "self-possession, a gentle manner," and gave constant attention to "the needs and desires of others before his own." And of course, as sure as he drew breath—or deserved to—the gentleman "is always respectful to women."

The constant coupling of manhood with words like *gentle, tender,* and *delicate* may sound effeminate to our ears—which is precisely what they were. The ideal Victorian male was neither a sissy nor a chest-pounding ape but the integrated creature that conflicted modern men claim they want to be. One of the century's Renaissance men, the great English critic and reformer John Ruskin stated his belief that a true gentleman combined "the strength of manhood with the delicacy of womanhood."

Many other writers of that sexually unthreatened era echoed these sentiments, and not just those who penned the rules of politeness for a living. In 1897 a prominent American physician and clergyman, Rev. Sylvanus Stall, said, "In the higher type of man the best and highest feminine characteristics have been fused with the best and highest masculine characteristics. The fighting instinct, for instance, has become moral courage." Ruskin also saw the distinctly feminine features of true manhood:

A gentleman's first characteristic is that fineness of structure in the body, which renders it capable of the most delicate sensation, and of that structure in the mind which renders it capable of the most delicate sympathies—one may say, simply "fineness of nature." This, of course, is compatible with heroic bodily strength and mental firmness; in fact, heroic strength is not conceivable without such delicacy.[6]

Take that, Iron John!

We've come a long way, baby, since women and "womanly qualities" were essential to defining manhood. Neither sex gained much from the journey. Women lost an incalculable power, and gentlemen devolved into mere men who grew increasingly rough around the edges. The currently prevalent image—with some roots in fact—of men as violent, selfish, commitment-phobic boors feeds conservative nostalgia for the 1950s corporate drone in a gray flannel suit who obeyed the law and supported his family. While he may have scored low on the warmth and personality meter, he was a dependable provider. But he was no Victorian gentleman.

His narrow scope of obligations began and ended with paying the family bills. And his sense of manhood—if one existed beyond his bank account and job description—had no social or spiritual connection to how well he treated women.

THE SEVENTIES SENSITIVE MALE

Since that "golden age" of the fifties, we have sampled enough brands of ideal men to fill the aisles of a Wal-Mart. The "sensitive" seventies male may seem Victorian at first glance, but as many women came to learn, he was more likely to be a glib, unprincipled wolf in sheep's clothing who schemed to get women out of theirs.

Sensitivity still "plays" for some men, whether they try to score with women or the legal system. One modern marshmallow recently sued the city of San Diego, California, for the "emotional trauma" he suffered at a Billy Joel concert when women grew tired of waiting in rest-room lines and boldly used the men's facilities. The presence of these anatomical aliens in plain sight of urinals was simply too traumatic to bear without financial compensation. Victorian men, who would have held their breath and a lot more to accommodate needy "ladies first," would have promptly flushed away this insult to their sex with all the other refuse.

The rebellious toughs of the 1980s proclaimed, "Real Men Don't Eat Quiche." Real men would never buy in to such slogans. The hodgepodge called the men's movement—a women's movement wannabe—helped men get in touch with their feelings but no one else's. Men are certainly entitled to explore their feelings, but did this emotional masturbation satisfy their "needs"? Not according to Bill Geist, a CBS news correspondent and the author of *Monster Trucks and Hair in a Can*. Geist calls men "dispirited. We've lost track of whether we're supposed to be acting more manly or more sensitive." Victorian men knew how to be both.

There are a few hopeful signs that men are recovering a sense of manhood that incorporates some of the Victorian ideals. The latest masculine flavors of the month are million-man marches and stadiums filled with Promise Keepers pledging to honor God and their family duties. Few would fault these intentions. Yet pledges, like diets, are easily made and broken in an era where only uncertainty is certain and the one constant is change. In 1962, Bob Dylan asked, "How many roads must a man walk down before you call him a man?" The answer is still "blowing in the wind."

The Ghetto "Man"

Ironically, today's only coherent concept of manhood—one that inverts and perverts everything Victorian—exists in inner-city ghettos. The renowned African-American scholar Elijah Anderson and the *Washingon Post* journalist Leon Dash have written painfully eloquent first-hand accounts of the rampant conscienceless brutality and crime committed by young men and boys with no respect for life, least of all their own.

In this Darwinian environment, the weak, including women and children, are not protected but routinely exploited. Manhood is still defined by females—but only in terms of how badly they are treated. Males gain status from their peers by publicly demeaning their mate of the moment. In his book *Streetwise,* Dr. Anderson describes an endless game of "hit and run" sex, where guys bed, impregnate, and abandon as many girls as possible, who are left with no hope of child support. These nominal fathers show up on "mother's day" to claim their share of welfare checks.

ADDRESSING MALE VIOLENCE AND HARASSMENT

Meanwhile, feminists urge women to fight for their rights, spurning any assistance from the "enemy," and they have even won a few lawsuits. But the victories often ring hollow in absence of social repercussions for vile male behavior. In 1995 the U.S. Equal Employment Opportunity Commission negotiated a record sexual harassment suit in which one million dollars was paid to fifteen female employees who had been fondled and otherwise assaulted by Dan K. Wassong, the chairman and president of Dell Laboratories. Although the male-dominated company agreed to institute mandatory sensitivity sessions, it added insult to assault by declining to fire Wassong. Apparently the impressive profits he earned during his twenty-year tenure at Dell carried more weight than his outrages against women. Before the advent of imposed sensitivity classes, Victorian males, sensitized by an entire culture of principles that honored women, would have boycotted the offender into professional and social oblivion.[7]

While this upscale barbarian was still enjoying his private-sector perks, four men in upstate New York were convicted of raping an unconscious woman. Their penalty? A plea-bargained misdemeanor charge and a $750 fine. You could get a stiffer sentence for kicking the family dog. The rapists were indicted on more serious charges only after women's groups protested.[8] But where were the indignant men? They may not wield canes or horsewhips anymore, but they still have mouths that might administer verbal lashings. Unfortunately, men's very free speech is more likely to offend women than to defend them these days.

What is worse, few women even expect male support on moral grounds anymore. In place of this lost power and privilege that women once enjoyed, they now have to fight for respect, resorting to the law to protect them from sexual harassment. But rather than concentrating on lawsuits designed to force men to show common courtesy to women, we should be asking ourselves: Is a civilized society possible when even nonviolent men have little moral stake in protecting the physical integrity of women?.

Where the Boys Are and the Men Aren't

A glaring example of modern men at their apathetic worst is the O. J. Simpson case. Quite apart from his double-murder charge and acquittal, Simpson was an acknowledged batterer. (He subsequently testified that his ex-wife's photographed bruises were self-inflicted. But that is another horror story.) Nicole Brown could have been any man's daughter, sister, or neighbor, yet after Simpson was sentenced to attend group therapy sessions to deal with his violence, he did not lose a single job as an actor, sportscaster, or company spokesman. When he decided to skip the therapy altogether, no judge or policeman enforced the sentence.

In a desperate effort to promote the kind of ostracism Victorian men would have imposed on Simpson, women's groups protested in front of the Los Angeles courthouse, carrying signs that reminded the nation he was "100 percent guilty of wife beating." In October 1995, a male reporter who was covering the demonstration was seen on the news asking the women what right they had to punish Simpson more than the legal system; he neglected to question the justice of a system that failed to punish Simpson for hitting his wife.[9]

Even before the verdict, a Columbia University professor wrote an article for *The New York Times,* entitled "The Morals of Marketing Simpson," in which he speculated on how the trial's outcome would affect the defendant's value as an advertising pitchman. Simpson's chief attorney, Johnnie Cochran, was just being a savvy (if swinish) lawyer when he sloughed off his client's 1989 spousal abuse conviction by telling the jury, "None of us is perfect." (Cochran should know, since his first wife also accused him of assaulting her.) But the good professor's article never even mentioned the abuse. Apparently, it passed beneath the threshold of his moral radar.

If patriarchy is a neat and tempting culprit for this drama of disgraceful actions and reactions, it is also a moribund institution that is as powerless as feminists to explain the rampant mistreatment of women. The problem is not men but modern men and their morally criminal contempt for the women those Victorian patriarchs protected and revered. This self-serving contempt even masks itself with makeshift morality, as we saw at George Washington University in 1995. A highly touted high school basketball star who had pleaded guilty to forcing a fifteen-year-old girl to perform oral sex and had been sentenced to a year's probation was given a full scholarship by the university. The school's male president, Stephen Joel Trachtenberg, justified this as part of its "mission to reclaim lost jewels." When questioned about his star recruit's brutal act, Trachtenberg replied, "I have neither the authority nor the inclination to try to impose my own morality on others." When a public outcry arose, the president tried the less-than-Solomonic compromise of offering a scholarship to the victim as well.

This mentality prevails from the halls of academe to the corridors of power. In 1995 a long overdue investigation by the Senate Ethics Committee documented a disturbing pattern of sexual advances by Republican Bob Packwood against his female staff. When asked to comment on the Packwood case, the Christian Coalition head Ralph Reed said it wasn't proper "to engage in witch-hunts of public officials based on personal or private behavior."[10] Just when are such hunts proper? When the sins are committed by liberals and other political opponents? If all private behavior is off limits to scrutiny, so are rape and wife beating, not to mention abortion. Either Ralph Reed needs a new Bible or I need a new religion.

Even seemingly innocent remarks by conservative politicians betray an anti-Victorian disdain for women that feels like a back-handed slap instead of a frontal assault. When *The CBS Evening News* profiled the Republican senator Richard Lugar during the 1996 presidential primary season, this upright, buttoned-down family man named *Animal House* as his favorite movie.[11] The brothers of this frat house showed as much regard for females as for the beer cans they crushed on their heads. They ogled naked coeds through dorm windows, bedded the dean's sex-starved wife, and left a passed-out underaged girl in a shopping cart on her parents' doorstep after a bacchanalian toga party. All in good fun, of course. Just a comedy. Boys will be boys.

High government officials routinely shrug at the abuse of women and even young girls. In 1995 the admiral who commanded all U.S. forces in the Pacific said three U.S. servicemen accused of raping a twelve-year-old Japanese girl in Okinawa could have hired a prostitute for the cost of the rental car where the crime was committed. Yes, and they could also have shown respect to women by not treating any woman or girl like an object for their use and abuse.[12]

And let us not slight former congressman Bob Dorman (R-California), a chief sponsor of the Defense of Marriage Act, which would allow states to refuse to recognize same-sex marriages. This advocate of family values has been charged by his wife with having "choked, struck, kicked, attacked, and harassed" her, according to documents filed in court.[13]

Our chivalrous national leaders had another chance to shine after the O. J. Simpson trial. *The Washington Post* noted that politicians on both sides of the aisle were reluctant to speak about the verdict for fear of inflaming racial tensions. They could have accepted the verdict, or even proclaimed Simpson's innocence, while still speaking up about domestic abuse. Aren't raped and battered women worth that much heat?

Politicians denounce crime with every breath, but none bothered to ask how men like Simpson can commit serious crimes against women without serving time. When we compare the legal and social penalties they would have paid a hundred years ago, can we doubt how much women have been devalued since then? Will national summits on domestic violence change that? (Simpson was acquitted during Domestic Violence Awareness Month.) The Navy developed a strict and comprehensive handbook on sexual behavior after women were assaulted at the 1991 Tailhook Convention. Yet outside experts doubted it would change the Navy's "ingrained contempt" for women. Meetings and manuals can only skim the surface; nothing runs deeper than contempt.

Shortly after the Simpson trial, Hillary Clinton went on television to urge everyone to participate in a Week Without Violence. This well-intentioned but futile gesture reminded me of the childhood pledge to give up sweets for Lent. What happens when this civilized week expires? Do we congratulate ourselves, then go back to battery as usual? We could build more rape crisis centers and battered women's shelters, as mainline feminists regularly demand. We could fund an infinite variety of after-the-fact Band-Aid measures, like the pilot program in New York City that lends cellular phones and pendant alarms to domestic violence victims fearful of future attacks.

Women Fighting Back

Alternatively, we could follow the increasingly popular practice of fighting fire with fire. These days Hollywood gives us an endless stream of tougher-than-thou role models, from Linda Hamilton's militant mom in *Terminator II* and Sigourney Weaver's warrior queen in *Alien* to the latest Thelma-and-Louise wannabe in a low budget made-for-TV movie. In real life, women are told to become more aggressive even as they demand that men become more sensitive. Millions of women are enrolling in martial arts classes and packing pistols. It may be a sign of these well-armed times that the National Rifle Association recently elected its first female president.

Those who remain too timid to karate-chop their assailants like a stack of boards, or blow a few holes in their egos and elsewhere, can resort to pepper sprays, stun guns, ear-splitting alarms, or plain old dime-store whistles, if pricier survival tools strain the budget. A farsighted woman with the means to splurge can even deter assailants with the aid of Safe-T-Man. For $99.95, plus $34.95 for his tote bag, you too can own a life-size blow-up doll to place in the passenger seat of your car to ward off would-be attackers. Since the genuine article is apparently too scarce or threatening, "independent" women must settle for a factory-model male. (With a little creative anatomical redesigning, he could do double duty as a lover, thus giving customers twice the "man" for their money.)

Safe-T-Man may fool a few gullible strangers, but the biggest fools are women who believe a bogus escort will offset the modern disadvantage of being the physically weaker sex. Life is not a round of golf. One way or another, crime takes a psychic toll on women. We live behind locked doors, choose a home in a remote but safe neighborhood, wait an eternity for a populated elevator instead of chancing a ride with a suspicious-looking male. If women can't feel safe at home, on a date, or walking on city streets, will they ever feel safe enough to "let go" in their romantic lives?

In this aggressively "liberated" age, it is far easier for a woman to act like a man than to find a man who makes her feel like a woman. The testosterone mind-set seems to be her only reliable security blanket. As Roseanne, the passive-aggressive patron saint of victims, was quoted in a July 1995 issue of the *New Yorker*, "Women should be more violent, kill more of their husbands." Compared to Roseanne's call for vigilante homicide, NOW's form of redress wears white gloves: The organization is currently seeking "test cases" for the 1994 Violence Against Women Act, which entitles victims of gender-specific violence—rape, battery, and assault—to sue assailants for financial restitution. But both throw in the towel on any hopes of reviving mutual respect and social civility.

Even when women "win," they lose by accepting the rules of a man's world. Civility takes a beating, whether the fight is physical, verbal, or legal. Why do we expect so little from men? Why can't women demand—better yet, assume—that men will discipline their own, as the Victorians did? Would we really halt the abuse of women or any other crimes by arming ourselves with guns and the itch to use them? Or do we just stoke the boiler? We should know by now that the brinkmanship of uncivilized behavior will never cure incivility.

The masculinizing of female behavior has resulted in the feminizing of violence and consequently our prison population. According to the National Center for Juvenile Justice, female arrests for robberies, assaults, and other violent crimes rose 23 percent between 1989 and 1993, and male arrests increased by 11 percent during the same period.[14] Recently, the Fairfax County, Virginia, juvenile court judge Jane P. Delbridge expressed surprise at the blatant defiance girls show to their families and the law. "Women wanted equality," she said. "Okay, now they're getting the handcuffs as quick as the men."[5]

Is this the sort of equality that advances the status of women? One probation counselor called this "a major emerging crisis." In Boston alone, girls now account for one in six arrests, but the tentacles of this trend reach beyond our inner cities. In Arlington, a "safe" Virginia suburb, juvenile court judge Joanne F. Alper reported, "There have been days when more than half the kids coming into my courtroom charged with crimes are girls. We've always seen girls not getting along (and lashing out against) siblings and parents, but what's surprised me is the increase in criminal activity the girls are now involved in outside the family circle."[16]

Video games provide a fertile training ground for females who want to kick butt just like the boys do. Game counselors who field calls for Sega and Nintendo say girls now account for 35 to 50 percent of the phone traffic, up from 10 percent just a few years ago. Rejecting the more sedate games that were developed for them, young girls are playing Killer Instinct, Virtual Fighter, and the Metroid trilogy. All feature Rambo-sized female war machines whose only "feminine" feature is their exaggerated breasts. Is this equal-opportunity violence what we want for our young women?

ENDING THE VIOLENCE

A national women's health group sells a BREAK THE SILENCE T-shirt, subtitled "Stop Violence Against Women." Yet there is no silence to break through anymore. Raped and battered women fill our headlines, movie screens, and TV talk shows. Every facet of this tragic fact of life has been graphically explored, especially since the murder of Nicole Brown Simpson. The phone numbers of crisis hotlines and other recovery programs for victims dot the information boards of libraries, schools, and grocery stores. And the "silence" is routinely shattered by widespread "take back the night" marches on college campuses.

The only silence that still requires breaking is the historical record. The fact is that in the nineteenth century, women did not fear such outrages because they insisted that men treat them with the utmost respect. Ladies set the standards of behavior and did not compromise them, or themselves. Individual women did not have to arm themselves to the teeth or practice martial arts to ensure their safety when all women were accorded respect.

We need to reacquaint ourselves with the idea that safety and respect for women can be more than a wishful slogan on a placard. Oppressed Victorian women had a freedom that we lack—freedom from the fear that anything in trousers was ready to spring like a panther. Even male strangers were regarded with a trust we can scarcely imagine. In her 1898 memoir, *Eighty Years and More*, Elizabeth Cady Stanton remarked that all women and girls could travel throughout America "with perfect civility and safety." Nearly a half century earlier, the educational reformer Catharine Beecher wrote in her book *Letters to the People on Health and Happiness*:

> There are few that have so much occasion as myself to render a grateful acknowledgement of this most chivalrous virtue in my countrymen; for during the last period of my life I have crossed from West to East, or from East to West, not less than thirty times, and have traveled in all Free States and five of the Southern; in all this varied experience—alone. I have never once known a coarse or disrespectful word or act toward myself, or witnessed one toward any other woman.

Even one of this country's harshest critics, Charles Dickens, gave chivalrous credit where it was due. In his famous *American Notes*, published in 1842, he looked down his very British nose at our speech, our clothes, and our manners. Yet he conceded that "any lady may travel alone, from one end of the United States to the other, and be certain of the most courteous and considerate treatment everywhere. . . . If a lady take a fancy to any male passenger's seat, the gentleman who accompanies her gives him notice of the fact, and he immediately vacates it with great politeness."

Perhaps a civilized society can dispense with the female prerogative for a seat on a crowded bus. But it absolutely cannot dispense with the masculine sentiment that once offered it, and allowed women to have a freedom of movement that we so envy today. If women are to regain their freedom, they must reclaim their power. They must demand that men treat them with respect.

PART 2

A SENSIBILITY
THAT
MAKES SENSE

6

The Benevolence of Manners

"There is no fundamental difference between man and the higher animals in their mental qualities," wrote Charles Darwin in his 1859 book *The Origin of Species*. Regardless of whether they rejected the theory of evolution outright as a godless doctrine, certainly on the whole the Victorians believed it was the duty and challenge of mankind to rise triumphantly from the primordial sludge. While our own age celebrates man's animalistic nature, the Victorians looked to manners, morality, and chivalry to humanize nature's most brutal law—survival of the fittest.

RISING ABOVE OUR NATURE

In 1877 the popular etiquette author Eliza Duffey aptly summarized her generation's frame of mind:

> Civilization . . . calls us out of the natural state in which we are most nearly allied to the brutes, and in which self-ish interests alone predominate, and places us in a condition where we may recognize ourselves as belonging to a common humanity, and in which the best good of each is

subserved by permitting many "natural" rights of individuals to be subordinated to the interests of all.

Nature teaches two savages to approach each other as enemies. Each, suspicious of the hostile intent of the other, maintains a natural right to kill that other in self-defense. Civilization teaches each man to respect the right of the other to live, and to refrain from killing him in the hope and expectation that the other will be equally considerate.

By this definition, we certainly have gotten back to nature. The Victorians would say we have regressed rather than evolved. In contrast to today's vague calls for civility, which leave us stranded in the wilderness without a road map, the Victorians' well-marked connection between social theory and personal practice gave strength and sparkle to both:

> Civilization has its laws, civil, religious and social, binding upon the community. Etiquette may be considered as the by-laws of civilization, binding upon each individual in the community. Arbitrary as many of these laws may seem, they are all founded upon some good and sufficient reason, and all intended to make our manners as agreeable and inoffensive as possible to people of refined and delicate tastes—those people, in fact, who have furthest escaped from the state of savagery natural to the [human] race.

The Victorians were proud, not ashamed, of being refined. To us, the blood and guts of savagery may be "real," but so are the deadly diseases we try to cure. You don't have to be a pinkie-crooking tea drinker to see why we need a little less "reality" and a little more refinement for both civility and survival. As Katharine Hepburn told Humphrey Bogart in *The African Queen*, "Nature, Mr. Alnutt, is something we were put on this earth to rise above."

The little courtesies that Ralph Waldo Emerson called "minor morals" were anything but minor. "The power of manners is incessant," he wrote. "It is the beginning of civility—to make us, I mean, endurable to each other . . . to get people out of the quadruped state; to get them washed, clothed, and set up on end.'" (The back-to-nature Woodstock generation retreated big time on this score. In retrospect, the mud that covered Yasgur's farm that weekend looks metaphorically appropriate.) Grace Dodge, president of the YWCA, wrote "Good manners are made up of little things, that taken separately seem very insignificant, but put together make up a very large whole."[2]

BEHIND THE DETAILS OF VICTORIAN MANNERS

The exhaustively extensive system of Victorian major and minor morals—which made life not just endurable but enjoyable—is legendary. From the prescribed way for a lady to treat a shop clerk to the equestrian rules of the road, all the rules of etiquette shared a logical thread: protection of the weak from physical or verbal exploitation. The rules of the Victorian road may seem overly detailed to us, but the powerful social stigma of breaking such rules served as an effective deterrent to antisocial behavior. With so many dos and don'ts, nineteenth-century Americans knew what to expect in social situations and didn't have to invent etiquette on the spot.

To navigate the complex terrain of Victorian manners required a detailed map as well as a compass. As Eliza Duffey noted in 1877, "Good sense and good nature suggest civility in general, but . . . there are a thousand little delicacies which are established only by custom."[3] But it was precisely these fine points of politeness, the "forms, ceremonies, and rules" that we have abandoned, which "establish and enforce . . . the regulation of the manners of men and women in their intercourse with each other." To the Victorians all this was deadly serious business. For example, ladies would grow apoplectic at the no-show guests we routinely endure with a frustrated shrug. In 1890 the bon vivant Ward McAllister wrote, "A dinner invitation, once accepted, is a sacred obligation. If you die before the dinner takes place, your executor must attend." He may have been joking, but only by half.[4]

WHEN ETIQUETTE IS DISMISSED

Of course, we don't have such courtesy crises anymore. Or do we? On a New York subway, one enraged rider slashed a woman's face with a boxcutter when the offender bumped into her and failed to apologize. A somewhat more sublimated example concerns the high-

ABOVE AND FOLLOWING PAGE: *These two "do" and "don't" engravings capture some of the specific rules of Victorian parlor behavior. The etiquette errors consist of (1) standing in the ungainly posture of hands on hips, (2) leaning forward in a chair, (3) sitting backward on a chair, (4) leaning against the wall and casually eating, (5) placing one's foot on a chair cushion, and (6) the three-fold error of tipping a chair, leaning one's head against the wall, and smoking in the presence of ladies.*

profile flap that erupted over an alleged presidential snub. House Speaker Newt Gingrich complained that during a long Air Force One flight back from a state funeral, Bill Clinton failed to invite him up to the front of the plane to discuss the budget crisis. Gingrich also had to use the plane's backdoor, while other officials exited through the front with the president. Journalists, pundits, and politicians cited this incident as an example of Gingrich's pettiness and complained that Newt's personal pique had stalled negotiations over the federal budget deficit. Amid all the finger pointing, no one suggested putting the issue of our national manners deficit on the table.

I received a first-hand lesson in the depleted value of this commodity—manners—during a recent visit to Washington, D.C.'s largest bookstore. In the midst of this bibliophilic extravaganza, the few books I found under the ETIQUETTE sign were bottom-shelf crumbs lying beneath the wedding planners. The sprawling children's section offered nothing on manners but an apologetic clerk. (I did, however, note an ample number of children's books on the subject of sex.)

Generation X–ers may find it difficult to imagine a time when pornography was sold under the counter and guides to good manners dominated the bookshelves. Etiquette manuals were so plentiful during the nineteenth century that one historian, John Kasson, called them "a major popular literary genre." Country peddlers and city department stores sold them in abundance, as did the twin giants of the burgeoning mail-order business, Sears Roebuck and Montgomery Ward.

Because learning good manners was the main Victorian route to self-improvement, the maxims in these books had the force of law— and more. "For instance, the law cannot punish a man for habitually staring at people in an insolent and annoying manner," said one self-proclaimed *Guide to True Politeness* published in 1866, "but etiquette can banish such an offender from the circles of good society, and fix upon him the brand of vulgarity." The recovery of civility depends upon reviving the stigma once attached to vulgarity and ranking it as high as "sexist" or "racist" on the scale of social and professional taboos.

CHIVALRY

But the crux of morality, civility, and the nicest of niceties—what we reduced to the phrase "gender relations"—was how well men treated women. Every advice manual on marriage, manners, or raising children contained the idea that a nation was judged by its citizens' attitude toward women. Even the era's robber barons, those ruthless Darwinian kings of the marketplace jungle, were servants to this sentiment. The English novelist Sir Walter Scott voiced the law of this land when he said that without chivalry—the high-minded and courteous treatment of women—"it would be difficult to conceive the existence of virtue among the human race. It is not what women do for themselves, but what men do for women that marks the true greatness of a people, and their real progress in Christian civilization."[5]

Can we conceive of measuring this nation's progress, no less its greatness, by what men do for women? All we do today is lament what men do *to* women. In the last century entire books were written on the daily courtesies men owed to women. Should we ridicule—or envy—the unquestioned female rights to chairs of choice, decent language, assistance into a carriage, a smoke-free environment, and countless other "ladies' first" privileges?

In the broadest sense, the superior strength of men entitled them to serve, not to be served. Chivalry required that men not only live for women but die for them as well. Chivalry's historic culmination—and its finale—actually occurred eleven years after the Victorian era officially ended. Yet that event was quintessentially Victorian in spirit.

Everyone knows the story of that fateful April night in 1912 when the "unsinkable" *Titanic* struck an iceberg in the North Atlantic. As Wyn Craig Wade recounted in his book *The Titanic,* only a third of the 2,235 passengers and crew survived; most who did were women and children. When one of the ship's officers was asked during a subsequent investigation if this "women and children first" policy was the captain's rule or the rule of the sea, he replied that it was the "rule of nature."

For Victorian men worthy of the name, making the ultimate sacrifice was the rule of nature, as well as civilization's triumph over the primal instinct of self-preservation. The fact that man was descended from the beasts was no excuse to act like one. On the contrary, the capacity for self-sacrifice was seen as a fulfillment of the truly human nature that raised us above our bestial origins. The behavior of the men who went down with the *Titanic* testifies to the power of these ideas to guide their thoughts and actions. We can give an ideal no greater testament than to die for it.

Sworn testimony revealed that several male passengers refused to enter lifeboats because they could not be certain all the women aboard had been saved. One man, when ordered into a lifeboat, not only went under protest but even made the ship's officer sign a statement describing the circumstances, to dull the stigma of surviving a calamity that claimed female lives. Among the few cowards who dashed for the lifeboats, one was evicted and beaten bloody by men who stood stoically on deck, facing death but spared dishonor.

The all-but-forgotten monument to the *Titanic* calamity, a relic of a forgotten chivalrous age, isn't even mentioned in many major guidebooks. Sadly, a similar tragedy today would likely have a less-than-inspiring outcome. By the modern laws of survival, only the fittest cross the finish line. Women would be left to sink or swim—quite literally—unless they were stampeded or pitched overboard by men racing for lifeboats. If push came to shove, no politically correct quota system could preserve a percentage of lifeboat seats for women. It would truly be every man for himself. (I'd like to believe the children would be saved, but I wouldn't bet my life on their chances.)

This scenario illustrates the misogynist peril of the strict gender equality that looks good on paper and makes for stirring sound bites. Victorian civility—not feminist consciousness—conquered the brutality of a kill-or-be-killed world. The twentieth century's march toward every form of liberation has often produced Pyrrhic victories that laid waste the best traditions of the past, and left us to do our atavistic worst.

The smallest gesture of "sexist" gallantry divides women now, and its crowning glory divided women in 1912, when suffrage was a deeply divisive issue. Radical suffragists rejected the chivalrous spirit demonstrated aboard the *Titanic*. One English socialist warned women on both sides of the Atlantic to "consider very carefully whether it is worthwhile to let men assume the entire burden of physical sacrifice in times of danger." But this view posed its own "danger"—making it "difficult to get men to relinquish their heroic ideals."

Modern women have been relieved of worry over men's heroic ideals. What is left of chivalry? Automotive bells and whistles, according to a recent glossy magazine advertisement from Nissan:

"For everyone who's said, 'Chivalry is dead'—we offer this rebuttal: The Nissan Maxima GLE. It opens doors for you, pushes your seat in for you, and adjusts the temperature for you. . . . It's time to expect more from a car."

A century ago, women expected more from men than any machine could deliver, even one that does its own windows. One suffragist declared it "preposterous . . . to confuse the issue of equal suffrage with the problems of the best methods to insure safety in times of panic, and the immemorial usage of seeking to protect the weak and helpless ahead of the strong." In fact, most suffragists praised the "heroic ideals" of men on the *Titanic*—perhaps because they saw the writing on a distant wall

However, the historic valor of those chivalrous men on the *Titanic* was criticized by the Chinese Merchants Association in a public statement issued shortly after the British liner sank. As Wyn Craig Wade recounts in *The Titanic*, a spokesman expressed contempt for a culture that placed the lives of women above those of men. Were the ship Chinese, he said, men and children—but no women—would have been saved. (Although the spokesman didn't press the point, little boys would doubtless have outranked little girls among the children on this survival scale.)

Feminists are still rightly outraged at the inhuman abuse China inflicts on its women. At a 1995 international conference on the status of women held in that country under United Nations sponsorship, vocal American participants denounced China's oppressive birth control policies that result in forced abortions and widespread female infanticide. The Victorians would eagerly join this chorus, while reminding their descendants that honoring women, in small and large ways, is a specifically Western, WASP, middle-class value.

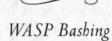

WASP Bashing

Unlike groups that are shielded from insults based on their past victimization or current minority status, WASPs are openly derided, despite the gradual loss of power that blunted whatever sting they once possessed. WASP bashing began in the 1920s, as Richard Brookhiser notes in *The Way of the WASP* (1991), when influential social critics of the day such as H. L. Mencken reveled in decrediting anything associated with WASP sensibilities. In the public mind, WASPs became "bad dancers," "lousy lays," a "font of pathology," and "an emasculated joke."

Once the arbiters of proper behavior, WASPs are now widely viewed as stuffy, stagnant, and spiritless. After generations of cultural backlash, the onetime high and mighty Episcopalian-born and prep school–bred Anglo-Saxon "ruling class" has been recast as the straight man who sets up a multicultural punch line. But this joke is no laughing matter. Brookhiser argues that iconoclasts like H. L. Mencken and Norman Mailer helped detach all classes from the nineteenth-century WASP principles of conscience, individual responsibility, and civic partici-pation, the very ideals we are desperate to restore.

Notwithstanding our love affair with film versions of Jane Austen novels and Ralph Lauren's preppy clothes, WASP bashing has become a national sport and the inalienable right of every minority. For example, by way of celebrating the growing influence of Latino culture on America, the late actor Raoul Julia could say off-handedly, "We're going to give the whole country salsa, spice. That cold, analytical computerlike Saxon men-tality is going out the window." Julia had no need to worry that an Anglo-Saxon Anti-Defamation League might take umbrage at his remark. Had one existed, its members would have been too reticent to criticize him publicly.[6]

Even those who appreciate spice might occasionally crave the taste of Victorian sugar coating. But that choice was struck off the menu decades ago. What is worse, we often confuse the Victorian WASP with Fawlty Towers–like parodies of their purely ethnic descendants. Awkward Basils, giggling Muffies, and tennis-playing Biffs are spineless shadows of a stalwart past. Today,

WASPs are too guilt-ridden over their "advantages" to understand or defend the moral heritage of civility that has been reduced to collecting matching china and silver services.

The politics of holding doors and giving up seats on the subway may seem irrelevant and petty compared to the drama of life and death on a sinking ship. But to the Victorians, even "petty" courtesies were part of life and death and the whole code of manly behavior. A man would "instinctively" sacrifice his life to save a woman only if he had spent it opening doors for her, tipping his hat, and otherwise expressing his deference and respect. A lazy lout or uncouth ruffian who was unaccustomed to giving up his seat in a train or parlor could hardly be expected to give up his seat in a lifeboat.

Chivalry—the respectful treatment of women—was always the shining centerpiece of Victorian etiquette, even though, of course, both sexes practiced the benevolence of manners. "The universal practice in this nation in thus giving precedence to women has been severely commented upon by foreigners," observed Catharine Beecher in 1869. But this was no apology to plaintive tourists. Beecher called female precedence "evidence of our superior civilization" that should "increase rather than diminish." Suffragist Mary Livermore reflected a widespread assumption of her day—not a gender wars hot-button issue—when she said, "Every boy should be trained to respect womanhood, and in our country this ought not to be difficult. For there are no men so courteous to women as American men."

Fast-forward nearly a century to 1995, when the feminist author and *Washington Post* columnist Judy Mann traced the abusive and disrespectful treatment of females to gender differences in how we raise our children. "Have boys do things for girls," she advised, "such as getting them a drink or fetching a book. The point is to have girls feel entitled to ask boys to do things for them and to develop in boys the capacity to do things for girls, as opposed to expecting girls to wait on them."[7]

Ms. Mann's column merely brushed the tip of the iceberg of all the entitlements her sex has gradually lost. These days mothers, daughters, and significant others grow giddy with delight when guys actually think to pour their mates a cup of coffee when they pour their own. In contrast, Victorian gentlemen rarely stopped waiting on women, especially at social functions. For example, one 1884 book described manly duties if music was on the evening's menu: "Any lady guest being invited to play the piano, it is courtesy for the gentleman nearest her to offer his arm and escort her to the instrument. While she is playing, he will hold her bouquet, fan and gloves, and should also turn the leaves if he can read music."[8] Modern males would undoubtedly label such public displays of attentiveness as unmasculine.

Lest they forget their due, *The Ladies' Book of Etiquette* reminded its readers of the welcome responsibilities a man assumed once a woman accepted his request for a dance:

> Recollect that your partner is for the time being your very humble servant and that he will be honoured by acquiescing in any of your wishes: for instance, you may wish to promenade, to walk from one room to another, to join your friends; you may require a jelly, ice, wine, or any other refreshment . . . in short he will feel honoured by receiving your commands, and he ought to anticipate your wishes on most of the above.

Only a man whose "manners were the index of his soul" would feel honored to be a woman's servant, eagerly accepting her commands and the chance to show himself and the world that he deserved the sobriquet of "gentleman." What modern woman would expect any guy not just to serve her but to anticipate her wishes? Henry James wrote of another time, not another planet, when he described in his novel *Washington Square* gentlemen guests who retreated from a room "in the best order"—walking backward, so as not to turn their backs on the ladies who remained. Now women are grateful if they don't get the backs of men's hands. Misusing those hands on a woman was once considered a sin beyond redemption. Consider the obligation to wear gloves while dancing. According to a 1901 etiquette book,

For a man to dance with a lady and leave the imprints of his fingers upon her dress is anything but creditable to him. . . . Above all things, men should bear in mind that women rule and sway society, and the man who incurs, in any manner, their dislike or enmity, is one of the most unfortunate of individuals who will find that the road he expected would be lined on either side with beautiful, blooming roses is in reality bordered by shrubbery of which the most conspicuous characteristics are sharp, protuberant and long thorns.[9]

Ouch! This painful botanical warning illustrates why the Victorians were so scrupulous about details that escape our notice or regard. The glove rule, which both sexes followed while dancing, is also a prime example of what Eliza Duffey called a "thousand little delicacies which are established only by custom." Yet there is plenty of sense in this custom, even if it isn't common. Wearing gloves allowed partners to comfortably share a dance, not the sweat of their hands.

The city streets, which have become a gauntlet for women, were another arena where civilized rules and ladies once reigned. Bowing and hat tipping were two ways in which men acknowledged and reinforced this fact of life. As Arthur Martine wrote:

The really well-bred man always politely and respectfully bows to every lady he knows. . . . If she expects no further acquaintance, her bow is a mere formal, but always respectful, recognition of the good manners which have been shown her, and no gentleman ever takes advantage of such politeness to push a further acquaintance uninvited.

Since this form of "ladies' choice"—and many others—were etched in stone, no woman had to worry about escaping from the men she knew but wished she didn't. Any man who hoped to win the favor of her further acquaintance had to properly wield his hat. A lazy tap or tickle of the brim was unacceptable. "A gentleman will raise his hat fairly from his head," *The Bazar Book of*

Decorum averred, "and not limit his salutation to a mere touch of the rim, like a coachman or a waiter."

A man was also obliged to salute even unknown ladies who were walking with any men he knew. If the man was honored with an introduction to the lady, he would not expect to hear that she was "happy" or "delighted" to meet him. Aren't such trite phrases just the sort we associate with courtesy-conscious Victorians? Not if they compromised a woman's supreme social power: "When a gentleman is introduced to a lady . . . the pleasure is supposed to be upon his part, the condescension upon her side," said Maude C. Cooke, the author of *Social Etiquette* (1866).[10] Hats were tipped to any woman on the street who requested directions or other information from a man. This assumed that women felt safe enough to act in a way we would consider potentially dangerous or provocative. Now there was freedom!

The removal of his hat provided a crucial test of a man's character, and woe unto him who failed it, even if the ladies he slighted

Hat tipping was serious business to the Victorians. Men acknowledged all ladies, regardless of age, beauty, or class, with this gesture of respect.

were those most likely to forgive the offense. The 1884 publication *Standard Book on Politeness, Good Behavior and Social Etiquette* reflected the prevailing standard on this issue:

> The man who stands with his hat on in the presence of his mother and sister, manifests thereby a want of apprehension of the requirements of filial and fraternal reverence and affection. . . . If circumstances do not combine to correct him, [they] will in the long-run render him fit for treason, stratagems, and spoils; he sets at naught feelings and principles which would interpose one of the most important barriers between himself and crime. It would not be surprising if such a man were to finish his career in the dock or the hulks; he lacks true nobility and elevation of sentiment without which he will not, and he cannot, come to good.[11]

No man since that time has ever carried such weight on his head. Those who valued their reputations constantly guarded their behavior on the streets. A full century before the song "Girl Watcher" hit the top forty, *Martine's Hand-book of Etiquette* decreed: "No gentleman will stand in the doors of hotels, nor on the corners of the streets, gazing impertinently at the ladies as they pass. That is such an unmistakable sign of a loafer, that one can hardly imagine a well-bred man doing such a thing." The popular imagination had stretched considerably by 1934, when etiquette books were pleading, "Girls, never, never turn at a whistle, to see if you are wanted. A whistle is usually to call a dog." This plunge in the evolutionary scale to canine status definitively demonstrates which gender lost respect, self-respect, and control of the streets when Victorian "delicacies" were swept into its sewers.

To the Victorians, civility depended not just on men who obeyed its rules but also on women who expected men's compliance. Women were entreated to continuously assert their "royal prerogative" in full, as Thomas Nelson Page wrote, and never to "accept with complacency the insolent indifference of the male sex . . . the scattered and scornful crumbs of attention that they deign to let fall before their eager eyes."[12]

If any crumbs are left, we need a magnifying glass to find them. Men are the generic scapegoats of choice—and often deserving ones. But it was women who put us on a starvation diet of manners and courtesies. The feminists who claimed they fought for all women's legal, professional, and economic rights never asked any women but themselves how they wished to be treated by men, or what rights they wanted revoked. Now, many women don't even know what female perquisites they have lost. Morbid curiosity prompted me to ask some Generation X women if any of their male peers still engaged in anti-quated rituals such as carrying their packages and holding chairs and doors. They responded with blank stares, as if I were a pointy-eared Vulcan who was just beamed down from a distant prime-time zone. One finally replied, "Like, when did guys ever do those things for girls?" This made me rethink the implications of Santayana's maxim "Those who cannot remember the past are doomed to repeat it." Women should be so lucky.

The perils of liberated living are familiar to every woman, but most of all to pregnant ones. I followed the nine-month odyssey of a colleague whose fate was all too common. After daily bouts of morn-ing sickness, she endured long commutes—on progressively swelling legs—with unencumbered yuppies who never offered her a seat. Twice she was knocked off the sidewalk by tardy young men sprinting toward the office. Frustration, fatigue, and fear compounded the usual burdens of her condition.

Understandably, such women, beleaguered by the death of chivalry, want someone specific to blame for the politically correct incivility that seems more like a crime against humanity. Without the essential chivalrous code that was once man's second nature—the code Lord Chesterfield called "the only protection [women] have against this superior strength of ours"—what laws could have given this woman the unequal treatment she sorely needed?[13] Will we draft affirmative action laws to protect pregnant, package-laden, or merely petite women on federally regulated sidewalks?

Victorian women did not need legislation to protect them from such public abuse and disrespect. In Henry James's short story "An International Episode," the obliging Willie Woodly is described as a man "whose mission in life . . . was to find chairs for ladies." Women today might not choose such a man as a life partner, but all our lives are impoverished when such men—and their mission—cease to exist.

At the turn of the century, Harvard president Charles W. Eliot implied the necessity of chivalry to the very existence of civilized life when he warned that "the chivalrous sentiments . . . of civilized men" would die if women became "coarse, combative, [and] rude."[14] Case closed—right in women's faces. If Victorian chivalry was a ruse to keep women in their places, it was equally effective at keeping men in theirs by defining a large measure of their self-worth and reputations. But as with all things Victorian, chivalry's purpose ran even deeper. Women were entreated to encourage and accept it because it demonstrated not manly "strength" but manly "honor," as Thomas Nelson Page wrote. If men still had this positive outlet for expressing their masculinity, perhaps they would stop verbally and physically brutalizing women and each other.

Echoes of the pathetic quest for chivalry's crumbs laced the controversy swirling around the Nation of Islam leader Louis Farrakhan and his 1995 "Million Man March" on Washington. He told the media one of its intended messages was "to atone to God for the way we have mistreated our women and girls." Unfortunately, he undermined this noble ideal by inviting the proudly unrepentant wife beater O. J. Simpson to the march.

Nevertheless, the sentiment is worth saving. What we need is a sincere national march of atonement by men of all races, and the female equalizers who triumphantly obliterated the sexist chivalry of macho pigs, and left us nothing but the sty. Consider the moral trade-offs made by unliberated women who don't want mud kicked in their faces. Despite Farrakhan's lightning-rod racist views and his "men-only" rule for the march, many black women supported it. Said one female African-American publisher, Frances Murphy,

> Actions speak louder than words. I have yet to walk into a
> room of Nation of Islam members where the men don't get
> up if a lady walks into the room. That's saying a whole lot.
> That makes you feel very, very good.[15]

Once upon a time, such behavior was a mere appetizer in the banquet of courtesy that awaited women. According to modern-day historians, however, women who stubbornly persist in regarding themselves as "ladies" have no right to feel good. For example, in a book called *Prudery and Passion*, Milton Rugoff asserts that the chivalrous Victorian gestures that "converted women into a figure on a pedestal" were not intended to make any woman seem special but were "an unction applied to an entire sex and . . . not a tribute to a particular woman." But current standards are blind to the reason why such "unction" applied to an entire sex. Victorian gentlemen had neither the moral power nor the luxury to choose which women deserved their deference by looks, youth, or any other discriminating criteria. Chivalry implied scrupulous equality. Women were objectified in the best possible sense, because all were entitled to chivalrous treatment. "Women—all women, of whatever age and condition— claim [a gentleman's] respectful care and tender reverential regard," declared the redoubtable Lord Chesterfield. "No provocation whatsoever can justify any man in not being civil to every woman; the greatest man would be justly reckoned a brute if he were not civil to the meanest woman." Many modern women would test even Chesterfield's gentlemanly mettle. But he understood that when a man's mood or hormones dictate his manners, most women will lose the struggle for survival of the fairest.

WASP SELF-RESTRAINT

The way of thinking that identified manliness with chivalry and self-control rather than self-assertion was characteristically Victorian. This sensibility was expressed in Henry Ward Beecher's maxim "Greatness lies not in being strong but in the right use of strength." But the idea that self-restraint was crucial to the functioning of society was also central to a WASP sensibility that has since been written off as ethnocentric. Never mind that such values served even non-WASP Victorians, who embraced honor and self-restraint as ideals that crossed cultural lines. The Victorians did not call themselves WASPs, although they recognized their religious, racial, and ethnic distinctiveness. Now we use this term pejoratively as a double-edged shorthand for the once-dominant culture of dead white males that we keep trying to bury. (Feminist sensibilities make us more ambivalent about all the dead white females who aided, loved, and inspired them.)

Ironically, even critics of WASP culture like Jesse Jackson have recently joined with such unlikely soulmates as Bill Clinton and William Bennett in calling for a revival of civility. Yet this civility is almost never linked to its distinctly WASP roots. The reason may be simple ignorance or a conscious historical blindness driven by the fear of re-imposing insulting customs on all the hyphenated peoples whom WASPs tried to "melt" before the melting pot was considered cultural homicide. In any case, a return to the central Victorian WASP values of chivalry and self-restraint in action and words is long overdue. "Letting it all hang out" has frayed our social fabric, yet we cannot begin to address our problems until we restore the rules of civil discourse that we abandoned so long ago.

7

Keeping a Civil Tongue

To modern materialists, we are what we eat. To existentialists, we are what we do. To the Victorian mind, however, we are as we speak. Our forefathers believed that virtue in words was intimately linked to virtue in deeds. Their concern for the niceties of language reflected their conviction that outward civility was an agent as well as a reflection of inner nobility. In this they followed the classical aphorism, "Speech is a mirror of the soul: As a man speaks, so is he."

FIGHTING WORDS

To the Victorians, the intersecting layers of language and life were complex. In 1837, the popular etiquette author William Alcott said:

> The individual who gives himself up to the use of improper or unchaste language, or even to the endurance of it unchecked, is giving up at the same time the out-posts of all human virtue. . . . The vices are all associated; and they who have been introduced to either, or especially to all of these, are likely soon to become acquainted with others, and perhaps the whole brotherhood of them. Let us there-

fore be aware of an improper or indelicate word or look . . .
for it is out of the abundance of these that not only the
mouth speaks, but the hands act.

Any who doubt that language drives behavior should consider a
recent case in which the effects of language were literally incendiary.
In 1995, a black man shot seven people at a Jewish-owned clothing
store in Harlem before setting it ablaze. In the weeks before this
tragedy, the gunman had joined picket lines outside the store, in
which protesters shouted anti-Semitic epithets such as "Bloodsuck-
ers!" The white "crackers" and black "traitors" who patronized the
store were also threatened.

No doubt the anti-Semitic atmosphere created by these epithets contributed to the crime. Few would contest the toxicity of a
link so overt and direct. We see the problem, but we flail about for a
solution.

SEARCHING FOR RULES OF DISCOURSE

It is no coincidence that "First Amendment absolutism" and "political
correctness" have both become familiar terms in the past decade. A
society that refuses to enforce reasonable restrictions on verbal
aggression will soon discover a demand for unreasonable ones. The
more we encounter egregious exhibitions of coarseness and tastelessness, the more sensitive some become to real and imagined linguistic
slights. Ethnic comedians tell increasingly ugly jokes about their own
groups, but they would be outraged at hearing even the mildest ethnic joke from someone outside their group. We are locked in a downward spiral, as extremists try to fill the void left by the loss of respect
for moderation.

The excesses of PC are easy to sneer at. The state of Massachu-
setts is replacing the traditional SLOW CHILDREN signs with WATCH
CHILDREN, to avoid offending youngsters with learning disabilities. In
the public schools of our nation's capital, there are no "poor" readers,
just "emergent" ones. Real estate agents afraid of being sued for bias
avoid advertising "master bedrooms" (which allegedly suggest slavery), while "spectacular view" or "walk-in" closet are taboo because
they might insult homebuyers who can't see or walk. In 1993, the *Los*

Angeles Times issued nineteen pages of *Guidelines on Ethnic, Racial, Sexual and Other Identification.* The offensive terms that were banished as unfit to print included "Dutch treat," "Chinese fire drill," "gypped," and "normal"—a term no one can use anymore without raising someone's ire.

The problem is that while liberals reflexively defend antisocial acts by the "oppressed" and want to repress the speech of loose-lipped "oppressors," conservatives chafe at the muzzle imposed by the sugary euphemisms applied to designated minorities and self-proclaimed victims. We wage our language wars through dueling committees, clogged courts, and last-ditch legislation like Raritan, New Jersey's 1994 effort to pass a blatantly unconstitutional ordinance prohibiting rude or indecent remarks.

The Victorians relied on unwritten laws to civilize language. Etiquette books, the Victorians' social bibles, devoted whole sections to "vulgarisms in conversation." But these tame offenses are a century and worlds away from ours. Unlike our slash-and-burn vulgarisms, which aim at the core of someone's identity, theirs were offenses against proper English, not people—unless you count "folks" for "people," and "old man" for "father." Notably absent were the four-letter word and demeaning names like "bitch," "whore," or their ethnic equivalents. Those who used them were too far down on the food chain to be recognized by readers aspiring to polite behavior.

Writing about her childhood, Edith Wharton recalled in her memoir that in her parents' circle, "Any really expressive slang was welcomed with amusement—but used as slang, as it were between quotation marks, and not carelessly admitted into our speech." Etiquette books, which were rarely amused by any form of slang, frowned on phrases such as "fly off the handle" (when angry, you flew into a "passion"), and "all to pieces" ("entirely destroyed"). And contrary to modern notions of fanatical Victorian prudery, "limb" was considered "a silly and affected expression for leg." Even saying the word "love" could be considered common and unrefined if that serious and venerated sentiment was used as a synonym for "like."

Such semantic quibbling may seem trivial to us, but the Victorians believed that even the smallest erosion of language would eventually result in a landslide of incivility and took steps to check any such downward slide as soon as it could be perceived.

FROM THE MOUTHS OF BABES

Unfortunately, in our culture the erosion begins in childhood. Researchers and educators lament the staggering rise of obscene and aggressive speech in America's schools. The Victorians assumed and insisted that children address all authority figures as "sir" and "ma'am," "miss," "mister," and "missus." At best, children now address their elders by first names. Moreover, *The Washington Post* reports that female teachers are accustomed to hearing "Shut the ——— up, you bitch," when they try to quiet disruptive students or simply greet them. "Every other word is the F-word," one Virginia school board member said.[1]

Experts cite the obvious culprits—rap music, movies, TV, and especially cable fare like *Beavis and Butthead*, which thrives on brutish and degrading humor. But the chief villains are parents. "Nasty language has become a second language," observes Ronald F. Federici, a northern Virginia school consultant and child psychologist. "Four-letter words are rampant. Parents are doing it at home. They won't admit it, but they do."[2] Richard Gelles, director of the Family Violence Research Program at the University of Rhode Island, has documented that one out of every two parents verbally abuse their children with profanity-laced outbursts at least once a month.

The publisher Madeline Kane cites the increasingly graphic language of today's parents for the widespread popularity among adults and kids of toilet-talk books. The titles of these inspiring works make further description redundant: *The Holes in Your Nose, Everyone Poops,* and *The Gas We Pass*. This last hot seller, which has gone through several printings, is used as a coffee-table book, according to Kane. (Imagine having coffee and cake on that table.)[3]

Susan Lammers, president of a firm that designs computer programs for elementary schools, defends the educational value of materials that make poetry of bodily functions. Since these poems helped her young son "learn rhyming and reading," she argued, "it's worth it." In the same article, Cyma Zarghami, an executive at Nickelodeon, the children's cable channel whose comedies have included *Salute Your Shorts*, says, "A tiny bit of naughtiness never hurt anybody."

Even those who don't turn a profit from hawking untraditional "toiletries" can barely muster a shrug over this trend. For example, *The Wall Street Journal* reported in 1995 that a professor of psychology at the University of Utah would put the brakes on kids' racist or sexist remarks but contends that "vulgarities are not going to harm any child." Besides, he believes, "other issues are more pressing." The same article quotes another credentialed critic, the psychologist Timothy Jay, author of *Cursing in America*, who objects to cleaning up media smut. "Who wants a sanitized, Walt Disney version of street life?" he asks rhetorically. Jay views indecent and coarse language as "a valuable tool for teenagers because it allows them to defy authority fairly harmlessly." But when does that "fairly" become fairly dangerous?

WOMEN AND COARSE DISCOURSE

Nowhere is the question of the relationship between verbal and physical abuse more apparent than in our ambiguity about the use of coarse and disrespectful language in front of, and by, women. The Victorians, male and female, were outraged by the verbal and physical mistreatment of women. But they would likely trace today's epidemic of abuse of women to women's lost social power and the general decline of civility, not the currently favored (and ahistorical) explanation of sexism.

The current penchant for public crudity inverts the Victorian notion that carefully weighed words preserved freedom, especially for women. Alexis de Tocqueville, our most insightful tourist, found it noteworthy that American men had such respect for women's "moral freedom that in their presence every man is careful to keep watch on his tongue for fear that [women] should be forced to listen to language which offends them" (*Democracy in America*). As the eighteenth-century English statesman Lord Chesterfield observed, the one thing women would never pardon was "a vulgar and awkward air." (Vulgarity was always considered awkward.)

Modern females have lost the vast but intangible power created by masculine fear of giving offense to ladies. Today, female ambivalence toward standards of civility gives off mixed signals that are more likely to confuse than frighten males. For example, a 1994 *Esquire* poll of 1,000 Generation X women found them almost evenly split on whether men should clean up their language in mixed company.[4]

The entry of women into formerly male-dominated careers has only intensified the confusion, as some women try to act like "one of the guys." A female midshipman at the Naval Academy in Annapolis recently complained to a reporter, "I've been called so many names that sometimes it doesn't even register as inappropriate. The lack of respect that the men have here for women is appalling." However, Navy Lt. Lynne Fowler expressed regret that her fellow carrier pilots had become more restrained around her since the infamous Tailhook scandal. "Loosen up," she tells them. "It's okay to tell a dirty joke around this woman at least."

This tug of war among women leaves them pulling both ends of the rope. In a similar case, a feminist college professor recently expressed outrage over complaints filed against a male colleague who opined freely about a student's breasts and often used "salty language." Writing in a *New York Times* essay, she ridiculed the women who objected as "Victorian damsels in distress." She also disparaged the college's grievance committee for its tone of "civility and high moral seriousness" with "echoes of Victorian melodrama." When virtue can be so readily redefined as vice, it is little wonder that women must constantly fight for the respect their great-grandmothers took for granted.[5]

The Victorians believed that social codes, not legal ones, should be used to police and prevent verbal offenses. This, however, requires reticence—the bedrock of Victorian civility that our culture has bloodied and muddied at every turn. Without the unwritten Victorian code that tamed the male tongue like a spirited show horse, women are left protesting, suing, and flailing about for the social power and "moral freedom" they lost by acceding to male standards, according to which refinement is a sign of weakness. The law court becomes the only resort when the sexes clash in the gray zones of behavior. Even if lawsuits and damage awards could solve the problem of our civil speech, the Victorians would have rejected the notion that civility and respect for women should be reduced to a mercenary matter.

Many women would agree with macho-fem Camille Paglia, who derides any attempts to return women to "their old status of delicate flowers," as she wrote in her 1992 book, *Sex, Art, and American Culture*. Paglia credits her beloved 1960s with breaking "the ancient codes of decorum that protected respectable ladies from profanation by foul language." Yet just how free are women who never had their say in revoking the rules of civilized language that once protected everyone from verbal guerrillas? Ironically, women are now accorded special workplace privileges in the guise of affirmative action, but woe unto those who drive trucks without talking like truck drivers. Is this what women want?

At the turn of the century, one social critic warned that women would always "lose more than they gain" by imitating uncouth men. He could not foresee the fat checks gender aping would confer on a few select entrepreneurs and entertainers like Roseanne. But most women gain neither comfort from nor compensation for such behavior.

Swearing Just like One of the Guys

Now that women can verbally swagger just like "one of the guys," they have lost their right to male respect. Ironically, feminists seeking freedom of speech helped break the last taboos that kept a civil lock on misogynist tongues. By adopting men's rude way of speaking, women lost the formidable power to set the standards that made language a tool of peace, rather than the offensive and defensive weapon we use in our daily wars of incivility.

Even consciousness-raising role models carry us into treacherous currents of uncivil speech, as they remain blissfully unaware of the whirlpool that lies ahead. When a crew from CBS's *60 Minutes* attempted to interview Gloria Steinem about her nemesis Camille Paglia, Steinem told them (and the audience she was lecturing) that she didn't "give a shit" about Paglia's views. Steinem's expletive hardly merits a blink in an age when even professional women, like the judge on the TV sitcom *Courthouse*, routinely pronounce themselves "pissed off." Perhaps that show's writer knew that Steinem was once voted one of the most "confident" women in America. It seems that crudity is now a badge of self-confidence.

Like many old-line feminists (as opposed to many of the young-Turk power-fems), Steinem believes pornography denigrates women and lowers their self-esteem. Connecting the X-rated dregs of "adult entertainment" to Steinem's simple expletive may seem like comparing a heart attack to a hangnail. Yet any woman who ever experienced a hostile environment knows what a wide range this thermostat has, and how easily both victims and aggressors can adjust it.

According to *The Portable Emerson* by Carl Bode, Ralph Waldo Emerson once wrote, "The corruption of man is followed by the corruption of language." Many of his contemporaries would have reversed the order. The Victorians believed that every coarse and demeaning bleep we utter knocks another chip in the crumbling ruins of civility, and invites other vandals to follow suit. So if women don't want to be treated like "shit" by men, they had better start being respectful when they assess and address each other. Their toxic emissions only worsen the hostile environments they encounter in the office, the home, and the street. If women on top of the heap must express themselves through terms for excretory functions, we have nowhere to go but down.

In contrast to today's frequent use of the F-word by women who think of it as a colorful modifier and verb, an 1837 manual on the duties of women (men had their own volume) by William Alcott warned them to avoid "coarse" expressions like "My stars," "By George," and "Good heavens." Those were the days! Fussing over these fusty but innocent exclamations may be a real knee slapper for us, but to the Victorians, they were not only "unbecoming"—a serious social sin—but also "savor not a little of profanity." In a century that noticed every nuance of good and evil, not just their blatant extremes, coarse language was the first rung down the ladder from the sacred to the profane.

If ever a declaration of social mores could seem a relic of a bygone age, it would be Sarah Josepha Hale's casual comment, "Swearing is considered so inadmissible in good society, or in the presence of ladies, that there is little danger of its being introduced in either." Mrs. Hale made that statement in 1868, when she was the editor of this country's most influential woman's magazine. Her misplaced confidence now seems more shocking than the gutter language that daily refutes it.

THE PROLIFERATION OF PROFANITY

The Victorians could not have imagined how insane profane could get. On a recent visit to New York, I noticed in Pennsylvania Station a souvenir T-shirt covered with silk-screened instructions on HOW TO USE THE F-WORD. The shirt suggests inserting this versatile expression into common phrases such as "Who are you?" and "Pass the salt." And why not? This is but a logical extension of our current approach to language. *Martine's Hand-book of Etiquette* (1866) compared polite conversation to silver: "useful upon all occasions." Now impolite conversation serves the same function.

In 1897 the English etiquette author Mrs. Humphry predicted the fate of "habitually using strong language. . . . It defeats itself; for if the forcible expressions are intended to express disapprobation, they soon become weak and powerless to do so, because they are used on every possible occasion. After a time they lose all meaning." As a good Victorian, Mrs. Humphry assumed that only the "low, arrogant, and ill-bred" used such language. Now the low, arrogant, and ill-bred are the entertainers of choice for the sophisticated, worldly, and well-bred power brokers who make a fine distinction between their dinner-party smut and the streetwise brand they profess to find reprehensible.

Of course, the Victorians had the luxury of assuming that everyone worth knowing would mind their P's and Q's as the rule, not the exception, so they could excoriate barroom language on the sole grounds that such rude discourse was a terrible insult to polite society. The stakes are much higher for us, because the "cream" of society has soured. Once-unspeakable speech is now so common among elite groups such as politicians, leaders, writers, and even educators that it threatens the very survival of the institutions that sustain a civilized democracy.

The great German writer Thomas Mann showed his Victorian-era upbringing when he wrote, "Speech is civilization." To the generation in which Mann was raised, civility meant striving upward in word and deed. Now civility is treated as a "downer," a restriction on our sovereign right to self-expression. The Victorians overruled verbal indecency on the once-obvious grounds that it attracts socially destructive self-attention and expresses disdain for others. The self-aggrandizing urge to shock has led us from the bon mots of Oscar Wilde to the wilderness of trash talk.

VERBAL FISTFIGHTS AND AMBUSHES

Once ribald language has been sanctioned in private conversation, it soon finds its way into public discourse. Indeed, among the arenas suffering most from the decline of civility are those in which words have the greatest power to inflict harm: politics and the law. Critics note that once-courtly rituals like legal depositions have degenerated into "Rambo-like tactics" aimed at intimidating witnesses and opposing counsels.

On the political front, the circus of TV talk shows is just a poor relation to the weekly televised shouting matches of educated journalists who know their politics but not their P's and Q's. Critics fault these shows for promoting conflict over substance and polarizing political debate. I would add the general debasement of everyday discourse to this list.

The Victorians believed in dousing angry sparks, not fanning them into an inferno. Being modern means acting or blabbing before you think, and never repenting. In 1855, over a century before the apostles of political correctness tried to selectively censor the raw emotions that break their rules, Catharine Beecher explained that the social obligations of civility required everyone to avoid

> . . . all remarks which tend to embarrass, vex, mortify, or in any way wound the feelings of another. To notice personal defects; to allude to others' faults, or the faults of their friends; to speak disparagingly of the sect or party to which a person belongs; to be inattentive when addressed in conversation; to contradict flatly; to speak in contemptuous tones of opinions expressed by another; all these are violations of the rules of good-breeding.

They are also the bread and butter of attack TV, bullet-tongued comics, poisonous music, and the scorchingly candid everyday atmosphere of our offices, homes, and streets that keeps daily life on the verge of boiling over.

In an article entitled "The Triumph of the Yell," the psychologist Deborah Tannen blamed our pervasive "culture of critique" for promoting extremism over compromise and stifling our search for truth. The Victorians were unusually blunt but accurate when they labeled perpetual critics "bullies." Whereas we celebrate the forthright rudeness of radio shock-jocks and tell-it-like-it-is politicians, the Victorians condemned brassy behavior as a barbaric lack of restraint. Even if one was able to win an argument with lungs and intimidation, "could" never justified "should." One etiquette writer scolded those skilled at sarcasm, barbs, and contempt, "Because you happen to have a razor in your possession, that is no reason why you should be allowed to cut the throats of the rest of us who are unarmed." Over a century later, Tannen noted how the Darwinian deck is stacked in today's verbal wars, writing in the aforementioned article that "opposition also limits information when only those who are adept at verbal sparring take part in public discourse, and those who cannot handle it, or do not like it, decline to participate." Can we truly have a democracy when our public, and private, discourse is dominated by bullies?

Blowhards did not fare so well a hundred years ago. The Victorians disapproved of people routinely rumbling like thunder. It was considered selfish, divisive, undignified—and therefore uncivilized—but it was also considered counterproductive. To be convincing, remarked Lord Chesterfield, always state your opinions "modestly and coolly." Losing your temper meant losing more than self-control: "A man who does not possess himself enough to hear disagreeable things without visible marks of anger and change of countenance . . . is at the mercy of every artful knave or pert coxcomb."

Cool-headed civil discourse may not play as well in the Nielsen ratings as getting one's nose broken in a discussion that has deteriorated into a brawl, but we sorely need to return to it if we are to solve any of our serious problems as a society. If we gave all ranters the Victorian treatment—stony silence—they would be forced to pipe down or be tuned out.

NO MORE SECRETS

Part of the reason we developed our high-volume style is our sadly mistaken notion that intensity, bluntness, and lack of reticence denote sincerity. Talk-show audiences doubt that dysfunctional guests have truly recovered unless tears flow, and reconciling parties are required to produce hugs and kisses. We applaud the "honesty" of bestselling memoirs that lay bare every dark family secret, from alcoholism to incest. Until fairly recently, mothers taught their children, "If you can't say anything nice, don't say anything." When I lamented the decline of this maternal wisdom, one devoted mother replied, "Then no one would ever say anything."

The reluctant renovation of Bob Dole is a prime example of the modern demand to prove that you have guts by spilling them. During the last presidential race, image makers convinced the normally reticent Dole to share in painful detail the pain and permanent debilities of the wounds he sustained during World War II, when his "I feel your pain" opponent was still in diapers. What was really accomplished by our learning that Dole's wife must peel his fruit or that he wears a shoulder pad beneath his undershirt to buttress his shattered frame—except the loss of the privacy and dignity this man had earned in his country's service? You don't need to be a Republican to admire either quality.

TASTELESS PUBLIC "HUMOR"

If we aren't demanding that people spill their deepest secrets to the general public, we are finding other ways to "democratize" ourselves by dropping our standards of public speech down to the lowest common denominator. Perhaps the saddest sign of our corrupted discourse is the willingness of self-described conservatives to adopt the tastelessness and rudeness that would have appalled their ideological forebears. Howard Stern would strain the needle on any vulgarity gauge. But where was the conservative decency brigade when Republican congressman Martin Hoke publicly remarked on the size of a TV producer's breasts, and talk-radio king Rush Limbaugh went on his television show in 1994 and defended Hoke as follows: "I'll tell you, we're in bad shape in this country when you can't look at a couple of huge knockers and notice it." If his listeners want to ditto that, let them try it in front of their wives.

This attitude illustrates how anti-Victorian modern conservatives can be. Limbaugh built a megabucks career on blaming liberals for America's moral decline, but his crude comment would never pass the most superficial Victorian moral muster. This persuasive preacher could begin his rehabilitation by learning a lesson from *Miss Leslie's Behaviour Book*, a popular manual published in 1859: "Persons who have no turn for humour, and little perception of it, are apt to mistake mere coarseness for that amusing gift; and in trying to be diverting, often become vulgar."

In our deeply politicized culture, crassness crosses all party lines. In 1995 President Clinton and a large collection of Washington's movers, shakers, and reputation breakers were entertained at the prestigious Radio and Television Correspondents' Association dinner by the comic Bill Maher, the longtime host of the humorous talk show *Politically Incorrect*. Putting that spirit into practice, Maher made a derisive ethnic joke about Senator Phil Gramm's Korean-American wife and peppered his racy monologue with four-letter words. Although a few boos were heard, no one walked out.

CNN's bureau chief, who had booked the controversial comic, declared the evening a success because at his table "there was a lot of laughing." Maher claimed, "The President was laughing the whole time . . . and he told me he enjoyed the performance." In addition to presidential accolades, "I got nothing but congratulations from people like Cokie Roberts, Sam Donaldson, Wolf Blitzer, John Sununu, and Ralph Nader." If anyone was offended, Maher said they should learn to take themselves "less seriously."

Compare this to the reaction to a notorious 1877 speech Mark Twain gave at a dinner attended by three cultural icons, Ralph Waldo Emerson, Oliver Wendell Holmes, and Henry Wadsworth Longfellow. The irrepressible Twain concocted a spoof, complete with his signature dead-on dialect, in which these honored guests became grotesque drunken tramps who invaded a miner's cabin. In his comic narrative, they ate the miner's food, drank his booze, cheated him at cards, and stole his only pair of boots.

Twain's wit badly misfired. Witnesses said the entire audience "turned to stone with horror." One attendee described the wall-to-wall silence as "weighing many tons to the square inch." Twain later said that the incident "pretty near killed me with shame." Although he wrote letters of apology to the three revered butts of his joke, one biographer said the event dogged him for the rest of his life. Ten years afterward, newspapers still referred to it as evidence that Twain had "no reliable sense of propriety."

Today professional insult mongers like Howard Stern can literally take their schtick to the bank. Not that the Victorians didn't appreciate humor—Twain was a legend in his own lifetime—but even legends were not excused when they broke the cardinal law best summarized by the late-nineteenth-century poet Will Carleton:

> "Careful with fire," is good advice, we know:
> "Careful with words," is ten times doubly so.

RELEARNING RESPECT FOR
THE POWER AND BEAUTY OF LANGUAGE

Propriety was not the only reason the Victorians took care in their choice of language. Like the seventeenth-century English clergyman Robert Burton, they believed "a blow with a word strikes deeper than a blow with a sword." But their posture was neither negative nor defensive. They simply loved and respected language, a loss that has cost us the most effective means of fulfilling our increasingly desperate quest to communicate. As a child, Edith Wharton learned "a reverence for the English language" that was "as authoritative an element . . . as tradition was in social conduct." Both language and friends, she said, were always treated with courtesy.

This sort of testimony belies the modern assumption that the self-censorship required by civility stifles creativity. If anything, it nourished the creative impulse by demanding discipline and discernment from Victorian-era writers such as the Brontë sisters, Edith Wharton, and Henry James. Even common folk spoke and wrote in language that would put to shame many modern writers who earn large sums and critical acclaim for their blunt and unrefined prose. Many people were amazed to hear the incredible richness and eloquence of expression in the letters between soldiers and their wives, which were featured in Ken Burns's PBS documentary on the Civil War. Would that such beautiful language were still a part of our common daily discourse.

Contemporary writers who use literature to shock or deconstruct, rather than to edify or ennoble, might well benefit from less candor and more self-censorship. Restricted expression can be a rewarding challenge, when the restrictions are self-imposed and widely accepted. We have been reduced to a literal but limited vocabulary. Too often, the beauty of tact and subtlety is discarded in favor of cold, brute honesty. In so doing, we have forgotten the value of graceful communication.

VICTORIAN SILENT LANGUAGES

Consider the lost Victorian legacy of silent languages, which once textured life with nuance. The only silent language we still vaguely remember was the most flirtatious, the language of the fan. The faintest movements of these lace, silk, satin, and feathery confections conveyed a world of meaning that was widely understood. But for the Victorians, life and love, like God and the devil, were in the details. Simply by touching the lips with the fan, holding it in one or the other hand, drawing it across the cheek, or fanning rapidly or slowly, a woman accomplished in its grammar could hold an extensive conversation with an equally literate suitor.

Between expressing the passionate extremes of love and hate, she could apologize for a tiff, ask for a kiss, or declare that her heart belonged to another. A right-handed twirl warned the hopeful swain he was being watched by a disapproving chaperone or parent. If a man requested the honor of escorting a lady home with an equally tactful cue—lifting his left forefinger to his left eye—she could accept the offer by resting her fan on her right cheek or reject it by resting the fan on her left. Tapping the fan with one finger meant an emphatic "My mother says no."

Even the fluttering motion held meaning. In 1832, the magazine essayist Joseph Addison wrote, "There is the angry flutter, the modest

Fans were not merely fashion accessories; ladies used them to convey the nuances of their emotions to suitors and would-be suitors.

flutter, the timorous flutter, the amorous flutter. . . . There is scarcely any emotion in the mind which does not produce a suitable agitation in the fan." Many of these gestures were too subtle for the modern eye to perceive. For all Martin Scorsese's attention to period detail in *The Age of Innocence*, he displayed a tin ear—or eye—for its silent languages. In a real 1870s drawing room, Michelle Pfeiffer's indecipherable fits of fluttering would have left Daniel Day-Lewis utterly befuddled.

Nowadays women must register their feelings with the bluntness of a sparring partner if they expect men to understand their intentions. As many women have discovered, the subtlety of a look, a frosty tone of voice, or body language is lost on most contemporary men. If women still had such a powerful and unambiguous nonverbal language at their fingertips, they could indulge their feelings and spare those of rejected men by avoiding mutually humiliating public clashes. The equivalent of a properly wielded fan might even prevent a few sexual harassment suits. It would certainly restore a picturesque and civilized quality to the often ugly exchanges between the sexes.

Before the bestselling author John Gray informed us that *Men Are from Mars, Women Are from Venus*, Victorian ladies and gentlemen shared a single planet, which they adorned with the comprehensive language of flowers. Dictionaries listed hundreds of flowers, plants, herbs, vines, and even weeds with their corresponding meanings. We have condensed this elastic art to the vaguely cheerful "Get well" bouquet, the funeral wreath, and the predictable dozen roses on Valentine's Day. By choosing the appropriate symbols, the Victorians expressed every shade of romance from "You are my divinity" (American cowslip) to "You will be death" (hemlock). One language might even soothe the wounds inflicted by another. Lotus leaves recanted ill-spoken words, while a gift of hazel pleaded for reconciliation. Without a breath of verbal confrontation, you could accuse someone of cruelty, deceit, coquetry, even misanthropy, or admire their bravery, wit, kindness, and the defining quality that separates the last century from ours—grace.

Gems provided an equally acceptable (if more expensive) public means for expressing private feelings. Before Marilyn Monroe taught us that diamonds are a gold digger's best friend, they symbolized the strength of eternity. As such, the diamond has long been a popular choice for engagement rings. But the Victorians also favored colored stones for both romantic and platonic gifts, because they symbolized diverse emotions. Emeralds and sapphires signified fidelity, while red gems such as garnets and rubies expressed affection. Coral was given to children to wish them a happy, healthy life, while death was marked by the bereaved with onyx for spiritual strength and jet for everlasting memory.

Particular combinations and sequences of stones provided a clever alphabet to "speak" in code through necklaces, earrings, rings, pins, and bracelets. In one version, the first letter of each stone's name spelled out a sentiment. Thus, a ruby, emerald, garnet, amethyst, ruby, diamond, and sapphire set in that order spelled "r-e-g-a-r-d-s." For a more impassioned attachment, a lavender amethyst, olivine, violet sapphire, and an emerald declared one's "l-o-v-e." Sadly, many of these bejeweled bouquets were dismantled when tastes changed early in this century. With their disappearance was lost a charming way to speak from your heart without smearing it on your sleeve.

Finally, the antique language that today is the most ridiculed and misunderstood involves the silent dialect of calling-card etiquette. In the Victorian ritual of paying calls, a visitor presented his or her card during the appointed hours when the lady of the house was "at home." Although business cards rule the world today, using one on a social occasion was once considered unpardonably tasteless.

After being admitted by a servant or other family member, the guest had tea with the hostess, an encounter garnished with light conversation. The all-occasion emotional gushing we call communication would have been thought rude and self-indulgent in an era when conversation was an art to be nurtured and savored. In learning to chitchat politely, the Victorians learned to be respectful to a new or casual acquaintance, not just those we gracelessly term "significant others." They did not take the liberty of inquiring about a stranger's religious or political beliefs, state of pregnancy, finances, or sexual behaviors, nor would they have proffered such information about themselves.

There is great need for these lost civilizing lessons in today's world, but it is hard to imagine how we could incorporate them into our modern lives. We regard "wasting" time as the greatest crime, and most Victorian habits would flunk our efficiency tests measured in computerized microseconds. Thus, the custom of calling has been reduced to call waiting. To modern critics, however, such old-fashioned customs even had an insidious side. According to one historian, they embodied the middle-class demands of "polished performance and emotional self-control" that "reinforced class distinctions" and "deference to superiors." Luckily, so these critics' thinking goes, we have since unmasked the authoritarian impulse lurking behind these repressive customs. Today members of all classes can be emotionally uncontrolled, and deference to anyone but oneself is considered dysfunctional.

Since the current mind-set is closed to the benefits of Victorian-style calling, it can hardly grasp the subtler but equal advantages of leaving silent messages via cards. If the Victorian hostess was not at home or unable to receive any guests, the latter could indicate the nature of their visit through the language of folding cards. Turning down a particular corner conveyed congratulations, condolences, or the courtesy of saying good-bye before leaving town. Most important, leaving your card was a safe way to approach someone socially who might not desire your acquaintance. If the person did not return the call, you were gracefully spurned. No one hung up on you or slammed a door in your face. Although today we have technologies such as answering machines and e-mail that could conceivably be used like calling cards, we have yet to develop a reliable and unambiguous system of using them. If a message is not returned, is it a snub or a software problem?

Gentlemen left calling cards when the ladies they were visiting weren't receiving visitors. An unacknowledged card was a clear sign that one's company was not desired.

THE POLITE SOCIAL DISCOURSE WE LEFT BEHIND

Today we talk endlessly of our failure to communicate. Our ancestors devised ways to communicate politely and precisely without speaking at all. Perhaps if we still practiced the subtle arts of silent conversation, we could do with less of the endless blather from pop linguistics experts and talk-show hosts who tell us how to understand and be understood. But the poignant eloquence of this other "hieroglyphic world" died in the 1920s. Coded Victorian jewels were melted down or reset. Mile-long cigarette holders replaced milady's fan. And flowers still pleased the eye but lost their ability to speak. In this same decade, people began to notice the accompanying decline of linguistic skills, as vocabulary became more restricted.

In her 1953 memoir *The Glitter and the Gold*, the socialite-turned-reformer Consuelo Vanderbilt later lamented the lost charm of the twilight Edwardian years she spent in England, when after-dinner entertainment meant Winston Churchill's distinctive recitation of Shakespeare's plays—which he knew by heart. But even the less oratorically gifted thrived on conversation:

> We talked so much more in those days than we do now, when I find my guests stampeding for the bridge table as soon as they leave the dining room. We talked morning, noon and night, but we also knew how to listen. There was so much to be discussed. . . . We talked endlessly, for the tempo of life was slow, gentle and easy; there was no radio to tune it up. . . . Our endless discussions on politics fostered a sense of civic responsibility, and I began to look beyond the traditional but superficial public duties expected of me.

It is fashionable to bemoan our declining sense of civic commitment; the Victorians would say we lack the words to inspire it. What replaced the spoken and silent communing arts our ancestors treasured? In *Only Yesterday*, one of the best memoirs of the Jazz Age, Frederick Lewis described the unisex taste for "strong language" that developed with the taste for strong liquors, as words like "damn" and "hell" became commonplace:

It was delightful to be considered a little shocking; and so
the competition in boldness of talk went on for a time . . .
a conversation in polite circles was like a room decorated
entirely in scarlet—the result was over-emphasis, stri-
dency, and eventual boredom.

We may have upped the four-letter ante since then, but our desperate attempts to shock are still doomed to end in boredom. Exple-
tives do not fill the void left by the Victorian eloquence that
disappeared. Since the 1930s, the courts have gradually narrowed the
legal boundaries of obscenity and indecency in entertainment, news,
and individual expression until the macho lingo of the meanest
streets became our de facto language of the land.

Recent years have witnessed a growing backlash against the
resulting debasement of social intercourse. We have a dim but growing perception that we need to establish some rules for discourse. But
the absence of a socially enforced consensus on civility has made
such efforts either marginal or misguided.

A RETURN TO CIVIL DISCOURSE

We only delude ourselves by assuming that free speech carries no
social costs. But the greatest delusion is believing that plain old
vanilla obscenities, which don't insult other colors, can safely slide by
without scarring our social fabric. Ever mindful that a deluge always
begins with a single drop of rain, one Victorian-era etiquette writer
warned, "If you pass over a thing today because it is slight, you will
pass over something else of at least—perhaps greater—importance
tomorrow."

Those who have recently rediscovered the wisdom of this simple
observation now find that studies are required to prove it. Very well.
"Language is the first symptom of conflict—the small stuff esca-
lates," said Ronald D. Stephens, executive director of the National
School Safety Center in Los Angeles. After two years of interviewing
fourth- to twelfth-graders around the country, the center's researchers
found that name-calling and cursing were among the most frequent
triggers of violent behavior. At the far end of this spectrum, according
to police records, homicides frequently begin with verbal provocation.

When mouthing off can lead to murder, we dare not dismiss crude or hostile speech as "fairly harmless."[6]

Julia Ward Howe possessed no scientific data, just the common sensibilities of her day, when she said that all "rude and selfish habits of mind" encourage "great social troubles and even crimes." Inhumane speech was and is a crime against our humanity, a misdemeanor from which felonies follow. Many modern women have been forced to relearn this lesson through firsthand experience. Feminists often insist that verbal aggression is as serious as physical aggression against women, despite concern that labeling verbal offenses as harassment or abuse diminishes the meaning of those charges. Our scant facility for nuanced language may exacerbate the tendency toward catch-all accusations, but women are grappling with serious problems that can threaten first the quality of life and then life itself. Without a common social agreement on what is acceptable speech and behavior, the lives and liberties of all Americans are diminished.

Hypocrisy,
Democracy, and Diversity

Even people whose image of the nineteenth century comes from Scarlett and Rhett think they know the problem with old-fashioned manners: They were phony, wooden, and stifling, reflecting the way the uppity upper crust excluded everyone who wasn't upper crust. At least that's today's party line. In truth, Victorian manners were anything but exclusive and exclusionary. Instead, well-mannered behavior, the great equalizer, was within the reach of all. The renewal of civility depends on our rediscovering how the democracy of manners once stabilized the nation and promoted true democracy.

THE DEMOCRACY OF COURTESY

In 1869, the very middle-class educational reformer Catharine Beecher defined manners as "the outward exhibition of the democratic fundamental principle of benevolence and equal rights . . . the same courtesy which we accord to our own circle, shall be extended to every class and condition." Victorians like Miss Beecher recognized that within such a democracy of courtesy, judges must exercise authority over their courts, teachers over their pupils, and bosses over their workers. This promoted "the general well-being." But even in distinctly unequal situations, respect and restraint were the rule at every level. This was because, as Miss Beecher wrote in *American Woman's Home*, "courteous address is required not merely toward superiors; every person desires to be thus treated, and therefore the law of benevolence demands such demeanor toward all whom we meet in the social intercourse of life."

American Manners

Many people's image of Victorian manners is based on toffee-nosed lords and ladies—like those in the novels of Anthony Trollope and the plays of Oscar Wilde—who lounge in the ornate parlors of *Masterpiece Theatre*. What is fiction for us may have been a matter of fact for Europeans, but American etiquette authors of the era scrupulously noted that more than an ocean divided us from the Old World.

Bootlicking and heel-clicking European customs were considered as outré in the New World as primogeniture. "Here the practice of politeness has in it nothing of the servility which is often attached to it in countries where the code of etiquette is dictated by the courts of monarchy," the etiquette author Arthur Martine wrote in 1866. In her book *Modern Society*, Julia Ward Howe criticized English or Continental manners which were "affected by those among us who mistake the aristocracy of position for the aristocracy of character." Similarly, Catharine Beecher, in *American Woman's Home,* emphasized that American civility relied on "gentility in mind," not "birth or fashion." Thus, even those to the manor born could be "vicious coxcombs." "Ruffians" were found "in the drawing room as well as on the street." And Thomas Nelson Page warned against those "vulgarians who use money, not courtesy, as a standard of pre-eminence." Etiquette writers were particularly critical of newly minted millionaires who tried to buy gentility by trading their marriageable daughters (and hefty dowries) to threadbare counts and lords in return for use of the family title.

Even top power brokers could be socially bankrupted if their uncivilized behavior went too far. A notorious example was the publisher James Gordon Bennett, Jr. Dixon Wechter recounted in *The Saga of American Society* how Bennett, the immensely wealthy owner of the influential *New York Herald,* was well known for being "brandied to his top white hat," a habit that eventually cost him his reputation and his wife-to-be. In 1877 the tippling Bennett attended a crowded reception at his fiancée's home. According to startled witnesses, "Suddenly it was apparent to those standing nearest the fireplace that the *Herald*'s publisher had mistaken the purpose of that fixture for a plumbing facility, and was extinguishing the flames in a most unconventional manner." Bennett promptly received a bum's rush into the street and was later forced to fight a duel with a young male member of the insulted household. Both men managed to miss each other, but the exchange of fire was required to rekindle the flames of family honor that Bennett had quenched in so unseemly a fashion.

Moreover, even though he was left physically intact, the offender's social position was mortally wounded. A Victorian-bred historian who later chronicled Bennett's antics matter-of-factly stated the only possible outcome in an era when rules were not made to be broken: "Obviously every private residence in New York was forever barred to him." Bennett's disgrace exiled him to Europe for the rest of his years. There his money bought him the high life, but it could never buy back his life in New York.

Even our own willful age has not changed its standards sufficiently to accommodate this kind of personal expression. But the penalties for such behavior have been drastically reduced. In 1995, when the drunken president of an investment banking company was refused additional drinks in a first-class airline cabin, he defecated on a service cart. Far from being tackled by the defenders of propriety, he assaulted a flight attendant. In this case the bum's rush would have been lethal, but I doubt the altitude would have stopped the outraged Victorians. The man was later arrested but quickly released on a personal recognizance bond. With or without the bond, a hundred years ago he would have lost all personal recognizance. Whatever fine this man had to pay, can we imagine his "disgrace" driving him from his country or even his country club?

Rules of Courtesy for All Classes

A truly democratic code of courtesy once preserved a civilized atmosphere for everyone by punishing anyone who flouted it. Its loss leaves us at the mercy of barbarians from every class, and especially those who can buy their pardons. Despite the egregious inequality of modern mayhem, however, contemporary historians deprecate Victorian etiquette for its alleged elitism. Of course, we have long since lost the emphasis on physical and emotional restraints that, in the words of the historian John Kasson, "assured the individual's deferential participation in the dominant social order." Unfortunately, what is left is neither social nor orderly.

This notion of deferential participation smacks of blatant or subtle coercion from the high and mighty. But it was nothing of the sort. In a study that traced how standards of proper behavior developed, the historian Arthur Schlesinger, Jr., called manners "one aspect of the common man's struggle to achieve a larger degree of human dignity and self-respect." Similarly, the social scientists James Q. Wilson and Richard Herrnstein note that working-class parents in Victorian America enrolled their children in Sunday schools to teach them not just religion but "respectability." They conclude, "The bourgeois world view triumphed in the late nineteenth century largely through consent, not force." At the end of the twentieth century, the brute force of public incivility revokes the very notion of consent. Victorian ideals of courtesy embodied equality and unity because everyone was entitled to learn them and live by them. Victorians of all classes strove to make etiquette habitual and ritualistic, understanding that manners, like discipline, can only be effective if they are applied consistently rather than treated like a set of fine china to be used only when company calls. As Catharine Beecher warned in 1869, "If good manners are not practiced at home, but are allowed to lie by until occasion calls upon their wearer to assume them, they are sure to be a bad fit when donned."

Courtesy at All Times

What a dreadfully unromantic image of civilized behavior Beecher's is, compared to the "random acts of kindness" movement that burst upon popular consciousness a few years ago. According to the authors, such acts are "those little sweet or grand lovely things we do for no reason." Spontaneous courtesy, the authors claim, means "the best of humanity has sprung exquisitely into full bloom." By buying lunch for a homeless man or a bouquet of roses for an elderly woman "you are not doing what life requires of you, but the best your human soul invites you to do."

Who but a misanthrope would rain on this blooming garden of philanthropies, which should make anyone's day this side of Clint Eastwood? Aren't random acts of kindness the perfect counterweight to our epidemic of random acts of incivility? Not a chance. Both live by the fleeting "I feel like it" factor, like dogs who might lick your hand or maul it. Both are dangerous—incivility for obvious reasons, spontaneous niceness because it leaves civility to the mercy of how merciful we feel at the moment. In contrast, the code of Victorian courtesy did not depend on our moods or biorhythms. It was a daily, demanding, universal obligation, not a whimsy that favored a chosen few. When courtesy was integrated in everyday life, one noticed its absence, not its presence.

Even the "random kindness" movement's founders concede that the main impetus for doing good is to make you feel good about yourself and promote personal growth. This brand of altruism offers another way to wallow in dysfunctions and justify self-indulgence, because learning kindness to others "begins by simple acts of kindness toward ourselves." Whatever window dressing it wears, me-first-ism is toxic to civility.

Our culture is rife with selfish and self-absorbed behavior. The Victorians believed in treating everyone with courtesy at all times. Instead we "treat" everyone to the juicy tidbits of instant intimacy that feed our egos and their ids. Respect and self-respect, not repression, made privacy what Lord Chesterfield called a "sacred right." He understood intuitively that private life would be cheapened and distorted if it became public fodder.

BARING ALL IN THE MODERN ERA

Baring our all compromises the humanity of those who gawk and those who are gawked at. Proper gawking was once confined to zoos and P. T. Barnum's freak-filled dime "museums." In the 1920s and '30s, disheartened Victorians pined for the days when notoriety was denounced as social nudism, and "people lived with more dignity and sinned more successfully than they do now," as Frederick Townsend wittily put it in his 1913 memoir. Citing the mounting number of divorce cases that the "cheap press" reported in "nauseating detail," he concluded that marriage was becoming "a joke." We need look no further than the tell-all divorces of Britain's royals or the videotaped near brawl in Central Park between John F. Kennedy Jr. and his live-in girlfriend. Royalty, real or presumed, looks uninspiringly plebeian when it goes naked in the world. (As for Kennedy's legendarily private mother, Jackie O., the astounding prices her personal belongings fetched at auction proved, as Maureen Dowd wrote in *The New York Times,* that "in an age of exhibitionism, coyness was a good investment.")[1]

Newsweek's Evan Thomas attributes our current fascination with Jane Austen—via movies and BBC series—to the mannerly reticence that we have lost. He noted that "people have become accustomed to vulgarity . . . and perfect strangers insulting them or, worse, confiding in them. Possibly they are growing sick of it."[2]

Possibly they are rediscovering the not-so-secret wisdom of buttoned lips. Charlotte Brönte wrote: "The human heart has hidden treasures / In secret kept, in silence sealed;— / The thoughts, the hopes, the dreams, the pleasures, / Whose charms were broken if revealed." We may relieve these hunger pangs for a few hours by watching period dramas, but Hollywood cannot bring celluloid civility to life. That requires recasting our modern virtues as the vices they were once considered.

Public Egotism

We are at our most anti-Victorian when we celebrate ourselves. Our ancestors didn't need the Bible to tell them, "Pride goeth before destruction, and a haughty spirit before a fall." Yet it seems that no fall is too great to dent the egos of today's "masters of the universe." For example, after reversing his business misfortunes, Donald Trump penned a paean to himself in a November 19, 1995, *New York Times Magazine* article. Far from teaching him humility, his brief experience of being down and out taught him that others were unworthy of his beneficence:

> Many . . . lives had been profoundly changed by me, in an extraordinarily positive way. Some had become rich, some powerful, but in all cases they would never have ended up in their high social or economic positions without the

influence of Donald Trump. When crunch time came, however, some . . . were not around when I most needed their help. . . . I view these people as being born with garbage in their genes.

Trump is hardly alone in publicly patting his own back, a trait than which, according to Lord Chesterfield, there was "no surer sign of vulgarity." In the decades since Norman Mailer aptly titled a collection of his essays *Advertisements for Myself*, a generation of self-promoters has learned to follow his lead. During the 1992 presidential campaign, Hillary Clinton told the Washington-based reporter Kathleen Matthews she had "no doubt" she herself would be a "terrific" governor or president in her own right. On the other side of the political spectrum, Rush Limbaugh calls himself "talent on loan from God." Mail-order catalogues offer mere mortals a similar chance to crow via a personalized $34.95 pillow that tells visitors, "It's Hard to be Humble When You're from 'X' college." Even cheaper are bumper stickers that advertise parental pride in having honor students. Advertisements for your children's accomplishments are deemed no more dishonorable than advertisements for your own. For good reason: The latter are extensions of the former.

Occasionally someone comes along to remind us that less is more. Air Force captain Scott O'Grady survived six days in the wilderness surrounded by hostile Serbian forces when his plane was shot down over Bosnia. When he was given a hero's welcome back home, he refused that tribute, conferring it instead on the marines who rescued him. In this "strut your stuff" age, journalists seemed genuinely perplexed by the modesty that used to be a common part of uncommon valor.

It is much easier for us to understand the self-proclaimed "courage" of Rachel Worby, West Virginia's first lady. In a book on the "private struggles" of "accomplished women," Worby revealed details of her extramarital romps, her progress from frigidity to orgasm, and the strategic location of a tattoo. When questioned about the propriety of this truly heroic act of self-revelation, her husband, the governor, seemed puzzled by the controversy, asking: "How can anyone be too honest?" How indeed? The Victorians lived by the adage "Pride and grace ne'er dwelt in one place"—not even in the "almost heaven" of West Virginia.[3]

Even as our popular culture screams for equality at any cost, it demands that we puff ourselves up to prove we are first among equals. "Nothing vilifies more than pride," wrote Arthur Martine in 1866. The Victorians, who recognized a deadly sin when they met one, knew how deadly pride could be to civilized relations, where all are entitled to feel valued, not inferior to big mouths and braggarts. We may call boasters healthy; Victorians such as Arthur Martine considered them "boa-constrictors spewing the vile saliva of selfish vanity." Their view of bragging, not ours, had a true egalitarian spirit. As the 1880 *Manual of Politeness* explained, "To shine in society is more frequently attempted than compassed; to please is in the power of all."

The Victorians believed it was impossible to please anyone but yourself if you turned conversations into rambling autobiographies. Not only was it "conceited" to brag and "make yourself the hero of your own stories," it was boring: "If you are full of yourself, consider that you and your affairs are not so interesting to other people as to you," proclaimed an 1891 etiquette guide, *Don't, or Directions for Avoiding Improprieties*. Alas, this assumption has become a dinosaur in this tell-me-all age. We prick up our ears for private affairs, not ideas. Our ancestors could never have imagined that we would actually boast of failures and dysfunctions along with achievements, or that we would reveal other people's intimate secrets without their consent.

A COMMENDABLE HYPOCRISY

But isn't this just the price we pay for truthfulness? We assume that honest people hold forth; only hypocrites hold back. We deride those tight-lipped Victorians with their starched-shirt fronts, their saccharine euphemisms, and their plastic compliments. Better to ruffle some feathers and feelings than compromise your own. The social philosopher Hannah Arendt summarized this "virtue" when she called any disjunction between feelings and their expression "the vice of vices." Those who don't tell it like it is are in denial, which always requires some liberating form of therapy. Civility and veracity are considered oil and water. For example, MTV's show *The Real World* was described by this introductory voice-over: "Seven strangers are picked to live in a house . . . to find out what happens when people stop being polite and start being real." Drama is guaranteed, but do not look for these seven strangers to experience a moment of the serenity of civility.

Yes, the Victorians were hypocrites and made no bones about it. Contrary to Arendt, however, there was virtue in this vice. The Victorians practiced what they called "a commendable hypocrisy." As Eliza Duffey wrote in *Ladies' and Gentlemen's Complete Etiquette*:

> We are called upon to make such minor sacrifices of sincerity as a due regard for the happiness and feelings of others demands. True politeness requires us to consider these before our own. A lady who shows by act or expresses in plain, curt words that the visit of another is unwelcome may perhaps pride herself upon being no hypocrite. But she is, in reality, worse. She is grossly selfish. Courtesy, which is the essence of unselfishness, would require her for the time to forget her own feelings and remember those of her visitor, and thus her duty is plain to make that visitor welcome and happy while she remains. If she really does this—forgets self and thinks only of her friend—there is no hypocrisy, but the highest order of Christian charity.

Certainly there is nothing commendable about the hypocrisy of certain public images and image makeovers. But the Victorian brand of social religion, which applied equally to each sex and to give and take alike, is a civilized alternative to using the truth as a bludgeon. Turning the high ideal of honesty to the lowest possible purpose— indulging ourselves—was, as Eliza Duffey wrote, cold-blooded and "only a pretext to introduce something that will wound your feelings." What is candor to us they denounced as survival of the thick skinned.

Most of us are walking wounded, courtesy of a culture that entitles friends, relatives, enemies, and strangers to act as self-appointed Solomons. Defining their opinions as truth, they may ruthlessly dissect every aspect of our thoughts, appearance, and actions as if we were laboratory rats. They generously give us a piece of their mind, even if it robs us of our own peace of mind. Brute truth is always a slippery slope, even when our footing seems secure. Your friend may tolerate or even appreciate being told her new dress makes her look like a parade float. But once the mouth starts its motor, where does it stop? With racial and ethnic slurs? Why censor yourself if that's what you honestly think? One rap musician dismissed complaints about his using the word "bitch" because "you call a spade a spade." If "bitch" is his heartfelt opinion of women, would we want him to sing false but flattering lyrics for the sake of civility? How could we trust his motives, his music, or our judgment if he did? Do we want to trade a "bitch" for "B.S."?[4]

The Victorians carefully distinguished between diplomacy—which used to be valued—and the fawning that Jonathan Swift called the "food of fools." Etiquette authors always vetoed affectation. "There is nothing more disagreeable in the intercourse of civil people than the deference which descends to flattery and obsequiousness," wrote E. H. Ruddock in 1899. Julia Ward Howe thought flattery an "offense against politeness"; those most susceptible to it were "already suffering the intoxication of vanity," she wrote in 1895. Because the Victorians were so attuned to character, the subtle cues of hypocrisy rarely escaped them. "When I hear the soft voice, a little too soft, I look into the face to see whether the two agree," said Mrs. Howe. "But I need scarcely do that. The voice itself tells the story, is sincere or insincere."

Moreover, chilly civility was considered as repugnant as stale hot air. The ideal social temperature was warm without being overly familiar. "Where kindness is rendered with cold, unsympathizing manners, which greatly lessens its value," wrote Catharine Beecher in 1869, it became nothing more than "the payment of a just due." Lord Chesterfield condemned "the mechanical observances of social for-malities . . . the courtesies of life are something real, and not a mere hollow form."

Did that mean you chucked the form if no real feeling filled it? Again, the Victorians had an answer that preserved both integrity and civility. They believed that like an arranged marriage in which love gradually grows, the duty that was an effort at first would become habit. Thus, you subdued your gloomy mood in company because, as Arthur Martine wrote, "To look pleasantly and to speak kindly is a duty we owe to others." But if we focus on their concerns, not ours, practicing selflessness we cultivate sentiments that fill those hollow

forms. This politeness was not phoniness, but "artificial good nature." Conversely, good nature was considered natural politeness.

If all this sounds like practice-makes-perfect fancy footwork, it was. But even Fred Astaire labored long and hard to achieve his look of easy grace. His performance was no less worthy for the effort that lay behind the impression of effortlessness. Victorian finesse was a labor of love whose essence lay in giving, not taking. Our ancestors loved the civility that cushioned all of us more than they loved the self that demanded expression. So they took pains—which spared others from feeling them. Lord Chesterfield urged his son to learn "how to conceal a truth without telling a lie."

Sometimes this finesse can be truly heroic. When the French president François Mitterand died in the winter of 1996, his widow revealed that he kept his cancer from her for ten years after it was diagnosed. "He didn't lie, neither to me nor those he loved," she explained. "He simply preserved our tranquillity of spirit."[5]

This secrecy may seem incomprehensible in an age when truth routinely tramples the spirit's tranquillity in the minutiae of daily living no less than the drama of life and death. The hardball business of gift giving provides a sad but fitting example. Miss Manners's and Ann Landers's columns are filled with hurt-filled stories of gifts blatantly unappreciated by the receiver, returned for cash or exchanged because they weren't liked or needed. Before detailed gift lists demanding material goodies of a specific size, color, and style number, gift recipients made the effort to sound grateful even if they weren't, because to all but the thoughtless the thought mattered more than the object.

Even in intimate matters, truth was a delicate balancing act. Arthur Martine urged his readers: "Speak from the heart when you speak to the heart; only making judgment prune the expressions of deep feeling without checking the noble sentiments that call them forth." So a commendably hypocritical lady gently rejected a marriage proposal by calling it an honor, even if wasn't. Now just asking for a date—where honor no longer figures—risks a range of bruising replies: a simple "No!," a more definitive "Not in this lifetime," or a selection from the menu of casual obscenities that have become our unofficial national language.

Our brutal honesty has become sheer brutality. The Victorians aspired to be, in the words of the seventeenth-century essayist Thomas Fuller, "cordial to the soul." We have lost our culture's soul, and even our ability to understand how simple cordiality sustained human dignity. This is illustrated in the classic Victorian novel *The Rise of Silas Lapham* by William Dean Howells. In this 1885 comedy of manners, the bumbling social climber Silas Lapham is invited to dine with the ultrarespectable Cory family. He frantically consults etiquette books to determine what color gloves and cravat he should wear. He becomes farcically obsessed with details, behavior the Victorians themselves derided as the "silver-fork school of etiquette." For all his sartorial pains, he gets roaring drunk at the dinner. He insults his hosts and mortifies his own family.

The next day Lapham bemoans his disgrace to the Cory family's son and asks what the senior Cory said about his boorish behavior after he left the party. The young man answers matter-of-factly, "My father doesn't talk his guests over one another. . . . You were among gentlemen." If Lapham had learned the spirit, not just the letter, of all the etiquette books he read, he would have known that "whatever passes in parties at your own or another's house is never repeated by well-bred people." The Corys' silence may have been hypocritical (just imagine what they were thinking!), but it was also soothing and forgiving.

LOWERING OUR STANDARDS

While we carry the banner of equality, we practice the reverse snobbery of forcing everyone to bring themselves down to the lowest possible level or risk being demonized as elitist. This is not just hypocrisy but a disaster predicted more than eight decades ago, when Thomas Nelson Page warned that a civilized society could not survive if the lower classes no longer took "their cue and tone" from middle- and upper-class ideals that stressed obligation over self-indulgence.

Today the mainstreaming of lower-class attitudes and behavior threatens to tear society apart. The prominent black columnist

William Raspberry worries about the role-model reversal among American youth, in which lower-class kids no longer mimic the styles of the privileged. Instead, he writes, "The downward pull of the 'bad element' is more and more evident in the pricey suburbs, even in the small towns of exurbia—and among girls as well as boys." Record industry executives report that middle-class white kids are bigger buyers of violent rap music than are blacks. Raspberry, no elitist, prays that "the slovenly dress, unsightly hairstyles and dismaying manners of our children" are not "a prelude to something far, far more deadly."[6] While I am reluctant to discourage any prayer, this one seems particularly futile if we continue on our current course.

Lower- and working-class crudeness also rules over TV's wasteland. Whether shows are set in the streets or corporate suites, they increasingly mimic the nasty edge of *Married with Children* and *Roseanne*. Both on and off the air, the blustery Roseanne torpedoes everyone who fails her down-and-dirty test of character. She has called top actresses like Jodie Foster, Susan Sarandon, and Meryl Streep "castrated females" who are "too middle class." She is clearly proud that more than talent separates her from these women.

While the growing ranks of civility preachers readily denounce her ilk, too few will openly tackle the sensitive but undeniable link between low class and no class. Bulldozers like Roseanne have plenty of defenders among the upper-middlebrow set. They range from the chic *New Yorker* editor who invited her to help "guest edit" a special issue on feminism to the *New York Times* critic who sees the newly belligerent style of prime-time TV as one of "honesty and sincerity, as opposed to the sneaky passive-aggressive style that goes under the name politeness."

The newly popular sports ethic of "in-your-face" is another example of how society's cream sinks to the bottom of the barrel instead of leading the way to the top. *The New York Times* describes the in-your-face approach as the "very fast, very physical, very vocal playground game that came out of the ghetto and now dominates the National Basketball Association. Half the game lies in the art of mercilessly taunting one's opponent during the game, then rubbing his face in the ashes of defeat afterward."

In a truly Victorian assessment of this unsportsmanlike approach to sports, the legendary Kareem Abdul-Jabbar warned that basketball is "moving back to the law of the jungle."[7] (In the last century, when sportsmanship was synonymous with sport, baseball prohibited sliding and stealing bases because they were considered "ungentlemanly tactics.") But life in and out of sports stopped being gentle when it took off the gloves and traded them for cleats. Criminologists note that the violence once confined to the inner city is now increasingly at home in the suburbs. Poverty is not a crime, but emulating the poor at their worst impoverishes our country's soul.

LOWER-CLASS MINORITIES AND MANNERS

Just as we must acknowledge the distinctly WASP flavor of Victorian etiquette, we must stop pretending to be colorblind if we hope to restore it. Race is the most explosive and divisive issue in America today. But only by discussing it candidly—something we claim to admire—can we reweave the threads of civility that will keep it from tearing us apart. Although civility's vandals come in every class and color, the young black ghetto male personifies the mocking antithesis of Victorian morals and manners.

The renowned African-American sociologist Elijah Anderson has extensively documented the "inability or unwillingness" of lower-class black males "to follow basic middle-class rules about dress and comportment." In his book *Streetwise*, he notes that their behavior is blunt, aggressive, and selfish. To establish dominance and turf rights, they rouse fear on the streets with their swagger, balled fists, boom boxes, cursing, loud spontaneous singing and laughter, and broadcasts about intimate matters. As Dr. Anderson puts it with some understatement, "All convey the impression of little concern for other pedestrians"—particularly women. Many women I know routinely negotiate a gauntlet of threats, dehumanizing comments on body parts, and proposals for their abuse. They will acknowledge this harsh reality only with reluctance and a don't-blame-the-victim dose of liberal guilt.

For all his insight, Professor Anderson faults people like me for clutching their belongings and making other instinctive defensive moves in reaction to any perceived threat. We are branded racists if we fail to distinguish between troublemakers and law-abiding black males, even when both wear the same clothes, such as gold chains, designer warm-up suits, and dark glasses. The logic of Victorian etiquette neatly resolved this problem, since it recognized—correctly—that such distinctions are impossible to draw during brief public encounters.

The Victorians believed that in work, as in life, "Graces do half the business," as Lord Chesterfield wrote. This is why job training programs, however well intentioned, will never make inner-city residents employable, unless they recognize that the right attitude is an indispensable skill. This has become painfully apparent in urban areas across the country. Despite the tax breaks and government grants that create employment opportunities for the poor, foreigners are often hired over needy locals. According to many employers, Hispanic and African immigrants have a strong work ethic, while native minorities lie about their qualifications, show up late if at all, and even assault their bosses. Rather than honestly confront this destructive and self-destructive behavior, urban experts pass this racial hot potato by blaming employer bias.

Basic civility is readily sacrificed to racial doubletalk in manicured neighborhoods as well. At one high school in an affluent Washington suburb, an African-American honor student said that "fear of crossing the PC line" smothers this essential debate: "There is a lot that people want to talk about [such as the fact] that black kids have been allowed to be rude, vulgar, racist because their parents and grandparents have suffered from discrimination. So no one holds them accountable."[8]

We must stop legitimizing the tyrannical, uncivilized minority of all races and classes, while stigmatizing those who want to reclaim safe streets and peace of mind for the majority. Jacob Riis, the great Victorian urban reformer, once said that to help the poor you must sometimes fight against them. Past wrongs and cultural diversity can never justify what Julia Ward Howe, writing in 1895, called "indifference to the divine and contempt for the human." Sixty-five percent of American adults believe "the world is out of control these days," a view shared by 79 percent of blacks—those most victimized by its brutality. In one way or another, we all have the scars to prove that "in-your-face" can never save face; it just leaves us to the mercy of time-bomb tempers.[9]

RAISING STANDARDS OF BEHAVIOR

Only recently have we rediscovered Victorian methods to diffuse hot tempers. In 1994, Harvard University's Jay Winsten, the creator of the highly effective "designated driver" strategy, turned his talents to the "squash it" antiviolence campaign." "Squash it" is a street-wise gesture based on the "time-out" signal used in sports. Winsten recruited entertainment industry leaders to help find ways "to communicate that it's cool and smart to walk away from a confrontation without a fight."[10]

In an acclaimed bestselling book, Daniel Goleman of *The New York Times* maintains that successful students need more than academic skills; equally important is what he calls emotional intelligence. This includes impulse and anger control, empathy, and harmonious interactions with others; in Victorian shorthand: self-restraint and respect. Students who lack these essential skills are more likely to get poor grades, behave violently, and experience discipline problems, teen pregnancy, and drug abuse. While all children with emotional deficits are at risk, African Americans suffer most. According to many inner-city teachers, those children who try to defy the stereotypes and the odds by pursuing academic excellence are often taunted by peers and accused of acting "white." Goleman's laudable book is another example of our inadvertently claiming past wisdom as our own. Back in 1852 Elizabeth Blackwell noted, "Knowledge alone will never make a people virtuous." Ralph Waldo Emerson put it even more pithily: "Character is higher than intellect."[11]

The growing number of "conflict resolution," "life skills," and "emotional literacy" programs in the nation's schools unwittingly promote this not-so-new idea. They teach the ABCs of civility so that kids won't pull a weapon on whoever bumps into them in the hallway. One largely minority high school in Washington, D.C., extends this approach to the next step by teaching girls to dress, speak, and carry themselves "like ladies." The Victorians understood that how you carry yourself is just as important as what you carry in your head. They believed that a person's posture and carriage expressed to others what sort of person she was. An upright citizen did not slouch and shuffle.

Another Washington-area program for mostly male minority juvenile offenders combines lessons in anger control with proper

English, grooming, and table manners. "I didn't realize how much better I would feel when people started looking at me with respect," said one gratified teenage participant.[12] Like Lord Chesterfield, he learned that "dignity of manners is absolutely necessary to make even the most valuable character either respected or respectable."

The Downside of Diversity

Ironically, even as we try to civilize (and, however unwittingly, Victorianize) our students, diversity training in the workplace is bucking that healthy trend. As our labor force becomes increasingly less homogeneous, we have an even greater need for shared standards of civility. Unfortunately, the current brand of cultural diversity that is popular in corporate America undermines its own stated goals—sensitivity, tolerance, and inclusion.

Over half of all Fortune 500 companies have diversity coordinators or directors. Business and government spend billions of dollars on such personnel and related programs. Diversity experts write that homogeneous values are "disturbing" and the melting pot is "destructive." The flaw in this approach is not its laudable goal of bringing more women and minorities into the workplace. But promoting the expression of diverse values guarantees continuous conflict by insisting that a wide range of cultural behaviors must be not only tolerated but celebrated.

The diversity consultants rely on a raft of management texts such as *Differences That Work: Organized Excellence Through Diversity, Cultural Diversity in Organizations,* and *Workforce America.* They teach that judging all workers by the "traditional white male yardstick" discriminates against racial and ethnic groups who see it as "foreign to their self-definition." Instead of minorities fitting into the organization, the organization must adapt until everyone has "the freedom and support required to be themselves." The racist whitebread yardstick is replaced by the inviolate assumption that "today's employees want to maintain their unique ethnic and cultural heritage while receiving the respect of their bosses, colleagues, and organizations." This new moral imperative is no less than "the key to solving our most pressing global problems."

There is so much surface sense in this argument that it is easy to buy it, especially if the open-handed buyers are white corporate executives who fear boycotts, bad PR, and lawsuits. Only by candidly assessing the diversity agenda can we see how it exacerbates the tensions, unfairness, and incivility it claims to cure. Consider the scenario, posed by one diversity trainer, of two female colleagues who disagree. A white woman has been socialized to be "conciliatory" in conflicts. As a "peacemaker," she always tries to "smooth over differences. Speaking with a New England regional accent, the volume of her voice will often drop as the pitch rises. She will exhibit more smiling behavior." In contrast, a black woman proudly describes herself as a "feisty battler." Research shows that her racially based behavioral preferences are "highly assertive, even bold by Anglo standards." With an "animated and challenging" style, she will emphasize points of disagreement, her volume rising with the pitch of her voice. "She will also frown or display more emotion."

These women are likely to "misjudge" each other. The white will be seen as "weak and cowardly," while the black will be wrongly viewed as "escalating rather than resolving conflict." The "direct approach" favored by many African Americans "may be perceived by others as inappropriately hostile or militant behavior, a perception that is reinforced by stereotypes of Blacks as being prone to violence." The proposed solution is to educate everyone to accommodate all stylistic differences, "with none superior or inferior." These clashing styles provide the added bonus of making the work environment "more stimulating and exciting."

Problem solved! Is everybody happy? Is everyone respected? Is everyone productive? Only if your ideal work environment is a free-for-all that drains time and money from the bottom line. Only if you believe that customers and clients, as well as workers, are equally "educated" and accepting of whatever behavior they encounter from those seeking to sell them a product or service. The seductive logic of diversity attempts to legitimize the "in-your-face" style that has turned schools, sports, and streets into battlegrounds. How absurd that we must be sensitive to a style that epitomizes insensitivity and obliterates civility.

Furthermore, there's an inherent contradiction in the message. Whites are expected to learn and uncritically accept all aspects of other cultural styles so minorities can be embraced as representatives of distinctive ethnic traditions without being stereotyped. Meanwhile, minorities are pressured to define themselves and be defined in terms of their ethnicity, whatever their personal preference. Is this progress? Isn't this pressure to conform, this compromise of individuality, the despised Victorian gospel we so proudly rejected?

Despite the lofty rhetoric about equally respecting all cultural styles, this stacked deck inherently favors "feisty battlers" over cool conciliators. The latter can either perish or adapt by abandoning their own cultural style to the heat of hostility—what the world needs now. By contrast, the Victorians believed that etiquette was "practical kindness" rooted in common sense. Common sense should tell us civility and hostility are inherently incompatible. Hostility is a volcano, exploding "in your face" at will. Civility presumes you "think before you act." This pearl of wisdom comes not from a present-day Ph.D., but from the quill of the fourteen-year-old George Washington. As a teenager, the future father of our country compiled over a hundred "rules of civility" to govern daily life. The Victorians often cited precepts from this list, which concludes with the all-purpose admonition, "labor to keep alive in your breast that little celestial fire called conscience."

Manners and Opinions

Victorian manners never precluded voicing opposing opinions, which can hardly be avoided in any workplace. But their artistry, born of necessity, was to keep conflict from destroying "peace and goodwill." Writing at the turn of the century, the educator Charles W. Eliot said, "Long experience among civilized men has proved that good manners are compatible with holding strong opinions and expressing them firmly on fit occasions. They cannot and should not prevent earnest contentions, but they can take the bitterness out of strife, and prevent personal animosities between sincere and strenuous opponents." Imagine how much less hostile and more productive our public and private debates would be if we followed Eliot's advice:

> If a gentleman advances an opinion which is different from ideas you are known to entertain . . . differ with him as gently as possible. You will not say "Sir, you are mistaken!" "Sir, you are wrong" or that you "happen to know better;" but you will rather use some such phrase as "Par-

don me—if I am not mistaken," etc. This will give him a chance to say some such civil thing as that he regrets to disagree with you.[13]

This approach not only preserves dignity and principled disagreement, it discourages the bruising insults that are often exchanged when people get in each other's faces.

AGGRESSION'S POWERFUL NEGATIVE EFFECT

Not only do manners, as Eliot put it, "take the bitterness out of strife," a value that can't be measured, but they are also essential to physical and economic health. In 1995 New York City launched a $150,000 five-year campaign to teach cab drivers and city employees to be polite to tourists. Why spend tax dollars to reform the rudeness capital of America? Because government surveys again ratified what was once Victorian common sense. Tourists named that legendary rudeness as a main deterrent to return visits to New York.

Etiquette is also good medicine, while hostility can be toxic. Medical researchers found that boiling tempers and loud, aggressive language contribute to coronary heart disease and death by raising testosterone secretions. Dr. Redford Williams of Duke University has characterized anger as a risk factor akin to smoking or high blood pressure. According to Dr. Aron Siegman of the University of Maryland, just speaking loudly can significantly raise blood pressure, while speaking softly eliminates "cardiovascular upheaval." Studies conducted at dozens of medical centers and hospitals show that among those who already suffered a heart attack, angry outbursts more than doubled the risk of having another within two crucial hours after the first. Can we really afford to promote any cultural style that shortens life expectancy and increases budget deficits?

Without the soothing coolness of manners, the Victorians predicted that society would fall apart. But patching Humpty Dumpty back together needs more than desperation and good intentions. It needs the glue of what Arthur Schlesinger, Jr., called the "nationwide consensus of manners" that defined nineteenth-century America. This consensus became more, not less, important as millions of immigrants diversified the country.

A COMMON COURTESY

The Victorians' rational response to widening class, racial, and ethnic divisions was the common currency of common courtesy that a fragmented country needs to peacefully settle disputes as much as it needs a common language. Imagine the chaos and traffic fatalities if everyone followed their own rules of the road. Responding to those who ridicule rules they had no part in setting, Schlesinger noted that the immigrants' willingness to imitate them "has in the long run had the effect of lessening artificial distinctions."

In 1895 Julia Ward Howe made a crucial observation that would be heretical today: "Perhaps our theory of the freedom and equality of all men leads some of us to the mistaken conclusion that all people equally know how to behave themselves, which is far from being the fact."

Unless corporate America has the courage to put the welfare of all above cultural coddling for some, what hope is there to civilize our streets with a unified code of manners? For business to function efficiently, workers of every racial, ethnic, and religious background must check some part of their identities at the door when they clock in each morning.

A nudist can't truly be himself on company time—and his means of personal expression is far less hostile than those celebrated and mandated by cultural diversity junkies. Not only do they balkanize society, they injure those they seek to help. In our candor-crazed age, we must bluntly admit what many only whisper—they don't object to working with people from different backgrounds, just those who display the brute, threatening, chip-on-the-shoulder attitude that coarsens everyone and drains the grace from everyday life.

The force-fed propaganda that justifies what the Victorians considered selfish and egotistical behavior fosters resentment and hardens whites to the laudable aspects of diversity—bringing more minorities into the labor force and encouraging everyone to learn about other cultures. This brand of diversity is a win-win goal, but diversity in manners guarantees adversity. There is little peace and even less pleasure in a world where equality equals anarchy. Without common rules of etiquette, we will continue to regress to the bullies' rule of the jungle.

Proponents of diversity often complain that their critics focus exclusively on the "here and now" while ignoring the history of past discrimination that unjustly devalued certain groups and cultures. I agree. The Victorian civility we have trashed for nearly a century deserves restoration and emulation, not as an exclusive privilege for a few but as a gift free to all for the taking. Polite isn't white or any other color. It is the key to the colorblind justice we owe each other in our daily interactions. When Lincoln said, "A house divided against itself cannot stand," he referred to the rift between slave states and free. Luckily, that house survived a bloody war. But it may not survive the continuing corrosion of its foundation—civility.

PART 3

PRIVATE INTIMACY

9

Babes in Toyland

If our new no-strings-attached sex is so great, why aren't we satisfied? . . . We wander down the aisles of a vast sexual toy store, filling up our carts with experiences and sexual gadgets and techniques but feeling unsatisfied and empty. Having destroyed the cultural climate that nurtures great love, we've been forced to settle for a great lay—if we can find it.

CAN'T GET NO SATISFACTION

Like shopaholics who try to buy that elusive high, we struggle in vain to fill the void of romance with racy paraphernalia and entertainment. Marketers invade our bedrooms with videos, books, and sex toys designed to cure our sexual ills. In place of poetry, we purchase our inspiration from 900 lines. Mail-order catalogs selling mops, mugs, and laundry stain removers also hawk his-and-hers glow-in-the-dark underwear "guaranteed to light up your love life." *Joy of Sex* author Dr. Alex Comfort tells his readers not to be afraid of reducing sex to a technique. Even conservative Christians Tim and Beverly LaHaye, in their 1976 book *The Act of Marriage*, describe the "art of love" as a product of "practicing mutually satisfying techniques." Yet for all our new moves and fancy footwork, we are still not finding passion.

In our desperate quest for ever higher erotic highs, we have scoured the kitchen, the toy store, the drug store, the burgeoning sex stores, and their mail-order spinoffs. We've had our love-ins, wife swappings, feminist consciousness raising masturbation workshops, scared-safe sex, man sharing, and man hating. We search everywhere but in the century that looks disapprovingly over our shoulders and are convinced there is nothing that we could learn from that era of "repression."

Animal Instincts

After all, isn't such repression of our animalistic instincts unhealthy? "It's scary for a feminist woman to acknowledge that she is also an animal," says Naomi Wolf in *Fire with Fire*, "because it is just our animal nature that a sexist society wants to use to constrain us. . . . At times, the critical mind has got to shut down; we have to become simply beasts, simply mouths, simply sex, even as men are known sometimes to want to be just sex. Let us make room for that need without being made to feel that we are abdicating evolution or revolution." This sounds like a strategy for putting women on top in the boardroom and the bedroom. But it is only another sad example of the delusional freedom that appropriates the lowest male standards. It limits women's choices rather than expanding them, and it normalizes a sexual conformity as sterile and severe as the relentless male bashing it opposes.

Like selfishness and crudity, animal copulation may be natural, but the female of the species naturally gets shortchanged by it. The Victorians knew that unharnessed primal instincts would turn courtship into a cold-blooded contest between the hunter and the hunted. *This* is what they deemed unnatural. Describing the "mean animal passion" of fornication, the physician William Acton wrote in 1875, "Its peculiarity and heinousness consist in divorcing from all feelings of love that which was meant by nature as the . . . intensest expression of unreserved affection to a mere momentary and brutal indulgence."

Sheer gratification of "natural appetites and passion" was never a sufficient reason to indulge. As Henry James, Sr., put it, "No man and woman can do that deliberately without converting themselves into brutes."[1] In her 1876 work, *The Relations Between the Sexes*, the ever-commonsensical Eliza Duffey specified which sex would be more brutalized by free love. [It] reduces man to the exact level of the cat, the dog, or the bull, which gratifies its animal propensities whenever or wherever it finds a willing female of its own race, and then goes away utterly oblivious of consequences. . . . As man dropped the mantle of responsibility in the matter of offspring, it would unavoidably fall upon the shoulders of women."

The current explosion of single mothers and welfare costs flagrantly proves her point. But the Victorians didn't need to experience such egregious consequences in order to reject sophistical doctrines of sexual equality. They understood biology's inherent double standard, but they responded by imposing women's standards on men. Their solution stands in stark contrast to our present-day practice of performing a mental sex-change operation on the female psyche. As with civility, "Women are especially called on to strengthen and guide the sexual virtue of a people," wrote Dr. Elizabeth Blackwell in *Essays in Medical Sociology*. The biographers Leon Stein and Annette Baxter note that Grace Dodge, first president of the YWCA, said any self-respecting woman "does not allow the sowing of wild oats in men." Now equality means matching them oat for oat.

WHAT'S GOOD FOR THE GOOSE

The Victorians, however, had a different sense of sexual equality. When a self-respecting Victorian woman declared, as Dr. Blackwell did in 1902, that "a man demands absolute chastity in a wife, and a woman should be no less in her demands," she was heard and heeded. In 1899, a prominent male physician, E. H. Ruddock, wrote in his advice book for husbands, "Society has no right to condone in man what it condemns in women."

This was no pipe dream or personal preference but a forceful cultural mandate of true manhood. Among the private period documents unearthed by the historian Karen Lystra is an 1898 letter from a middle-aged widower seeking to reassure his new love interest of his honor. During the fourteen years since his wife's death, he wrote, he "loved no woman," although passions "blaze in my blood as fiercely as volcano fires [but] break forth only where I love. I will look into your eyes with a clear, unchallenged soul, Clara, when I meet you." Subsequent letters confirm that their eventual marriage was both physically and emotionally rich.

Despite Mark Twain's raucous youth, he was a virgin when he married at thirty-four, according to his biographer Resa Williams. Did inexperience equal deprivation for this man who was an embodiment of worldliness? Not a chance. Always deeply reverential toward women, Twain still sounded like a smitten schoolboy when corresponding with Olivia, his wife of fifteen years. He mourned nothing so much as her grievous loss. The painfully romantic epitaph he spoke at her graveside was not just a tribute to one couple's boundless love but a reflection of masculinity fulfilled in his time: "Wherever she was, there was Eden."

Teddy Roosevelt, according to his biographer Edmund Morris, proudly wrote that he remained "perfectly pure" throughout his bachelorhood. Now onetime basketball star Wilt Chamberlain boasts in his memoirs of bedding twenty thousand women. Which man was more manly? Current NBAer A. C. Green doesn't play the macho game Chamberlain's way. This self-proclaimed virgin intends to remain one until marriage. He preaches chastity in schools and on talk shows, hoping to inspire youngsters, especially those who worship sports figures. He also wants to teach young men to respect young women.

Perhaps if there were more men with an attitude like A. C. Green's there would be fewer women who think their only option is to adopt the male attitude to treat the opposite sex like something to be consumed, used up, and thrown away. Coldhearted consumerism is a sorry substitute for passion.

In retrospect, how many women found sexual satisfaction in the much lauded "zipless fuck," a phrase coined by Erica Jong in her 1973 book *Fear of Flying* to describe an emotionless, guilt-free sexual encounter? Yet the mentality that girls-must-be-boys continues to find its supporters. In a 1994 *New York Times* Op-Ed piece, Celia Barbour claims she has a solution to such sexual dissatisfaction and women's resentment of "men's easy access to sexual arousal," to wit: "[m]ore good pornography for women" to "even the score."[2]

Ms. Barbour is no fringe academic theorist but an associate editor at *Martha Stewart Living*. Now we know the real sublimated yearnings of all those Martha-ites who crackle-glaze floors, renovate lamp shades, and make spun sugar. Tough luck for women who can't or won't follow Barbour's lead. They are the ones who need renovation, says advice guru Ann Landers. Responding to an angry woman who signed herself "disillusioned" after discovering her husband's porno collection, Ann declared that wife, not hubby, needed counseling to get over her "obsession." The Victorians understood that evening the score on such sorry terms guarantees men will still keep score.

At best, this validation of male standards, or the lack of them, blurs acceptable sexual boundaries for everyone. The resulting confusion produces the kind of hair-splitting rules that have taken sex from the sublime to the ridiculous. For example, Antioch College issued a dating code that sounded like a parody and became instant fodder for stand-up comics. Thirteen pages of legalistic dos and don'ts required students to obtain explicit consent for each act of touching and disrobing. This would make sex stilted and awkward, critics complained—as if it isn't now. Not surprisingly, male students were especially concerned that "asking means not getting what you want."

If women are not getting what they want, some experts blame anatomy. The biologist Robert Francoeur of Fairleigh Dickinson University claims that women's brains are better integrated: Their left and right hemispheres are more intimately connected. Thus female sexuality is "whole body," whereas "the male orgasm is much more penile-centered."[3] This helps explain *Women Who Love Sex* author Gina Ogden's finding that women view sex "more holistically, more as a whole person proposition, body, mind, and soul, than men do."

Having reviewed over 200 studies, the University of Vermont psychology professor Dr. Harold Leitenberg has found that women's fantasies focus more on emotional connections, unfold at a slower pace than men's, and involve more nongenital caressing than genital contact. In a poll of 1,000 women, two out of three women said they would choose hugging without intercourse, twice the number who preferred humping to holding each other. Not surprisingly, men's fantasies are more genital, graphic, and impersonal, including strangers as well as friends. One researcher called these scenarios a pornotopia where "sex is sheer lust and physical gratification, devoid of encumbering relationships, emotional elaboration, complicated plot lines, flirtation, courtship, and extended foreplay, where all the women were easily aroused and willing."[4]

Biology may tempt us to capitulate to this soulless, self-centered, penis-centered pleasure principle. The prisoners of this century's hundred-year war between the sexes include all the women who settle for the best they can get, as well as those who make the best of being manless. Yet the Victorians would not allow the worst of nature to trump the best of nurture. The holistic sex we term "female" was their unisex ideal.

THE TRUTH OF CONSEQUENCES

All sides in the current sexual debate are destined to keep talking past each other, if they remain blind to the fundamental Victorian insight that sexual relations are social relations. Doing your own thing—even in the ultimate privacy of bed—is never just your own business. Free sex is never free, because its salespeople indirectly impose their expectations on conformists and dissidents alike. Just as passive smoke pollutes the lungs of nonsmokers, casual sex poisons the atmosphere that nourishes romance. This equation cheats all lovers of sublime loves, not just superb lays.

Victorian women and their sentiments reigned supreme during the century of romance. The loss of those sentiments reduced most ordinary women to the status of powerless pawns, even as the favored few play at being mistresses of the universe. When Madonna slides a whip between her legs, she is degrading all other woman, regardless of whether they have a penchant for leather. When rapper Adina Howard sings, "I want a roughneck brother who can satisfy me," she invites guys to play it rough even when their partners want it soft and slow.

Among those seeking an alternative route is Christina Kirksey, a teenage intern at the National Political Congress of Black Women. In a newspaper interview, she described Ms. Howard's music as a roadblock for African-American women, not a liberating force: "The lyrics were nasty and vile. I'm striving to get an education and make something of myself. I have to constantly fight against catcalls and sexual harassment on the street and here comes Adina Howard [with] 'I need a freak in the morning.'"[5]

The infamous Tailhook convention also made an entire gender fair game. Although the media focused on female officers and civilians who were forced to run a groping gauntlet and were otherwise assaulted by drunken Navy fliers, a Defense Department report concluded that "many women freely and knowingly participated in gauntlet activities." Some bared their breasts so they could be pasted with squadron stickers, or encouraged men to drink shots of tequila from their navels. Some performed simulated fellatio on a dildo attached to a booze-dispensing rhino.[6]

The women who reveled in this orgy breached the bounds of self-expression (never mind decency) by compromising the choices, the welfare, and the credibility of women with less expansive views of sex and recreation. Those who say they were assaulted are easy to doubt, precisely because others volunteered their bodies to the assaulters.

Although it is men who directly violate a woman's body and peace of mind, other women unconsciously conspire in those crimes. Demi Moore received $12.5 million—the single highest fee ever paid an actress—to unveil her artificially enhanced breasts in the movie *Striptease*. Defending her nudity and her salary, she told a reporter, "The strongest feminine statement I can make is: Be supportive of women who make conscious choices for themselves." It is certainly a commentary not only on Ms. Moore's mentality that this is "the strongest feminine statement" she can make, but also a sad commentary on the milieu in which she thrives.

In this "get mine any way I can" mode of liberation, Moore and her ilk bank the loot while other women get taxed. "We need sluts for the revolution," Naomi Wolf told *Esquire* magazine.[7] But all women who ever shared a neighborhood with streetwalkers know that every woman becomes not only a target for prowling men but also a compulsory competitor in feeding the furnace of male pleasure. Women who feel empowered by appearing nude or seminude in public will never lack for partners, however fleeting, in an era that has drastically defined down romantic expectations from their Victorian peak. Only women who believe in the tooth fairy could imagine themselves in the place of Ellen Olenska, when Newland Archer kneels to kiss the tip of his beloved's satin shoe. You say such scenes could only have existed in fiction? Then imagine receiving a birthday gift like the one the composer Richard Wagner gave his wife in 1870. He assembled a group of musicians, whom he had secretly rehearsed, on the stairs of his house, and directed the first performance of his famous Siegfried Idyll, which he had written for her.[8]

Men do not express such sentiments toward strippers, porno mimics, or sluts, be they pro- or antirevolution. The cold truth is that whatever politically correct mantras men feel compelled to voice, we all know that "slut" is precisely what they're thinking and what they snicker to each other when safe from the propaganda police.

Prisoners of Sexual Freedom

Moreover, modern women who desire the attention and affections of a man must struggle with new standards of attractiveness. Forget character, bearing, and personality. Beauty is our bait, and the more we see airbrushed, near-naked females on every television screen, magazine cover, and public street in the summertime, the more impossible it seems to be to measure up to this ideal. Current studies by psychologists show that anorectic, computer-corrected images of Barbie Doll models foster unrealistic body images that contribute not only to widespread eating disorders but frigidity among the many women and girls who feel hopelessly flawed. No feminist needs science to validate the destructive effects of "normalizing" impossible standards of beauty, which have bound women to the Stairmaster and the plastic surgeon's table.

Women create for themselves a "falsely styled freedom," as Dr. Elizabeth Blackwell said in 1902, when they lower themselves to the level of male standards, instead of raising men up to their own. When enough women hit the sexual fast lane, others are pressured to keep up speed if they want a second date. But just how free are women who express relief (in private) that the fear of AIDS provides a convenient excuse to abstain from "casual boinking" in their search for the Holy Grail of Mr. Right?

The Victorians believed a woman deserved far more than fidelity and a ring on her finger. Respecting her bodily integrity and freedom was a sacred if implicit vow that a husband took in marriage. However difficult it was to uphold, a gentleman's personal honor and a couple's joint happiness depended on his sexual restraint just as much as social stability depended on controlling the selfish instincts of brute force. With roots in this rich soil of loving monogamy, trust, intimacy, and passion blossomed.

10

When Life Was Foreplay

Nine out of ten people, if asked what "Victorian" means, will include "prudish" or "sexually repressed" somewhere in their answer. It's something everybody "knows," even if they don't know exactly where they learned it. They probably picked it up partly from the popular culture—all those Hollywood films and Harlequin Romances that feature nineteenth-century heroines breaking free of rigid social conventions to find true romance. But this is one point on which Hollywood agrees with most history books.

Generations of historians have taught us to ridicule the Victorians' attitude toward sex as a token of our own enlightened perspective. According to some of these scholars who created today's conventional wisdom, such as historian Ronald Pearsall, our benighted ancestors regarded sex as "vulgar," "deplorable," a "deed of darkness." Desire was "something the well-bred man and woman should not have." Women in particular were supposedly sexless creatures, mere "child-bearing vegetables" who could only "lie still and think of the Empire."

At a time when we are willing to question just about every other piece of received wisdom, and "revisionism" runs rampant among historians, no one ever seems to question the priggish and

THE BENEVOLENCE OF MANNERS

puritanical image we have of the Victorians. And why should we? After all, one of the most frequently quoted passages on the Victorians' thinking comes from an 1865 work, *The Functions and Disorders of Reproductive Organs*, in which Dr. William Acton wrote, "The majority of women (happily for society) are not very much troubled with sexual feeling of any kind. What men are habitually, women are only exceptionally."

VICTORIAN SENSUALITY UNCOVERED

Unfortunately, it turns out that Dr. Acton was very wrong about Victorian sexual mores. In 1974 the eminent historian Carl Degler discovered an unknown but extensive survey of married women born between 1850 and 1880. Until Degler found this unpublished gold mine, it was widely assumed that such surveys did not exist before the 1920s. Yet the Stanford University professor Dr. Clelia Mosher, a highly respected female physician, began this research on sexual attitudes in 1892. Even more surprising is that most of Mosher's subjects were the picture of sexual health by modern standards. These ordinary middle-class women freely admitted that they had sexual feelings, enjoyed intercourse with their husbands, and usually experienced what they called "voluptuous spasms"—a term far more evocative than the more prosaic and clinical "orgasm." One claimed that sex rendered "a sense of completeness, a spiritual oneness, which is not gained in any other way." Another described intercourse as "the extreme caress of love's passion," whose "habitual bodily expression has a deep psychological effect in making possible complete mental sympathy, and perfecting the spiritual union."

The spiritual importance of sensuality was not lost on Henry James, Sr., either. In what may sound like blasphemy to some but was a tribute to the supreme importance and scope of Victorian love, he wrote, "The more perfect the oneness" husband and wife attained through sex, "the more like God."[1] Similar sentiments were expressed in the correspondence analyzed by the historian Karen Lystra in her book *Searching the Heart: Women, Men, and Romantic Love in Nineteenth-Century America*. One young husband's awed description for intercourse with his spouse was that it was "solemn and sublime." Another called the act of physical love simply "a sacrament."

In fact, numerous Victorian marriage manuals, all aimed at the general public, celebrated intercourse and female sexuality. *Excessive Venery: Masturbation and Continence,* an 1887 work by Dr. Joseph Howe, described sex as "one of the essentials to perfect health." A generation earlier, Dr. James Ashton wrote in *The Book of Nature* that sex was "essential for good health"; he prescribed lima beans, mushrooms, and shellfish as aphrodisiacs. And in his 1899 book *In Health,* Dr. A. J. Ingersoll called the sexual life "the sustaining life of the mind, as well as every organ of the body" that "controls all actions of humanity." Ingersoll counseled his patients to "love and reverence sex," and he warned that suppressing it "could lead to disease, even the lunatic asylum."

Dr. Ingersoll's tribute to sexual expression appeared in the same year that an unknown young physician named Sigmund Freud published *The Interpretation of Dreams.* The book sold fewer than 200 copies that year, and it would take another decade for Freud's theories to find more than a narrow audience. A century later, it is easy to forget that Freud was not the first medical authority to notice the importance of sex to personal health and marital satisfaction.

Even the prototypically prudish Dr. William Acton believed that "to ignore the bodily and secular aspect of married love would be false and unwise," as he wrote in *The Functions and Disorders of the Reproductive Organs.* Despite his notorious pronouncement on female frigidity, he also commented that some women "have sexual drives so strong that they surpass those of men." Other physicians of the period noted that women often experienced more intense orgasms than men. By mid-

Victorian prudery has been much exaggerated. Couples expected and experienced passion within marriage.

century many, such as Charles Knowlton, M.D., asserted (as post-Freudians rediscovered generations later) that the clitoris is "the principal organ of sexual pleasure in the female." In an 1897 work with the provocative title *What a Husband Should Know*, Sylvanus Stall may have stoked more fears than he allayed by describing sex as a "ruling passion" for some women, who should marry only men with "large powers of endurance or risk ruining their health."

Nor did the passionate cravings felt by wives die along with their husbands. Dr. Elizabeth Blackwell recalled witnessing "the severe and compound suffering experienced by many widows who were strongly attached to their lost partners [which is] also well known to the physician, and this is not simply a mental loss that they feel, but an immense physical deprivation. It is a loss which all the senses suffer by the physical as well as moral void which death has created."[2]

Speaking for themselves, both famous and ordinary women affirmed the deep deprivation of an empty bed and the joys of a shared one. In 1835 one lonely Southern wife wrote her husband that she would "drain your coffers dry" when they were reunited. He in turn wrote of anticipating "unspeakable delight in your embrace," as he imagined her "caressing hands" and "voluptuous touch."[3] The English author Beatrix Potter experienced similar exquisite torture, recording in her journal in 1889 that "God knows celibacy is as painful to a woman as it is to a man. It could not be more painful than it is to a woman."[4]

On the other side of the Atlantic, a bride wrote in her journal in 1879, "I am most deeply grateful to God for giving me in my husband a man whose fresh springs of deepest tenderness and love grow fuller and fuller every day, encompassing me with the sweetest life-fountains that a woman's life can ever know."[5]

These warm-blooded women were anything but frigid mummies who were stoically doing their duty to posterity. Even confirmed spinster Emily Dickinson promised some imagined lover, "Wild Nights—Wild Nights! / Were I with thee / Wild nights should be our luxury." And the era's icon of prudery, Queen Victoria, was less repressed than most have supposed. She and her husband, Albert, bought each other nude portraits, and she even drew some. Biographer Louis Auchincloss wrote that the intensely passionate nature of the queen "may explain her near insanity on Albert's death."

Women's consuming yearnings were no surprise to the men who were their object. In an 1853 letter to his intended, one man wrote that he assumed his wife would be his "equal with flesh and blood, with magnetism, electricity, passion." Another gallant swain assured his fiancée that he would not take premarital advantage of "the roused and throbbing nature of your woman's heart, which in its sweetly awakened passion might feel tempted . . . to throw all reasons to the wind and give life, love, thought, being, destiny—everything—to the lover who holds you in his arms."[6]

After his own extensive survey of revealing letters between Victorians of all ages and relationships, the historian Peter Gay concluded in *Education of the Senses* that "the bond that mattered, surpassing all others, was that between spouses. The nineteenth-century middle class wife who pours all her affection into her children and denies her husband all sexual warmth is largely a myth." Gay found that shared sensuality—something we think of as a tribute to our own "enlightened" sexual attitudes—was considered an "indispensable element" of marriage. Many couples undoubtedly found it, for as de Tocqueville noted in the 1830s, America above all countries "is the one in which the marriage tie is most respected and where the highest and truest conception of conjugal happiness has been conceived."

So why has the twentieth century so severely misrepresented the sensual Victorians as fanatical prudes? Carl Degler faults twentieth-century historians for failing to fully survey all the available literature. But the Victorians' artistic legacy is difficult for even the laziest scholar to miss. We needn't read the Victorians' letters and journals to know that nude statues were displayed throughout the century in parks, public buildings, and homes. Copies made in Paris of Hiram Powers's classical undraped maiden, *The Greek Slave*, were among the most popular ornaments for parlors. Another Powers masterpiece, *Eve Tempted*, also celebrated voluptuous female nudity. And what could be more erotic than the embrace of naked lovers in Rodin's *The Kiss*?

Peter Gay, in *Education of the Senses*, blames present-day ignorance of Victorian sexual realities on the legacy of Freud, "a professional skeptic" who based his observations on sexually maladjusted people rather than healthy ones, and was therefore inclined to "underestimate the opportunities for erotic happiness available in the bourgeois world, for women and men alike." Even though revisionists have since made Swiss cheese of Austrian psychotherapy, we still accept the Viennese doctor's dismal view of Victorian sex, or the lack of it.

Our drastic differences from the Victorians feed our suspicions of their ways, along with our occasional awe at their accomplishments. Perhaps it is inevitable that we should judge them on our terms rather than their own. Because sexual reticence is as alien to us as high-buttoned shoes, we erroneously assume, as Gay puts it, that ordinary people in the nineteenth century "did not know, or did not practice, or did not enjoy what they did not discuss."

A PRIVATE PASSION

In contrast to our own "open-book" attitude, the Victorians drew sharp lines between the public and the private. Sexual intimacy was regarded as just that—intimate, personal, and very private. It was not fodder for budding exhibitionists or salivating voyeurs. William Wordsworth wrote: "Strange fits of passion have I known: / And I will dare to tell, / But in the Lover's ear alone, / What once to me befell."

By contrast, contemporary practice now favors an approach that might be called the public gush. For example, tennis star Martina Navratilova could not confine her sweet nothings to her lover's ears. In an article that appeared in the Style section of *The Washington Post* in July 1996, she announced to the press that she and the L'Oréal model Hunter Reno, a niece of Attorney General Janet Reno, were an item. "I've never been one to hide," Navratilova explained. "I love Hunter in a way I haven't loved before." The Victorians would score this advertised "love" just as tennis does—as zero.

There was far more than finger-wagging prissiness to the old etiquette rule "Make no public exhibition of your endearments." As Karen Lystra noted, "Forbidden expression in Victorian public life . . . attained a special and privileged meaning in private precisely because of public prohibitions."[7] This gave a "special aura" and "heightened meaning" to romantic love that eludes us today because of, not in spite of, our loose talk, loose sex, and celebration of technique. We announce our sexual needs and our bedroom conquests and failings with the boldness of cheap cologne. Victorian passion was an exotic perfume made all the more alluring by its subtle presence.

While we presume that other hidden facets of private life, like wife beating and child abuse, were rampant in the not-so-good old days, we don't apply this "given" to sex. We define sexual extroversion as healthy and diagnose as "sick" an age that loved to love under the covers, not in the spotlight. But making a spectacle of sex not only clouds our historical judgment but also cheapens a treasure, draining it of the intriguing secrecy that once raised passion into the stratosphere of desire and imagination. "Its very mystery," observes Peter Gay in *The Tender Passion*, "often taken as a symptom of the shame with which prudish bourgeois approached the marriage bed, was something of a tribute to their high regard for loving," and for "erotic pleasures" as well.

Mysteries make us wary in this age of nonstop communication. We demand that our potential bedmates put all their cards and transmittable diseases on the table. Anything less is a bluff that derails the brutal honesty essential to building a solid relationship. Didn't the Victorian veil of privacy compromise this candor? Weren't people condemned to marry strangers who revealed their true—and worst—selves only after they tied the knot? Wrong again. The Victorians believed in absolute mutual premarital candor, with full disclosure of every flaw and folly. "To be natural is the great secret of success in love making," advised "An American Gentleman" in his book *Good Behavior for Young Gentlemen* (1848). "To disguise your character and study affectation in courting is the very error of the moon."[8]

It was precisely because the lovers' bond was intensely private that they could reveal all their imperfections to each other. Since they regarded marriage as neither a passing fancy nor a phase of self-development but a lifetime commitment, its stakes were as high as you could go. America's first ordained female minister, Antoinette Brown Blackwell, quoted in *Hands and Hearts*, told her future husband, "You must always say everything to me, darling. Nothing but the utmost confidence can make us quite happy, and nothing but the want of it can destroy happiness."

Victorian lovers often risked all for love by baring their souls—only to each other—so their marriage would not crash on the rocks of false ideals. This theme appears repeatedly in letters and journals from the period, many of which were collected by Karen Lystra: "I have rather ruthlessly shown you my worst traits in a sort of passionate desire to have your love founded in realities and not on dreams," wrote one young woman to her fiancée. Looking back on a misunderstanding with his sweetheart, an attorney offered this defense: "I am not sorry . . . to have let you see whatever you have seen. I want you to marry me and I am unwilling to win you under false pretenses."

Revealing your darkest side was a dangerous test of love. But true love had to be tested with truth, and this was both acknowledged and appreciated. Responding to his fiancée, an architect wrote, "I am very glad you did send me your downhearted letter instead of destroying it as you thought you ought to have done the next morning. . . . It is good to know and share our innermost consciousness and we need more than anything else to get acquainted—to really know our own and each other's true selves."

THE DEATH OF INTIMACY

In contrast to these sincere confessions, Ellen Rothman found a striking change of attitude in correspondence from the 1920s. As she wrote in *Hands and Hearts,* in that decade "a growing emphasis on personality and physical attractiveness made self-exposure a risky proposition. 'Catching' a mate had become a matter of wearing stylish clothes and knowing the latest dance step, rather than of demonstrating certain attributes of character."

For example, Rothman reports, one disenchanted young man wrote his mother that he "wasn't very favorably impressed" with a girl he met at a dance. She wasn't "a looker" and "her line was weak," he complained. "At a time when young people were expected to woo each other with the right look and the right line, candor and openness were outmoded virtues," Rothman concluded. "This was the message of popular fiction, movie romances, advertisements. Even the marriage counselors of the period advised young lovers to 'get over any habit of thinking that they must be frank and tell everything they know.'"

For all the lip service we pay to letting it all hang out and urging others to follow suit—without hanging them out to dry—we have inherited the line. When sex is the goal, honesty is easily sacrificed to the self-serving sound bites that ease the way into bed. Women especially expect to hear the right noises before they hit the sheets, an exercise that often taxes macho patience beyond its narrow limits. This

gender war raged in a much-debated February 1994 *Esquire* article on the rise of the postsensitive male who rejects female standards in the mating game. As one man admitted, "It used to be . . . that you didn't date, you screwed. And when the drugs wore off the next morning, if you could still remember the woman's name, you had a relationship. Today they all expect you to remember their name. . . . I spent most of the last twenty years trying to make the right, enlightened sounds, and there were times I was so convincing, I believed what I was saying."[9]

Cynicism and Male Bashing

This man's psychological swindle might explain his failed marriage, not to mention the male bashing that has become a national sport among women. No wonder women feel cheated, deceived, and disempowered by all the frauds who made the right sounds. No wonder they are so wary that they increasingly rely on private investigators to "check him out." One advertisement for such a service warns, "He may have a wife, an embellished resumé, a criminal record, or the potential to be a 'fatal attraction.'"

This wholesale mistrust of the opposite sex (which seems more like another species these days) breeds an embittered contempt that is toxic to mutual respect, much less romance. One painfully humorous T-shirt illustrates the seething frustrations of women who keep kissing toads in hopes of finding a prince. The shirt features "The Perfect Man" in the shape of a gingerbread cookie. The caption reads, "He's quiet. He's sweet. And if he gives you any crap, you can bite his head off."

The problem is not that men are inherently deceitful, but that they no longer accept the Victorian ideal that candor in love enhanced their masculinity. Where women now have to dig for the truth through calcified layers of masculine muteness, Victorian men were expected to be willing and equal partners in the give and take of truth. But why should we care about this missed historical footnote and the mincemeat unscholarly scholars made of intimacy in bygone days? What could we possibly learn from a society that lacked vibrators, flavored condoms, and illustrated manuals to sexual acrobatics?

We could start by recognizing the hunger that exists in the midst of plenty. For all our vaunted openness and freedom to experiment, sexual relations seem no better than any other relations between the sexes today.

NO SATISFACTION

The widespread absence of sexual satisfaction has been documented by numerous surveys in recent years. Women are especially dissatisfied with their lot, which they regard as far too little. A 1994 poll conducted by the University of Chicago found that only 29 percent of women always experienced orgasm with their primary partner, compared to three quarters of men.[10] (If only Woody Allen's orgasmatron from *Sleeper* were more than a futuristic prop.) And over half of 1,000 women age 18 to 25 surveyed by *Esquire* magazine in 1994 admitted to doing what Meg Ryan so ably demonstrated in the movie *When Harry Met Sally*: They fake orgasms.[11] So much for candor. No wonder the popular book *Why Women Need Chocolate* claimed this always satisfying treat outranks sex on the female priority list.

For those who place their faith in the future, there is little hope that the next generation will bridge this intimate divide. A Roper poll of 503 ninth- through twelfth-graders found that nine out of ten boys called sex a pleasurable experience, compared to only six out of ten girls. Even more telling—and disheartening: 62 percent of all girls surveyed regretted not waiting until they were older to become sexually active. These once tender years have become very tough, and the toll this is taking is anything but equal.

Since the 1970s surveys have shown that early intercourse predicts lingering sexual dissatisfaction for females. With the lost age of innocence steadily dropping, their prospects are dim for getting what they want or deserve from men. In a recent public-service ad broadcast on television, a remorseful pregnant teen wishes she had waited for "real love," and girls are urged to believe "you're worth waiting for." At this late date, such efforts are likely to have less effect on unwanted pregnancies than on our sense of irony that the Advertising Council has belatedly discovered the joys of abstinence.

Increasingly, though, it is grown women who have lost their patience. Movies like *Waiting to Exhale* explore a growing intolerance of men's emotional and sexual deficiencies, which range from the Felix Ungers who take forever to unwrap a condom to the bedroom growlers who make women feel like zoo keepers. Yet a generation after Dionne Warwick addressed her pleas to "anyone who had a heart," some experts tell women to settle for anyone who has a pulse. The prominent black sociologist Audrey Chapman advocates *Man Sharing* (the title of her book) for women who lack the energy to fight "reality." Reality means using available men for sex and having no "romantic illusions" about this scarce and undependable commodity.

Ms. Chapman is addressing the plight of a particularly put-upon group of women whose rivals for potential mates all too often include drugs, violence, and the criminal justice system. Yet such concerns are not just "a Black thing." This was evidenced by a national Harris poll of 2,002 adults, in which 70 percent of the men were honest enough to admit that birth control is a "woman's problem" because men are too irresponsible to choose and use a method.

Feminine disenchantment runs deep. "Love," like "soul," has become a four-letter word long since milked of its meaning by modern neglect and our penchant for cruder expressions. This soul, an intangible spiritual essence that transcends any religion, fired Victorian love and passion with a consuming intensity we can scarcely imagine.

Just as we have lost the civility that graced and ordered Victorian public life, so have we lost the mystique that elevated sex and romance beyond a bunch of roses or the almighty orgasms we tally like beans. This loss has impoverished the inner lives of men and women alike, but even as women are the prime victims of modern incivility, women have suffered most from the loss of soulful sensuality. We long to recapture the sensuous rhythms of the dance of romance we left behind. To do so, we must first listen to the lyrics of its swan song.

Backseat Follies

Like the demise of civility, the death of romance came after a lingering illness. Contemporary conservatives see romance as a hit-and-run victim of the 1960s, the decade that whetted our appetites for loveless love-ins and letting it all hang out. But the sexual revolution merely euthanized an invalid whose fate was sealed long before, when the world stopped waltzing and started spinning out of control.

WHO NEEDS THAT OLD-FASHIONED ROMANCE?

The devotees of twenties café society and the denizens of speakeasies aspired to "do it" like Cole Porter's amorous birds, bees, and educated fleas. Instead of making love, the bright young things of the Jazz Age just wanted to make whoopee. From the first herd of Miss America contestants parading in bathing suits through Atlantic City in 1921 to the new sensational movies that featured Max Sennett's bathing beauties, sex was suddenly everywhere, and no one wanted to miss out.

In *Only Yesterday*, his devastating chronicle of the Jazz Age, Frederick Lewis Allen described how its new, more permissive mores robbed love of its power and panache:

The intellectuals believed in a greater degree of sex freedom—and many of them found it disappointing when
they got it, either in person or vicariously through books
and plays. . . . Love was becoming too easy and too biological to be an object of respect. . . . The heroine of a postwar novel . . . indulged in 259 amours, if I remember
correctly, without getting the emotional wallop out of any
of them, or out of all of them together, that the lady of Victorian literature would have derived from a single compe-
tently completed seduction.

In his book *Haven in a Heartless World*, the social historian
Christopher Lasch traced the decline of romance that "set impossibly
high standards of devotion and loyalty" to sex manuals of the 1920s
and '30s that prescribed techniques for "stage-managing quarrels, the
technique of mutual agreement on how much adultery the marriage
could tolerate, the technique of what to do in bed and how to do it."
Lasch noted that in the same period the literature of grand fantasies,
consumptive heroines and impassioned suitors went out of fashion,
along with the "unhealthy" music of Wagner, Strauss, and Puccini.

Henceforth, sex, like work, was considered a pragmatic task to
be mastered by adopting a set of practiced skills. Sacraments had no
place in this budding science. "Sex does not need to be elevated into
something else after the fashion of those who advocate spiritualizing
marriage," opined Ernest Groves, a pop psychologist of the period. So
sex traded its magic and its mystique for the thrill of notoriety.[1]

Sex quickly degenerated from a class act into a sideshow. As
Frederick Lewis Allen noted: "Almost every human motive was attrib-
utable to it; if you were patriotic or liked the violin, you were in the
grip of sex—in a subliminated form. The first requirement of mental
health was to have an uninhibited sex life. If you would be well and
happy, you must obey your libido. Such was the Freudian gospel as it
imbedded itself in the American mind."

Modern Girls

The new looser sexual mores of the twenties cheapened what the Victorians esteemed even more than sex—the worth and self-worth of
women. Hutchins Hapgood observed in his 1939 book, *A Victorian in*

the Modern World, that "the future mothers of the race no longer had that self-preservative instinct which is extremely difficult to maintain without the tradition of right living." In the guise of liberation, sexual license was only a means to exploit them, a legacy that lingers like a recurring infection. Then as now, notes the historian Linda Gordon in her 1976 book, *Woman's Body, Woman's Right,* women were offered and often accepted ersatz unions based on "arguments designed to show that love without marriage was infinitely superior to the other kind, and that its immediate indulgence brought the world, night by night, a little nearer to freedom and Utopia."

The Victorians believed that in morals as in manners, man would—and did—follow woman's lead. Our century revoked that feminine privilege when it legitimized the notion of love as a passing fancy. This was accomplished with the aid of a divide-and-conquer strategy, in which some women pressured others to conform to sliding standards. This compromised both all women's honor and the freedom of choice that has become our own religion. Early surveys quoted by Ellen Rothman in *Hands and Heart* show that women born after 1900 were twice as likely as their elders to "forego the sweetness of waiting." Holdouts were derided as "mid-Victorian." Ninety-two percent of Jazz Age coeds engaged in petting, and those who abstained were chronically dateless or on the defensive.

With STDs becoming an adolescent rite of passage as commonplace as acne, our grandparents' concern over petting may seem quaintly anachronistic. But getting to this base and all the others began turning sex into a game in which scoring eventually got boring. By 1936 *Forbes* magazine declared that on blasé college campuses "sex is no longer news."[2] (This same story line, suitably updated and embellished with details of contemporary practices, has proved a hardy perennial of weekly newsmagazines ever since.)

Out of the Parlor

The key that unlocked the door of the sexual closet was a novel institution called dating. You don't have to be a prude to consider "date" a four-letter word. With the advent of this practice, women traded social power for physical pleasure. Feminist historians who regard women's loss of "virtue" as a gain in freedom should think again. Long before date rape became a movie-of-the-week cliché, the date established an

insidious strain of male control that has been fluffed over by the innocent veneer of prom queens, sock hops, and beach-party movies.

Women were literally driven down the garden path. The automobile—that shining symbol of modernity and mass consumption—
made dating, and parking, possible. When women began rutting in
the rumble seat, it was only a matter of time before men would
demand that they do it in the road. The historian Beth Bailey notes,
in *From the Front Porch to the Back Seat,* that when wooing exited
parlors and porches for restaurants, theaters, and dance halls, "One
had to buy entertainment. . . . Money—men's money—became the
basis of the dating system and, thus, of courtship. This new dating
system, as it shifted courtship from the private to the public sphere
and increasingly centered around money, fundamentally altered the
balance of power between men and women in courtship."

During the previous century, it was women who, once they
came of age, designated their "at home" days to receive gentlemen
callers. In this female-governed world, a man needed permission to
call, and undesirables were promptly turned away, like the luckless
Freddie Hill in *My Fair Lady.* Despite repeated attempts by Freddie,
flowers in hand, to see Eliza Doolittle, Professor Higgins's vigilant
gatekeeper-housekeeper informed him that Miss Doolittle was "not at
home," even when she was. The closest he came was the consoling
joy of knowing he was "on the street where you live." Today only stalk-
ers get a high from that knowledge.

If admitted callers stayed too long, made inappropriate remarks,
or otherwise behaved rudely, a hovering chaperone would indicate that
their behavior and future visits were unwelcome. Describing how the
dating system abruptly shifted power between the sexes, Bailey writes:

> "Calling," as either a simple visit or as the elaborate late
> nineteenth-century ritual, gave women a large portion of
> control. First of all, courtship took place within the girl's
> home—in women's "sphere," as it was called in the nine-
> teenth century—or at entertainments largely devised and
> presided over by women. Dating moved courtship out of
> the home and into man's sphere—the world outside the
> home. Female controls and conventions lost much of their
> power outside women's sphere. And while many of the con-

ventions of female propriety were restrictive and repressive, they had allowed women [young women and their mothers] a great deal of immediate control over courtship. The transfer of spheres thoroughly undercut that control.[3]

Women retained the prerogative to refuse a date, but once they consented, the man controlled the wheel, the purse strings, and the moves. At this late date, it is easy to forget how unthinkable this once was. The etiquette author Eliza Leslie explained in *Miss Leslie's Behaviour Book*:

> In her intercourse with gentlemen, a lady should take care to avoid all pecuniary obligations. The civility that a gentleman conventionally owes to a lady is a sufficient tax— more she has no right to expect, or to accept. A man of good sense, and of true politeness, will not be offended at her unwillingness to become his debtor. On the contrary, he will respect her delicacy and approve her dignity; and consent at once to her becoming her own banker on all occasions where expense is to be incurred.

Pay Up or Else

The feminist version of the Dutch treat revived this arrangement but not the power women once enjoyed. Men no longer feel obliged to pay the tax of civility. Yet for many women, paying their share of the bill is not a choice but a presumption that is as awkward to negotiate as safe sex. Splitting a check won't change the way a guy treats a chick. That will require resurrecting the old esteem for women whereby they were treated as ladies first and lovers later. Like all matters of heart and conscience, this kind of change cannot be legislated, bought, or sold.

Even gifts from Victorian admirers, however well intentioned, were returned if their extravagance or implications compromised a woman's sovereignty. Eliza Leslie wrote:

> Young ladies should be careful how they accept presents from gentlemen. No truly modest and dignified woman

will incur such obligations. And no gentleman who really respects her will offer her any thing more than a bouquet, a book . . . or a few relics or mementos of memorable places—things that derive their chief value from associations. But to present a young lady with articles of jewelry, or of dress, or with a costly ornament for the centre-table (unless she is his affianced wife,) ought to be regarded as an offense, rather than a compliment, excusable only in a man sadly ignorant of the refinements of society. And if he is so, she should set him right, and civilly, but firmly, refuse to be his debtor.

Like so many other aspects of life and love, the Victorians treated gifts as deeply symbolic. So without a permanent commitment (what used to be called "an understanding"), perishables like flowers and candy were the most acceptable tokens a man could give. Only then could a woman reciprocate. Even then, her gifts had to be "handmade and inexpensive," like a "drawing or a trifle from a needle." Like the rules of civility, these norms protected a woman's integrity, a man's solvency, and the uncorrupted value of what they shared. But dating, like prostitution, made all potential mating a balance sheet that debased and commercialized relations between the sexes and set the stage for our endless gender wars. Even old tokens of endearment lost their "sweetness and light." According to one person in the 1920s who reminisced about earlier days:

> The coal dealer and the gas man may fear the coming of summer—but florists aren't much worried over the fact that spring flowers will soon be growing in every front yard. . . . The days have gone by when a young man may pick a bouquet of flowers from his own yard and take them to his best girl. Nowadays she demands a dozen roses or a corsage bouquet bearing the name of the best florist.[4]

Girls lost far more than the gift of sentiment when their suitors began picking the florist instead of the flowers. Men began to grouse about unfavorable rates of exchange from women who reneged on their tacit obligations to those who purchased their meals and entertainment. Popular magazines from the Jazz Age routinely printed male complaints to this effect. The bluntness with which correspondents expressed these sentiments reminds us that women who accept the economic model of courtship had better be ready to give value for money.

For example, in 1924 one unsatisfied customer wrote a letter to a magazine to declare a "one-man buyer's strike" after estimating that, as a "buyer of female companionship" for the previous five years, he had "invested" about $20 a week—a grand total of over $5,000. Finally, he wrote, he had realized that "there is a point at which any commodity—even such a delightful commodity as female companionship—costs more than it is worth." The commodity he had bought with his $5,000 had been priced beyond its "real value," and he had had enough.[5]

Comparing the 1890s and 1920s in the seminal study *Middletown*, the sociologists Robert and Helen Lynd analyzed how such bluntly mercenary relations pressured women and priced them like cattle:

> Necking and petting were integral parts of the dating system, and to participate in the system, one had to meet its requirements. Furthermore, the dating system promoted sexual experimentation not only through the privacy it offered but also through the sense of obligation it fostered. Dating was an unequal relationship: the man paid for everything and the woman was thus indebted to him. According to many, boys and men were entitled to sexual favors as payment for the debt; the more money the man spent, the more petting the woman owed him.[6]

Back then male revenge may have been limited to dumping recalcitrant dates or smearing their reputations with locker-room tales of easy conquest. But the imagination doesn't have to leap very far to see the same perverted sense of entitlement in a Washington, D.C., man who recently unleashed his pit bull to attack a teenage girl who refused to undress on command. Indeed, the crude economics of woman's demands and her relative worth became a staple of advice columns down through the decades:

One late–1940s book for men suggested techniques for winning various "types" of women. For the "prom queen" (which the author considered an overpriced commodity), one must "spend money like water. You don't win prom princesses," he said, "you buy them—like show horses." Public sources, over and over, emphasized that women should be evaluated as if they were show animals. Women's value as dates—so far as they had individual value—lay in the impression they made, in how the possession of them made men look.[7]

Grading women from prime cuts to by-products reversed the cherished Victorian ideal of elevated womanhood. Christopher Lasch noted that sociologists who studied campus life in the 1930s saw "formal modes of true courtship" yielding to "dalliances" that exploited women. Social prestige took precedence over character in choosing a date or a temporary mate. Like smart clothes, smooth lines, fat wallets, and nimble feet that could jitterbug the night away, the human ornament on your arm was another way to gauge your popularity. However much fashions and dances have changed, we are the fruit that fell from this tree and has been rotting ever since.

The Battle Lines Are Drawn

Lasch wrote that the equally ruthless and mathematical "rating and dating complex" that weighed so heavily in this equation fed the growing yen for thrill seeking at the cost of romance. There were no more Ralph Waldo Emersons to pen poems with titles such as his "Give All to Love." Making your mark on the social scene depended on using the opposite sex and avoiding emotional attachment.

Lasch also notes that the sociologist Willard Waller, who studied collegiate behavior between the two world wars, found fraternity "bull sessions" in which those who displayed dangerous symptoms of old-fashioned romance were "repeatedly warned that they are slipping, those who have fallen are teased without mercy, and others are warned not to be soft."

Waller could have been recounting tales from the trenches of any modern campus when he wrote, "Wary is the only word that I can apply to the attitude of men and women students towards each other.

A fundamental antagonism exists between [them]." One male student Waller interviewed described the cynical shell women developed to protect themselves from cold-blooded males. "They're out for what they can get. That's fine. So are we. Everything is one grand big joke. Many of the girls really fight against liking a boy. . . . One way in which they do this is the use of ridicule." Sound familiar?

This bitter joke turned the sweetness of romance into a struggle for survival of the fittest. Thus Christopher Lasch concluded, "The dating system repudiates those who make the mistake of falling in love and awards its highest prizes to the cynical."

INTIMATE NEGOTIATIONS

Rather than liberating women, the changing rules left them in a position of being damned if they "did it" and damned if they didn't. By 1948, Kinsey was applauding widespread necking and petting as an essential part of high school and higher education. But then as now, girls remained understandably ignorant of how to cave in to sexual pressures, as popularity demanded, without losing popularity and self-worth by being labeled cheap. John D'Emilio and Estelle Freedman, in *Intimate Matters: A History of Sexuality in America*, report that one teenage girl summarized her dilemma this way: "The girl who permits

liberties is certainly popular with boys, but her popularity never lasts very long with any one boy. You know the saying 'Just a toy to play with, not the kind they choose to grow old and grey with.'"

The progression from women setting the sexual parameters to men making the rules began benignly enough, according to D'Emilio and Freedman. In 1905, the *Ladies' Home Journal's* "Lady from Philadelphia" advice column received a letter from "Sadie" asking what to do "when a man persists in holding your hand in spite of all that you can say." The answer: "No man, who is fit to be welcomed in your home, would refuse to release your hand if you asked him as if you meant it." This advice is the formula that persisted for decades, but with one important difference. Here, the man's liberties are not necessarily the woman's fault. If the woman is truly virtuous, and the man does not comply with her wishes, it is because he is not "fit to be welcomed in [her] home." That conditional term soon disappeared.

D'Emilio and Freedman also note that by 1914, the author of a later *Ladies' Home Journal* advice column, "Girls' Affairs," largely ignored men's possible role. A girl wrote from a coed college asking what to do about boys who refused to date girls who didn't allow "privileges." The adviser, Mrs. Parks, replied: "I think that girls are largely responsible for the attitude of boys in this matter; for if, whenever fun merged into familiarity, the girls would instantly check such conduct, the boys would soon learn what to expect whenever they dared trespass the barrier of a self-respecting manner."

The sagacious Mrs. Parks failed to mention that the maintenance of this barrier presumed not just self-respect from women but also male respect for women—which was steadily eroding in both the private and public spheres. Other historians noted how this devious double standard and the budding gender war persisted through the next several decades, while acceptable boundaries of casual sex kept stretching from necking and petting in the twenties to premarital intercourse by the fifties.

During the *Happy Days* era, girls still set the sexual limits but boys routinely pushed them, according to D'Emilio and Freedman. In turn, many girls were pushed into petting or coitus by "subtle pressure" or "outright aggression." They note that one pregnant sixteen-year-old who was seduced and abandoned poignantly summarized the dangerous rift between the sexes, even as they rocked around the clock together, and the resulting position of women—up against the wall: "How are you supposed to know what [boys] want? You hold out for a long time and then when you do give in to them and give your body they laugh at you afterwards and say they'd never marry a slut, and that they didn't love you but were just testing because they only plan to marry a virgin and wanted to see if you'd go all the way."

The Victorian ideal of sex as a sacred expression of devotion and elevated love became a distinctly female adjunct of virginity. As such, it was doomed to fight a losing battle against the duck-tailed conquistadors who enhanced their prestige among their buddies by cutting notches on their belts. No, I haven't forgotten the "good clean fun" of relatively sublimated traditions of the 1950s such as panty raids. But collecting lacy briefs or running them up a flagpole is hardly the twentieth-century equivalent of Newland Archer's attempt in *The Age of Innocence* to steal Ellen Olenska's parasol just long enough to kiss its handle.

The rituals of twentieth-century coupling replaced the sentimental passion that filled the yearning soul with a system that was designed to scratch an itch. By the 1940s and '50s, Beth Bailey reports, "relationship" experts were telling sexually inexperienced girls that "frigidity" was as bad as promiscuity and were urging them to find a middle way: "The person who is over-inhibited, excessively prudish, or unresponsive to the extent that he or she cannot or will not tolerate overt expressions of affection from a member of the opposite sex has just as great a problem as the person who aggressively goes as far as possible in petting on all dates."

In theory, this was a gender-neutral critique, but every teeny-bopper knew that the gropers and the gropees came equipped with different hormones. Young women learned this lesson every time they watched Doris Day play a repressed ice maiden who only needed the right man to melt her. The male version of this message was made explicit to moviegoers of the following decade, who saw James Bond use his virile charms to redeem a character named Pussy Galore from her lesbianism in *Goldfinger*.

Girls were told to stop complaining about male aggression and instead ask themselves how they had provoked it. Now we call this blaming the victim—the double whammy Victorian women were spared when they encountered cads, rogues, boors, reprobates, scoundrels, and other such swine. The varied pejoratives that were used to describe these offenders demonstrates where the blame was placed. The demise of these labels bespeaks how a serious moral crime became a misdemeanor that eventually required sexual harassment legislation and judicial intervention to restore its punch.

NOT-SO-NIFTY FIFTIES

Today's conservatives yearn for a counterfeit "age of innocence" dating from the days of their own youth. They cannot look back far enough to see how much power women (along with love and decency) lost when wooing to the slow lyrical creak of a porch swing devolved into make-out sessions in the backseat of a T-bird. As Stephanie Coontz observed in *The Way We Never Were,* the halcyon fifties were no model for abstinence and deferred gratification: "'Heavy petting' became a norm of dating in this period, while the proportion of white brides who were pregnant at marriage more than doubled. Teen birth rates soared, reaching highs that have not been equaled since. In 1957, 97 out of every 1,000 girls aged fifteen to nineteen gave birth, compared to only 52 out of every 1,000 in 1983."

Bed hopping went mainstream in this era, however subtly it was portrayed by current standards. "Wink wink nudge nudge" was the formulaic response of popular entertainment to a public culture caught between an old order that was gone but not forgotten, and the first stirrings of the "anything goes" ethic that we now take for granted. On television during the late 1950s, for example, *The Bob Cummings Show* featured a swinging bachelor whose career as a photographer allowed him to caress his models as he positioned them for shots. His job also gave him the opportunity to play the field, sometimes juggling two or three dates in one evening. His promiscuity was not officially admitted, because he never took the "girls" home to bed in the house he shared with his widowed sister and her teenage boy.

Of course, this offstage denouement was leeringly implied in every episode of the *Cummings Show* (which was later syndicated under the title *Love That Bob*), just as *Three's Company* relied on the sniggering subtext of an unconsummated threesome two decades later. Soon thereafter, the leers began giving way to hoots on the laugh tracks of television's lascivious sitcoms. In the 1990s television gets its yucks from sex-starved newlyweds humping on the kitchen table while their dinner guests wait in the dining room. (All that distinguishes this scene in *Mad About You* from most of the prime-time competition is that the couple was married.) But what is explicit today was already implicit back in the not-so-innocent 1950s.

While television introduced winking innuendo to every family lucky enough to have a set, postwar America was bursting with pornography as well as prosperity. D'Emilio and Freedman point out that the demoralized youth of the land returned from World War I with the first pinup girl posters and cartloads of pornography acquired abroad. By the 1940s, corner drug stores for the first time openly sold cheap paperbacks with cheesecake and beefcake covers. In 1948 Popular Library tempted readers with its lurid "nipple cover" on the book *The Private Life of Helen of Troy*. Pornographic books, photos, movies, and records blossomed into a billion-dollar business by the mid–1950s. In 1952 Marilyn Monroe posed for her famous nude calendar. According to Russell Miller's book *Bunny*, the following year a shrewd Hugh Hefner bought the rights to it for $500 and published the first issue of *Playboy*. Summarizing the creed of the magazine and its founder, Miller wrote,

> Most of *Playboy*'s articles and ads were devoted to the idea that since women were only out to catch a man, men needed to learn how to get as much sex from them as possible without getting trapped. *Playboy* invited men to take over editorial areas of domestic and personal consumption formerly managed by females: food, clothes, wine, and body scents. Men didn't need a "purchasing agent for the home" anymore; all they needed was a nubile partner for the bedroom.

So much for the fabulous fifties. The emblem of this idyllically wholesome decade inverted the entire Victorian philosophy of women by pinning bunny tails on them. Hefner taught America that manhood meant living in silk pajamas surrounded by sex toys and accommodating babes that you proudly collected and displayed. An increasingly permissive culture opened a welcoming door to once-secret lives, making venereal disease (the dreaded "VD") the only remaining risk. If men no longer had honor, at least they had none to lose.

D'Emilio and Freedman note that "after World War II, pornography, as well as other media products that titillated males by sexually objectifying women's bodies, moved beyond their customary place in a marginal underground world." This was exactly where Victorian respectability, obscenity laws, and the veneration of women once kept them, even as purity crusaders like the notorious Anthony Comstock tried to expunge them.

Sex as a Science

Sex was further brought out into the light of day by Alfred Kinsey and his apostles, who claimed that sexuality was a natural human function on the order of eating, drinking, breathing, and defecating. They waved the banner of animal sex, charted its different outlets like electric sockets, and taught us the importance of frequency, position, and technique. Directly or indirectly, this emphasis on performance justified casual sexual encounters, guiltless affairs, and quantity over quality of sexual experience. Orgasm was no longer seen as a shared glimpse of heaven but an end in itself—a mere physical function, not a transcendent experience.

By the Ozzie and Harriet era, women and men had abandoned the ideal of transcendent love. Ironically, as Christopher Lasch noted in *Haven in a Heartless World*, women's lowered expectations produced a rare gender consensus you could take to bed: "They no more wished to revive the nineteenth-century ideal of the lady than their husbands wished to pose as patriarchs. Both sexes, repudiating the mystical exaltation of womanhood formerly associated with the cult of romantic love, tried to ground marriage in . . . 'charm.'"

Behind the doors of those charming aluminum-sided homes and seemingly happy marriages, however, were some very unhappy women. According to doctors interviewed by Betty Friedan in the early 1960s for *The Feminine Mystique*, many wives were so sexually ravenous that their husbands couldn't sate them. Without a high-octane career—the new-feminist panacea—frustrated females had meaningless affairs, popped pills, or became psychoanalysis junkies. Sex stripped of old-fashioned romance was not a panacea, as Friedan observed:

> Instead of fulfilling the promise of infinite orgiastic bliss, sex in the America of the feminine mystique is becoming a strangely joyless national compulsion, if not a contemptuous mockery. The sex-glutted novels became increasingly explicit and increasingly dull; the sex kick of the women's magazines has a sickly sadness; the endless flow of manuals describing new sex techniques hint at the endless lack of excitement.[8]

The Victorian sexual mystique that led to women being treated with respect and even reverence had been replaced by a "Playboy philosophy" that confused mere rutting with the art of romance. But women lost far more than window dressing when intimacy became a gender impasse instead of a shared religion. Modern marriage was viewed as a sexual partnership, yet husbands and wives often approached the conjugal bed with widely divergent expectations about the meaning of sex. Many women hoped for love and affection; their partners sought orgasmic relief. The companionate ideal posited equality between spouses, yet wives remained economically dependent, aware that failure in marriage spelled disaster. As D'Emilio and Freedman wrote in *Intimate Matters*, in the fifties

> ... marital ideals prescribed that [a wife] be an erotic companion to her husband, that the happiness of marriage would grow in proportion to the sexual magic generated between husband and wife. By the 1960's ... wives could look with concern at the sexual competition they faced from women who did not have to change diapers or cook for a family. For her part, the single woman might forever question her own femininity, lacking as she was the central attribute of motherhood. Whether dutiful wife or alluring single, the American woman was left to wonder whether she made the grade.

Some of the conflicts that American women faced were embedded within the new system of sexual liberalism. As the birth control pill lessened the dangers of pregnancy and the media portrayed the glamour of the single life, young women who had helped shape an ethic of "permissiveness with affection" found the rules suddenly altered. Placed on the defensive, they rapidly lost the right to say no that nineteenth-century feminists had struggled to obtain. We have not, it seems, come a long way, baby.

A COMMENDABLE HYPOCRISY

Of course, Victorian bashers love to point to the hypocrisy of those Victorian "gentlemen" who secretly indulged in dirty books, French postcards, and local prostitutes, disdaining a society that looked away from moral slumming to keep its petticoats clean. But such hypocrisy had a commendable purpose: The Victorians followed La Rochefoucauld's sage maxim "Hypocrisy is an homage vice pays to virtue." We modern sophisticates would eliminate hypocrisy by lowering our virtues until they correspond to our vices. But the Victorians were consummate strivers who kept reaching for the heavens, even when they slipped and lost their footing. They knew that rewriting the script to make ideals conform to reality would only destroy the ideals and degrade the reality.

Even the most inveterate debauchers understood the need to sin discreetly and pay severely if they were caught. For example, the eminent architect Stanford White never dared parade his sweet young things—some of them very young—through the parks and reputable parlors of New York. His was the classic double life. His wife and family resided in the country, while he enjoyed his paramours and his erotica collection in a carefully chosen urban hideaway equipped with mirrored ceilings and a red velvet swing.

White came to what the Victorians considered an appropriate end. In 1906 he was shot and killed by the millionaire Harry Thaw. This self-appointed avenger discovered that several years earlier, White had unceremoniously deflowered Thaw's wife-to-be, the showgirl Evelyn Nesbit, after allegedly rendering her unconscious with champagne. After White's various escapades were exposed in the ensuing sensational trial, denunciations of his behavior issued from the pulpit, the press, and even the presidency. These were the days when death did not redeem a sinner. A resolution introduced in Congress denounced his "loathsome and licentious acts" for their "demoralizing influence on the youth of the land." Today, Mr. White would be driving to the bank to deposit his $2 million advance against royalties for a tell-all autobiography.

Sadly, after all these years of mechanical tinkering with the relationship between sex, love, and passion, we have stripped the gears of romance and left women to walk home. Our flashy new vehicle of casual sex somehow does not work as well as the old reliable romantic monogamy did and we can't figure out what went wrong, or how to get back to where we started.

12

The Religion of Romance

The Victorians looked at love in the same way they looked at life—as a holistic fusion of one's body, mind, and eternal soul. It was this transcendent fusion—as opposed to a narrow focus on physical or even merely mortal love—that made their passion so gloriously great, consuming, and complete. This is why we mistake great sex for grand passion.

The Victorians made a religion of love, believing it lifted them up into a transcendent realm of experience. This exalted ideal was commonly expressed in inspirational terms of endearment far richer and sweeter than any "honey"—the best we can muster. To Nathaniel Hawthorne, his wife's love letters were "spiritual food." So ardent was his veneration of the feast that his adored Sophie supplied, writes the historian Karen Lystra, that he wrote, "I keep them to be the treasures of my still and secret hours, such hours as pious people spend in prayer; and the communion which my spirit then holds with yours has something of religion in it." Among the courtship letters of ordinary Victorians studied by the historian Ellen Rothman was that of a college student who told his fiancée, "You have been my very soul."

Today's woman can choose from models of masculinity that range from the sensitive "postfeminist" male to socially sanctioned sides of beefcake. But can we imagine any of them, from Tom Cruise to Fabio, describing sex like the Victorian swain Austin Dickinson, who, when writing to his beloved Mabel, called it a "consecration" and "the white heat that engulfs my being"?

NOT-SO-GREAT EXPECTATIONS

Indeed, while Victorian passion thrived on great expectations, we bring cynical and dispiriting apprehensions to the tentative venture of love and marriage. This wet-blanket attitude was rampant among welfare mothers recently profiled in an article in *The Washington Post*. "I don't know what people get married for," said one resigned twenty-something woman. "For stability or security or what? That would just make you co-dependent on some man."[1]

Declining marriage rates among rich and poor alike reflect the deep disillusionment with any chance that love is forever. In her book *The Hearts of Men*, the journalist and author Barbara Ehrenreich warns women that their relations with men will be brief, "punctuated by emotional dislocations, and seldom offering the kind of loyalty that might extend into middle age." So use men for sex, she counsels, but rely only on women for friendship, support, and every other human need men are too inhuman to meet. Better yet, rely completely on yourself and the insurance company whose ad tells women to "Be Your Own Rock," presumably with suitable investments. This unchallenged gospel touts the mental equivalent of safe sex—protect yourself at any cost or it will cost you plenty.

We may steel our hearts and bank accounts against assault, but steel is no substitute for poetry, passion, or the love we are supposed to learn to live without. Since Gloria Steinem compared the utility of men to women as that of a bicycle to a fish, women have asserted that they don't need men to be happy or fulfilled. Some actually believe it—independence is loneliness that learns to smile. Many settle for the warmth of whatever hairy body they can find, but I have yet to meet any woman who could imagine a religion of love. "[H]ow can you make the sexes act as if they needed each other to survive when they don't?" asked *Nation* editor Katha Pollitt in a *New York Times* article. "All they need each other for is love, and love is hard to find."

To reweave all the threads we have severed—love, marriage, children—Pollitt says, "We would have to bring back the whole nineteenth century." This threat is supposed to send shivers down your unnostalgic spine, so that you keep the world secure for all the commitment-challenged hedgers and vacillators who cover their rears even when they're naked. Otherwise you might crave the old-time religion, with all its rules and demands, its unbreakable bonds, and its bared and vulnerable hearts.

Till Divorce Court Do Us Part

Even if you have the best modern knockoff—a sustained relationship—take care to treat it cavalierly. No more "white heat that engulfs my being." Even the Hollywood celebrities who have turned yesterday's "alternative" lifestyles into today's norm can't handle the heat of that kitchen. For example, the actress Susan Sarandon, a sex symbol for the over-forty set, enjoys a long-term live-in relationship complete with children. In an interview with *Cosmopolitan* magazine, she offered this verbal shrug on infidelity: "If someone is very special to you, is it really that important if every now and then he takes off and has a liaison with someone else? I mean, is it really a great catastrophe?"

Yes, but only if your love life is something more than a mutually satisfying arrangement between independent contractors. Not everybody in Lala-land goes along with this enlightened approach. Still, there's no question which values set the tone for the town that sets the tone for towns around the country. Closet monogamists tread lightly in the land of the cutting edge. Even professional tough guy Bruce Willis avoids bruising the feelings of his fellow celebs by not imposing his own lifestyle choice on them: "I believe in monogamy for myself, although it works for very few people."[2]

Cynical about their future, many up-to-date spouses are deadly serious about protecting their possessions and their precious space. Separate finances, separate vacations, even separate homes protect what's "yours" and "mine" from becoming "ours." In the process, they protect you and me from becoming us. Promises that were once etched on the heart are now inscribed in the dry legalese of prenuptial agreements. These contracts provide an escape clause for those who fear being locked into what was once quaintly termed "holy wedlock." One prudent young couple featured on *World News Tonight* specified every particular, from who will keep the budget and fill the gas tank to how often they will have sex. Any breach of any clause extracts a fine—picking up the tab for dinner. Should these parties of both parts ever permanently nullify this agreement, they can take comfort in the current catchword that terms a first union a "starter marriage," where you learn the ropes for the second.

COMMUNING VS. COMMUNICATING

Unlike today's pop psychologists, who pontificate about how hard it is for "partners" in a "relationship" to really "communicate" with each other, it is hard to imagine Victorian couples expressing their feelings in terms of "soul communing." When souls failed to commune, their failure was not shrugged off as a mere bust in the bedroom or a bad experience to be brushed off like dandruff. It was seen as a moral disaster. Because sex was "the highest part of your nature and should be held sacred," observed Henry C. Wright in his 1855 book *Marriage and Parentage,* sex devoid of spirit was "coarse, selfish, polluted, and necessarily tends to denigrate and profane both body and soul."

This message squarely hit the broken home of an embittered Elizabeth Cady Stanton. According to her biographer Elizabeth Griffith, after separating from her husband, Cady Stanton wrote to a cousin lamenting that she and Henry Stanton no longer shared "the joy of a deep soul love." During their long marriage she relished "connubial relations," but scorching the sheets was not enough. "Soul union should precede and exalt physical union," she said. "Without sentiment, affection, imagination, what better would we be in procreation than the beasts?"

We still ask that question, though the sad state of modern love and the ongoing war between the sexes renders it prophetic rather than rhetorical. It is not only Hollywood hedonism that turns the rhapsodic into the prosaic. While we might expect more talk of souls and sentiment from the religious right, they too offer an erotic wasteland. For example, Tim and Beverly LaHaye's bestselling seventies marriage guide gave this tediously literal take on sacred sex: "Be fruitful and multiply." Keeping up with the times, the LaHayes assured their readers that conception is not the only legitimate purpose of their God-given plumbing: Intercourse is also for pleasure and "marital communication." Where is the poetry in this pious benediction of bodily delights? Where is the passion? This Bible-thumping brand of therapeutic psychobabble is as estranged from the Victorians' "spiritual food" as the low-rent epicureanism of *Melrose Place*.

We have so desecrated sex and love that we find it appropriate instead to consecrate their dissolution. Some ministers now perform divorce ceremonies so couples can feel that untying the knot is divinely condoned. This four-hundred-dollar package includes personalized prayers, a ritualistic burning of the marriage certificate or other related items, and a perverse exchange of rings. For those determined to erase all evidence of their connubial blunder, a service called Divorce X will use the wonders of modern technology to edit your former spouse or any other undesirables out of your wedding pictures. In the ultimate denial of what was once a union "till death do us part," you can even order a pure self-portrait.

A RICH TAPESTRY OF LOVE

Those serious young couples in Victorian wedding photographs, on the other hand, understood dying for love, as Sidney Carton did in *A Tale of Two Cities*, or dying from its loss, as the eponymous Anna Karenina did. They would not, however, have understood either the Hollywood inamoratas who love and let love or the lawyerly lovers who begin their romance with contingency plans. To our ancestors, love that was ephemeral and divisible was unworthy of the name. But the only eternity left to today's lovers is the one that has elapsed since people fervently believed in the title of the William Morris poem, "Love Is Enough."

In an age where love has become a high-wire act that requires the safety net of divorce and the services of plaintiff's attorneys, we experience a gulf between the Victorians' cup-runneth-over faith in love and our own cup-is-half-empty cynicism. Nowhere is this clearer than in the enormous change in the valentine card.

Forever Yours
Victorian valentines were so lavish and expensive, they were often gifts in themselves. Although simple printed cards like ours could be had for pennies, men tried to buy the best, and women often made their own.

During the Civil War, when many soldiers made about fifteen dollars a month, a smitten suitor would spend as much as ten dollars on a single card. By the 1890s, the price of luxury cards topped twenty-five dollars.

Those costly tokens of love, and the feelings they expressed, became treasured keepsakes that both sexes displayed in the privacy of the bedroom, despite their distinctly feminine look. These intricate confections of filigree lace paper could be painted, gilded, or silvered, even fragranced, and were often so thick they came packed in presentation boxes. Trimmed with silk, satin, feathers, leaves, or dried and wax flowers, they featured universal symbols of love such as hearts, doves, cupids, or bows and arrows. Some unfolded like fans, while mechanical valentines had levers or disks that made figures dance, hands move, and birds flutter their wings. These unique and memorable cards remained popular until the 1920s, when morals, manners, clothes and interior décor converted to a new religion: Less is more. Its believers got less than they bargained for.

The lyrics printed on Victorian valentines were as effusive as their appearance. Whether sent by a steady beau proposing or a secret admirer finally confessing his feelings, these cards were unabashedly sentimental, pleading for the affections of "my sweetheart" or "my one and only." They pledged undying devotion happily ever after, and delighted in complete surrender to the rule of love.

Victorian valentines were often elaborate and unabashedly sentimental in their verses.

The sweeping amorous certainties that impassioned the past have dissolved in the ephemeral, evasive, fence-sitting emotions that give modern valentine cards the solidity of a cloud. According to researchers at Hallmark's Val Lab, love is such a traumatizing gamble that the "L-word" is used sparingly, if at all. There is a "real need for a more guarded message," according to one company rep, so cards are designed more to soothe the nervous giver than to please his partner. Such cards "talk about waking up beside you or your touch. Something like that." Alternatively, flippancy or ridicule are easy fallbacks that save face and mask the fears of wading into love's deep waters. "Be my Valentine," says one such card. "I've already told people we're sleeping together."

Even admissions of love are neutralized by turning every body part except the heart into the object of affection. Cards that rhapsodize over a well-shaped butt may be the perfect way to express affection in a Beavis-and-Butthead world. The next logical step is the proliferation of smutty "love" cards, whose sentiments don't bear repeating. All these cards represent the ultimate out for a culture that prefers the upper hand and cool detachment to the terrifying risk of surrender.

The Lost Language of Love

Today's language of love ruthlessly demeans the intimate experience the Victorians cherished. All the beaux, swains, admirers, the admired, the beloveds are gone. Sweethearts have become the squeezes we wring dry before moving on to fresh ones. Instead of courtship, we have relationships, as we do with hairdressers or tennis partners. Even the meaning of making love has narrowed from all the feelings, stages, words, and gestures of wooing to specific physical acts that lump us in with any other mating beast. How appropriate that sexual malaise drives us to shrinks who help accommodate us to our emotionally downsized culture.

Like prayer, the Victorian language of love was exclusive to itself. By contrast, our present-day sexual vocabulary borrows from the lingo of animals, mechanics, and sports. It seems only too appropriate that scientists are debating the presence of higher emotions in animals while they study the mating behavior of humans. If we share a mailbox and a bed, we "cohabit" like any other domestic animal.

When we copulate, we "perform" like seals. When we do so frequently, the appropriate reference is to minks. An attractive male is a hunk, a female is a piece. Both are available postmortem from a butcher.

THE SENSUOUS—AND SENTIMENTAL—MALE

Victorian men relished the full menu of tender words and touches that really light a woman's fire. "Days and weeks go by when it would be wine to see even the hem of your dress," one man wrote to his sweetheart in 1883.[3] Women's hands were considered intensely erotic in an age that did not measure arousal in the stretch of a string bikini. Smooth, shapely feminine hands were reproduced everywhere in the form of candy dishes, card holders, ring stands, even drapery tiebacks.

In the days before groping was socially acceptable dating behavior, women expected their hands to be lavished with a lover's kisses, especially as his first physical display of devotion. Thus, at the turn of the nineteenth century, a middle-aged widower launched his courtship of a widow with a letter revealing his desire to kiss her fingertips. Subsequent correspondence shows that they maintained their charms for him even after marriage. Elizabeth Barrett Browning later described in one of her sonnets from the Portuguese the "First time he kissed me, he but only kiss'd / The fingers of this hand wherewith I write; / And ever since, it grew more clean and white."

Every woman knows the earth-moving power of subtle sensuality, even if she knows it only by its absence. Women crave the little things that mean a lot. They want love as a total experience of all the ways and reasons one is loved, like those in this breathtaking letter that still pulses with passion a century after it was written: "I kiss your cheeks, dear Little Girl, and that's for friendship. I kiss your brow, sweet Lady Violet, and that's for reverence. . . . And I stoop to cover the soft warm lips with a lover's kisses—many and long—and lingering Lover's kisses, dear. . . . No one in the world—no one else, can kiss you as I do. My darling."[4]

Men are still enthralled by women's body parts, though not as parts of a glorious whole. We have butt men, breast men, and leg men, like those who favor particular pieces of roast chicken. Fan magazines rate the specific parts of Hollywood stars, while family newspapers like *The New York Times* routinely run steamy clothing ads that zoom in on bare cleavage, half-unzipped crotches, and peek-a-boo rears. Ignored are the feminine features once cherished by literature, art, and life. In his lush poem titled "Ruth," Thomas Hood rhapsodized over the assets that are now shortchanged: "Round her eyes her tresses fell, / Which were blackest none could tell, / But long lashes veil'd a light, / That had else been all too bright."

When men loved women piece by piece, rather than regarding them *as* a piece, their love was exalting rather than degrading because its object was always esteemed as far more than the sum of its parts. A woman was a work of art—rather than an orifice—to be admired from every angle, in every light. Passion was stirred by what seem like "nothings—by an untied shoe-lace, by a glance of the eye in passing."[5] The loss of these sweet "nothings" stripped women's worth to bare meat and bones. By the same token, it deadened men's sensibilities to a treasure trove of pleasures. Today, the mere turn of a feminine ankle no longer turns the heads of males who can go to the movies to look up Sharon Stone's skirt. We have to take Bill Clinton's word as to whether he wears boxers or briefs, but viewers of *Basic Instinct* could see for themselves that Ms. Stone wears neither.

Part of croquet's immense popularity during the last century was the chance the game offered to glimpse a lady's petticoat or ankle when she placed her foot on the ball.

When sex is treated as nothing more than a bodily sensation—as "only the thrill of boy meeting girl," in the words of a popular song—the quest for that sensation becomes an addiction in which ever-increasing doses are required to produce ever-diminishing effects. As a character in the crossover soft-core porno flick *Showgirls* observes coolly during a Las Vegas strip-show scene, "In America every man is his own gynecologist." In a society that has ruthlessly physicalized feminine allure, the religion of love is reduced to the physiology of lust.

Explaining the appeal of the aesthetically alien film *The Age of Innocence*, one critic, Andrew Delbanco, noted that in the movie, "The only removal of clothing comes in an intensely erotic scene when Archer, pressed close against Ellen in a narrow brougham, unbuttons and peels back her tight, calfskin gloves and kisses her exposed skin and wrists." Because Newland Archer ventures no further, "He touches a nerve in us."[6] Would a carriage quickie with Countess Ellen Olenska have been as resonant or arousing as these nuanced gestures?

Even sounds have been deromanticized and disimpassioned by our painfully literal view of sex. We understand the grunts and groans of bumps and grinds. But can they fire the imagination like the music of an unseen petticoat? "Drapery but enhances the estimation in which men hold the female attractions of the person," wrote the physician Nicholas Cooke in 1870. "The rustle of a woman's garment is more potent to charm than the lavish exposure of the proportions of a Venus." The fashion historian Alison Gernsheim noted that in 1902 some fashion arbiters decreed that audible petticoats were "vulgar." Yet, as Gernsheim notes, women refused to relinquish their glacé silk and taffeta lingerie for quieter satins and brocades, because husbands enjoyed such suggestive sounds. Can we say the same for the snap of a Spandex body suit?

A SENTIMENTAL JOURNEY

The open sentimentalism of Victorian men makes their descendants seem like another species. Yet the culture of sentimentality that once nourished great romance has long been a target of historical and rhetorical scorn. Consider our contemporary understanding of this onetime Victorian virtue. *Webster* tells us that a sentimentalist is "unduly" influenced by tender feelings, and *Roget* reminds us that its connotations include the sappy, the syrupy, and the maudlin. The psychoanalytic pioneer C. G. Jung called sentimentality "a super-structure covering brutality." And the historian Milton Rugoff claimed, "There was a tendency to gloss over such primal urges [as sex], to veil, to gild, prettify, idealize or sentimentalize them, or sim-ply push them into the cellars of the mind."

By this myopic logic, sentiment is lethal to sex. But since when did heat preclude warmth? The Victorians had their ultrarich cake and ate it too because both men and women savored every taste of love. The ladies were legendary for collecting immense albums of romantic keepsakes such as pressed flowers and souvenirs of excur-sions. Favored gents eagerly contributed a sketch or a few lines of poetry. This was an age that courted by the faint flickers of light given off by small domed glass or ceramic fairy lamps, even though gaslight and eventually electricity made candlepower obsolete. An historian of decorative arts calls this nostalgic ritual "incredible." But if we accept the Victorians on their terms, this practice is hardly as surprising as the escalating value of those bewitching little lamps.

The allegedly repressed Nathaniel Hawthorne possessed a sin-gular literary talent, yet his expression of sentiment was far from unique when he slept with his wife's letters next to his heart while away from home. Like knights who took their ladies' scarves into bat-tle, Victorian males carried women's locks of hair or pictures in their pocket-watch cases. You won't find such sentimental tokens on a man's Timex.

Gone are the men who cherished what contemporary males now dismiss as female stuff. In love, as in civility, true manhood melded what John Ruskin called delicate sympathies and fineness of nature with masculine strength.[7] Victorian men lived and died for love in ways as tragically poignant as the heroes who went down with the *Titanic* after escorting their wives and children into the lifeboats. The crusty newspaper editor Horace Greeley died of a broken heart shortly after the death of his wife. When consumption claimed James Tissot's adored young model, the artist took refuge from the world in an abbey, where he died.

Jilted men also bore deep scars. Even love lost was so impor-tant that wounded hearts could never grow blasé. The English poet

Arthur Symons wrote: "And I would have, now love is over, / An end to all, an end: / I cannot having been your lover, / Stoop to become your friend." Now sundered couples and spouses boast about remaining friends, and the television series with the name *Friends* celebrates friends who are sometimes sexual partners but never lovers. Our casual attitude toward friendship and love alike would make romantic Victorians cringe. To them love was not a mood or a pair of ships that docked together at their mutual convenience; love, in the words of poet George Henry Boker, was "the orbit of the soul."

Real Men Say I Love You

How the mighty feelings have fallen. Today talk-show shrinks are constantly urging men to emulate women by expressing their intimate feelings. Although we assume that men have always by nature been emotionally challenged, our national religion of communication is determined to convert them to sissies, despite biology, dysfunctional backgrounds, or whatever else has greased their flies but stitched their lips together. For example, in the hit film *Ghost*, Patrick Swayze can respond "I love you" to his significant other, Demi Moore, only at the end of the movie. Until then, he can only mutter an aloof "Ditto" when she voices her affections.

Like Ms. Moore's character, women know they must pull teeth for something more than a "Ditto" or a grunt. Our impoverished males desperately need a history lesson. Even the manliest Victorian males reveled in pouring out their passion to the women who inspired such sentiments in them. This is one equal right and shared pleasure that women have lost, thanks to the shifting cultural sands whereby true confessions were once encouraged but now "sensitive" men are scorned with peer pressure and ridicule for sounding like the clown-ish characters in Harlequin novels.

Letters from the Heart

In private love letters, middle- and upper-middle-class Victorian males fairly exploded with feeling, manifesting as much emotional intensity and range as their wives and sweethearts. In the extreme privacy of romantic relationships, men's emotional expression flour-ished, contrary to the stereotype of the emotionally constricted Victo-rian male. The historian Karen Lystra writes, "The range, depth, and intensity of masculine emotional expression in love letters challenges any unqualified generalization that nineteenth-century men were less emotional or less forthcoming about their feelings than nineteenth-century women."

Our minimalist approach to love has had its day in the sun, and it has left us parched and singed. Victorian love was effusive and ageless, not the sole province of smitten young studs with abs of steel. In 1890 the staid sixty-year-old college bureaucrat Austin Dickinson sent this torrential letter to his mistress:

> I must tell you ... that you are my love, that I love you with a wild, passionate love, with all the love there is in love—the finest, the tenderest, the sweetest, the highest, the greatest, the most dependent, with all my heart, and soul, and mind and strength. . . . That in you in our eight years of closest intimacy, in which we have penetrated the most veiled recesses, each of the other—always with delight—I have found you only fresher, more charming each day—ever new.[8]

A definite step above "Ditto," especially for an old warhorse whom our youth-crazed era would put out to pasture. The fire of this amorous missive cannot be brushed off as a relic from a letter-writing age—writing letters being a lost art that enhanced every part of life—or the thrill of adultery. Only a bloodless cynic would believe this impassioned couple, or any couple, "penetrated the most veiled recesses, each of the other" just on paper. Victorian love existed in the flesh as well as in the imagination.

Mark Twain's connubial affections for his "better half" never cooled through three decades of marriage. In the correspondence that bridged their long separations, this old-school "man's man" bared his captive heart without ever doubting the potency of his other organs:

> I do love you, Livy—as the dew loves the flowers; as the birds love the sunshine; as the wavelets love the breeze; as mothers love their first-born; as memory loves old faces; as the tides love the moon; as angels love the pure in heart. I

so love you that if you were taken from me it seems as if all my love would follow after you and leave my heart a dull and vacant ruin forever and forever.[9]

This was no idle prediction. Losing his beloved Olivia devastated the aging Twain and severely darkened the last phase of his fiction. Recounting the wrenching moment he found her dead after a long illness, he wrote that she was "unresponsive to my reverent caresses—a new thing to me and a new thing to her that had not happened before in five and thirty years." Marriages made in heaven may be a rarity in every century, but without a religion of love, love remains as hopelessly stuck on earth as the tongue-tied young lover in *Ghost*.

Even Presidents Get Smitten

According to his biographer Edmund Morris, Teddy Roosevelt, the quintessential man's man, publicly and privately indulged his obsession for his first and greatest love, Alice Lee. Before she accepted his pressing proposals, he so feared someone would steal her that he carried a pair of French dueling pistols around with him. When heart sickness sent him on endless insomniac wanderings through frigid winter woods, his alarmed Harvard classmates appealed to the Roosevelt family for help.

It would sorely tax modern minds and male egos to envision this rough-riding big-game hunter reading poetry to his wife or mooning in his journal over his "sweet queen." One critic, reviewing a PBS documentary on Theodore Roosevelt, marveled at TR's ability to combine "the soul of a poet and the hide of a rhinoceros."[10] But Roosevelt's blend of outer toughness and inner tenderness was precisely what men of his time aspired to and admired in him. TR may have been a fool for love, but in his day, only jealous fools would have mocked him. What manner of "today's man" could fill this Renaissance man's boots?

Another Oval Office occupant displayed the same dual nature, although he and Roosevelt were cut from different cloth. The reserved and bookish Woodrow Wilson also suffered the untimely loss of his adored wife. But when an attractive widow caught his fancy, this bespectacled midlife widower sent her countless boxes of orchids and amorous letters, as many as three or four a day. We might label such surface contradictions as hypocritical or crazy, but this duality was fundamental to Victorian romance. As Robert Browning wrote: "God be thanked, the meanest of his creatures / Boasts two soul-sides, one to face the world with, / One to show a woman when he loves her."

TWO SOULS UNITED AS ONE

The public soul and the private soul were equally real, and equally vital to protecting the exalted creed of love. We too draw lines, but they compromise love's power and uniqueness by exalting individuals above the bond that unites them. Even committed mates jealously guard their space. Women especially are warned by relationship experts that subsuming their identity to a man's promotes low self-esteem and male dominance in the endless gender wars.

This war was as alien as singles' bars in the world of Victorian love. "Men and women . . . viewed each other not as useful performers in the drama of survival, not as antagonists in the battle of the sexes, but as two-in-one, a united being," writes Karen Lystra. Thus, couples reveled in "the deep silent look in each other's eyes . . . the consciousness of nearness, even to the absolute unison of being."

Passion was not a product of contests or separate checks. As civility and morality presumed some sacrifice of personal freedom by each that repaid all a hundredfold, the solid gold ring of love required both the emotional and ritual wedding of two becoming one. Yet there was no short change in this bargain. Although wives were legally subservient to husbands during the nineteenth century, it was men who longed to experience feminine sensibilities. As Ford Maddox Ford wrote in *The Good Soldier*:

> The real fierceness of desire, the real heat of a passion long withering up the soul of a man is the craving for identity with the woman that he loves. He desires to see with the same eyes, to touch with the same sense of touch, to hear with the same ears, to lose his identity, to be enveloped, to be supported . . . to come to her for the renewal of his courage, for the cutting asunder of his difficulties.

This is quite a contrast to the his-and-hers standoff of women anxiously policing their turf and macho watchdogs who could never imagine relinquishing theirs. The most politically correct couples would believe, or at least parrot, this especially progressive 1870 definition of marriage as an "alliance [where] neither is superior, neither inferior. Their qualities mingle by exchange. The wife is strengthened by the husband, who in turn is made better by the wife." Victorian men knew that woman was the key to a sublime high—the kind that men now seek in fast cars, drugs, and sports. Mark Twain wrote, "My whole being is permeated, is renewed, is leavened with this love, and with every breath I draw its noble influence makes of me a better man."

Because women were so exalted—emotionally, sexually, and spiritually—they alone could provide the magic carpet ride that exulted men beyond any other thrill. Masculinity was fortified, not diluted, by the loved and loving woman who fulfilled what Austin Dickinson called "the sweetest, richest dreams of my boyhood, youth, and early manhood. That I found in you what a woman may be to a man, hope, courage, joy, inspiration, rest, peace, religion!"

Victorian men who knew the meaning of true masculinity embraced the wisdom expressed in this line from a poem by John Ruskin: "Lay thou thy soul full in her hands, low at her feet." Now the only entity willing to stoop to those depths is Nike Inc. "You are not a goddess," proclaims their magazine ad for a woman's walking shoe, "and most likely you never will be a goddess, but just because you are human that doesn't mean we can't worship the ground you walk on."

Today most women would jog barefoot over broken glass if only their love were returned in kind. But for Victorian men, simply reciprocating love was paltry gratitude for the precious gift they lived for and would die for. During his dogged pursuit of the suffragist Lucy Stone, Henry Blackwell said that he felt so ennobled by her affections, he would constantly strive to prove himself worthy. "I reverence you, as well as love you," he wrote a few months after their marriage in 1855. "I long for opportunities to manifest to you the love which fills my soul." His forty years of devotion to her and her cause redeemed that promise.[11]

If heaven turned into hell, some Victorians did divorce. But that comparative rarity was not only a personal tragedy and a social disgrace, it was also the morally devastating fall of religious ideals that nourished the highest romantic expectations. For us divorce seems as permanent as roadway gridlock. We will never reduce its frequency or its toxicity to the heart so long as it is plumbed into the architecture of life and love.

An entry from Theodore Roosevelt's journal illustrates the delicious tension and thrill we have lost by divorcing sex from the sacred. Meeting Alice after a long separation, he noted that she had "a certain charm that I do not know how to describe; I cannot take my eyes off her; she is so pure and holy that it seems almost a profanation to touch her, no matter how gently and tenderly; and yet when we are alone I cannot bear her to be a minute out of my arms."

At the core of this antimacho sentiment was an ideal that all men ought to treat all women respectfully, in gestures small and large: chivalry.

13

Wives and Lovers

It was not only maidens who were protected by Victorian notions of chivalry. In an age that venerated women, romance, and the unsundered bonds of those joined by God, even marital sex was regarded as prostitution or outright rape if it was dictated purely by male demands. The author Eliza Duffey forcefully stated this case in 1876, over a century before its belated rediscovery became a talk-show staple: "I see . . . women who feel that they bear the brand of the prostitute within their souls, because they are forced to yield their bodies unwillingly to gratifying that which they can regard in no other light than selfish lust, hallowed as it is by no mutual desire, nor exalted by self forgetting impulse."

To the woman who wondered what to do when her husband wanted sex and she didn't, Duffey advised that she "should give or withhold her favors according to her own best judgment, uninfluenced either by fear or over-persuasion," for a man's only marital rights were "to take what is granted to him freely and lovingly. A woman is no more bound to yield her body to her husband after the marriage between them, than she was before, until she feels that she can do so with the full tide of willingness and affection."

MUTUAL AFFECTION

Duffey was not alone in condemning what was called the "phallic worship" that threatened the physical and moral integrity of women. Many male physicians and clerics advocated full equality of bedroom perks. Sounding distinctly modern and even politically correct, Rev. Sylvanus Stall wrote in 1897, "As mutual affection is the heavenly bond of marriage, so mutual pleasure should also sanction its earthly bond. . . . No sorer punishment could be inflicted than to be deprived of the right of ruling over one's own body." Any breach of that rule was "conjugal debauchery" and a "gross insult to womanhood."

In his 1881 work, *Sexual Physiology*, Dr. R. T. Trall accused carnally selfish men of turning spouses into "mere machines." Likewise, Dr. Nicholas Cooke asserted in 1870, "Nothing should induce a man to gratify his own desires at the expense of his wife's comfort or inclination." Only rapists engaged in "unreciprocated passional indulgence," wrote Henry Wright in his 1855 book on marriage—a crime deserving of "the gallows or the dungeon."

While shared desire was both expected and considered ideal, the Victorians believed the female psyche and the burdens of pregnancy made woman first among equals. Men might rule the world, but women ruled the bed. (Now, having been liberated, they rule neither.) "The wife must decide how often and under what circumstances the husband may enjoy the passional expression of his love," said marital adviser Dr. Denslow Lewis. In 1902, Dr. Elizabeth Blackwell called woman "the natural regulator of sexual intercourse." The more poetic Dr. Joseph Howe regarded her as "the true guardian and priestess of the temple of marriage."

The undisputed sexual authority of wives was not just preached but widely practiced, as journals and letters from the period reveal. In 1853, one man wrote his fiancée to assure her that "you will be my law" in intimate matters. This was no obligatory promise to some cold fish. The author assumed his life's partner would possess "human passion and susceptibilities . . . [of] a warm blooded girl" who would "lie in a warm blooded man's bosom."[1] Historians cite steadily declining birth rates throughout the nineteenth century as evidence that Victorian gentlemen, unlike their less gentlemanly ancestors (and descendants), understood the meaning of "No." (Fertility rates dropped from 7.04 children per family in 1800 to 3.56 by 1900.[2])

Just as civility depended on curbing brute instincts, "true manliness" meant taming the libido without breaking its spirit. "A strong sexual nature is not a curse, but a blessing," said Reverend Stall. "God made no mistake in making man what he is; but He never intended that the lower nature should rule over the higher and better nature of man." A prominent physician, Dr. Trall, also reflected the Victorian respect for sex as a double-edged sword: "It is very true that nothing can be more vulgar, indecent, and degrading than its abnormal or merely lustful indulgence. But it is equally true that, normally exercised, no act . . . is more holy, more humanizing, more ennobling."

The Victorians believed this humanizing and civilizing view of sex distinguished them from the misogynists and self-centered savages who felt "no moral obligations . . . which compel them to abstain from a natural gratification of their passions." Unless a man could transform his lust to love instead of the other way around, he became his wife's master but not his own.

In those pre-pill days, it was essential for a man to spare his wife from frequent and often dangerous pregnancies—what Queen Victoria, an amorous mother of nine, called "the shadow side of marriage." But in love, as in life, sacrifice was its own reward. Refraining from constant intercourse not only proved a man's love and deepened his reverence for his spouse. By placing her needs above his own, as Bernarr MacFadden, a married female author of several marital guides, wrote in 1918, "his happiness proportionately increased."

THE MIND-BODY CONNECTION

The Victorians' moral instruction on sexuality was reinforced by the scientific thought of the era, which held that expending an ounce of semen was equal to losing forty ounces of blood. Definitions of "excessive venery" varied widely. In general, however, more than weekly copulation was believed to risk depleting the male's "vital life force." Among the dire consequences invited by overindulgence were muscular degeneration, mental enfeeblement, headaches, nervousness, blindness, heart disease, sterility, and impaired resistance to epidemics.

A few physicians believed that during intercourse, the expenditure of "nerve force" was replenished by the magnetism (energy) of the partner. Yet there was no hope of recharging the batteries of those who descended to the level of "beastliness" by engaging in the "subversive and degrading" practice of "self-pollution" (masturbation). While physicians debated the extent of "physical, moral, and mental" damage inflicted by "self-abuse" (as Dr. Elizabeth Blackwell put it in her book *Essays on Medical Sociology*), all agreed that it violated the essence of sex: emotional and spiritual connection.

The Victorians believed that no artificial substitute could replace this link, a conviction that would put a crimp in the growth of today's burgeoning sex tools industry. For example, amid such articles as "No Mistakes Guide to Home Hair Coloring" and "Trim Down Tune Up in 7 Days," the aptly titled *Self* magazine recently carried an ad for a product its manufacturer calls "The Tongue." The copy reads, in part, "Designed by a woman for women. This incredible product duplicates oral sex with absolute perfection by providing REAL MOVEMENT and tireless rhythm. . . . This amazing wonder has 5 orgasmic speeds . . . is erotic, soft and lifelike." Even if this little wonder did windows as well as women, the Victorians would have questioned the amount of "life" in the cheap thrills it offers for only $39.95, plus shipping.

Because "the God-given relationship is two-sided," even coupling was not regarded as fully legitimate when the sexual act hit for one partner but missed for the other. "It becomes mere masturbation to the body and mind of the one who alone is gratified."[3] Lust was considered toxic to love. The Victorians would not be surprised that in our increasingly macho culture, selfishness is a national disease, although men still take the lion's share, especially in bed.

A WOMAN'S SENSUALITY

Gory theories about enervating ejaculations may sound like a quack rationale for penis control. They certainly provide a convenient excuse, which many historians use, to dismiss all Victorian notions of sex. But before we start snickering, we should remember that twentieth-century science has spawned its share of junk studies and embarrassing retractions, from the Piltdown Man to cold fusion. Whatever the limitations of their biological knowledge, our ancestors understood and honored the unique intimate needs of women. For all our apparent enlightenment and superior science, we are still struggling to recover that understanding from our own flirtations with the unisex ideology and Pygmalion mentality that impose male standards on women.

Long before researchers discovered that biology makes women more likely than men to contract sexually transmitted diseases, the Victorians recognized the handle-with-care feminine sense of sensuality. They were correct (if not politically correct) in openly admitting the inherent gender inequalities that leave us conflicted and uneasy today. Physically and emotionally, a woman is more vulnerable than the man between her legs. Thus his sensitivity—the hallmark of chivalry—determined her fate in the street and in bed. Elizabeth Blackwell wrote in 1902:

> All that concerns the mental aspect of sex, the special attraction which draws one sex towards the other, is exhibited in greater proportionate force by women, is more steady and enduring, and occupies a larger amount of their thought and interest. . . . Words spoken, slight courtesies rendered, excite a more permanent interest in women. That which may be the mere passing thought or action of the man, at once forgotten by him, obliterated by a thousand other intellectual or practical interests in his life, often make a quite undue impression upon the woman.

Men were expected to emulate women's superior qualities, not to belittle them or subsume them to basic biological mechanics. This was more than a question of moral high ground. It was a choice between the heat of a once-struck match and that of a well-stoked furnace. Eliza Duffey noted in 1876 that women, unlike men, "do not love lust for lust's sake." For women, she said, passion and love go together. Furthermore:

> This bud of passion cannot be forced rudely open. Its development must be the work of time [or] the bud will be blighted. The husband will have only himself to blame, if he is bound all his life to an apathetic, irresponsive wife. She will be wounded in her deepest feelings, and dis-

gusted and sickened. The apple of pleasure will turn to ashes in her taste. She will become convinced, as this apathy extends through the years, that she was denied all passional feelings by nature. . . . She will feel deep regret that she should have lost out of her life something so essential, which of right belonged to her.

Exactly one hundred twenty years after Duffey issued this warning to men who were "utterly selfish and rapacious," instead of "practicing in lawful wedlock the arts of the seducer," a letter to Ann Landers confirmed the timeliness of Victorian wisdom that so many unsatisfied women still want their partners to learn. A reader explained to men who wondered why their wives were so turned off by sex that women are tired of men's demands after having been ignored, yelled at, and deprived of loving affection: "Do you ever hug or hold us? If you get close enough to touch us, do you grab a part of the anatomy that may have been an erogenous zone in another lifetime? We are not trying to punish you by withholding sex. We're just trying to salvage a shred of decency." Where, the reader asked, did the premarriage tenderness, kissing, and caressing go?

Ann Landers's published reply reflects the widespread sexual illiteracy of males in our sex-soaked society: "Your letter is going to be taped to a zillion bathroom mirrors and placed on a lot of pillows tonight."[4] Zillions of men would not be sharing their pillows or morning shaves with a newspaper clipping if they understood how women ticked as well as those "repressed" Victorians did, and relished the manly challenge to keep the clock running smoothly. Those too egocentric or too lazy to try received blame and contempt from other Victorian men, rather than a friendly poke in the ribs reaffirming that they were one of the guys. Dr. Charles Knowlton observed in 1878:

Passion is forever killed, or, if capable of resuscitation, it is not at the hands of him who destroyed it. It may be that another can reawaken the slumbering spark, and the flame be all the wilder for the rights it has been denied. This is the reason for the fall of married women. . . . You should never forget that this passion is ordinarily slower of growth and tardy of excitation in women than in men, but when fairly aroused in them it is incomparably stronger and more lasting.[5]

Advice manuals of that era, such as *The Gynecologic Considera-tion of the Sexual Act* by Dr. Denslow Lewis (1900), consistently urged bridegrooms (who were presumed to be gentlemen) to be "delicate, attentive, and forbearing" toward their brides (who were presumed to be virgins), even if days or even weeks were required to "cultivate womanly passion" and consummate the marriage. Talk about foreplay! Not only was such saintly patience "due the woman he loves," said Dr. Lewis, but following her sexual tempo was the only way to win her trust and ensure that "perfect and reciprocal happiness would crown the act." To the Victorians, true happiness, like marriage, had to be shared—it never flew solo. Although virgin brides are now as rare as honest politicians, can anyone imagine a "forbearing" modern man enduring days of false starts, even for the woman he claims to love?

In an age when selflessness was a precondition of self-fulfill-ment, any man worthy of the name did not resent his wife's sexual reserve. On the contrary, he cherished it, even as he searched for a way to light her fire. As a Bernarr MacFadden wrote early in this cen-tury, "Responsibilities are a joy to one who has the courage to meet them, and the greatest pleasure in the world comes through sacrific-ing oneself for those whom one loves." Yet even when finally reaching "the fullest abandon . . . and highest exaltation and desire in a physi-cal union," the "female impulse" still determined the frequency and pace of intercourse: "The real lover waits upon every word and look and gesture of the beloved."

The previous century, unlike our own, taught men that it was bet-ter to give than receive both in society and between the sheets. Victo-rian romance had no place for horny hubbies who rolled over on their wives like logs. Whether newly wed or old, an "impetuous husband" who satisfied himself but not his spouse was guilty of "defrauding womanhood," in the eyes of the indignant clergyman Sylvanus Stall. This lesson might have spared John Wayne Bobbitt the ultimate vengeance of his defrauded wife, who told the police she castrated him because "he always have orgasm and he doesn't wait for me to have orgasm. He's selfish. I don't think it's fair, so I pulled back the sheets then and I did it."[6] Feminists who treat Lorena Bobbitt as the patron saint of revenge fantasies miss the point: The problem isn't men, it's modernity.

Quality, Not Quantity

The Victorians considered anything that compromised what Dr. Nicholas Cooke called "the pleasure to which woman is entitled" to be a "cruel injustice." This included contraception. They had spermicidal douches, condoms, primitive diaphragms, and a flawed notion of the rhythm method. But the most common form of birth control was withdrawal. Many objected to this practice for depriving women of, as Dr. Cooke put it, "full satisfaction." Periodic abstinence was favored as cultivating reverence for women and the sexual act, and most Victorians feared "mechanical methods" would make women "playthings of men."[7]

Few women today would relinquish the modern mechanical methods that make sex possible without making babies in the bargain. But we have yet to solve the stubborn problem of keeping women from becoming male playthings, and the condom hasn't been invented that can separate frequency from mediocrity. The Victorians believed that habitual copulation risked degenerating into sheer habit and boredom. While we can no longer imagine quality without quantity, this was one realm of life where our ancestors thought less was more.

In the 1880s Dr. Joseph Howe voiced the conventional wisdom when he warned that sexual gluttony would ruin "the real charm and zest of married life." As Rev. Sylvanus Stall put it, intercourse was meant to be "an overpowering passion, not simply a source of physical gratification." Because sex was so important, "It belongs only to the hour of highest spiritual communion, when heart and soul are merged in the consciousness of but one existence, one life, one eternity," said Stall. "Then, the whole being may and must thrill in unison with such harmony. Passional intercourse is meant to be an ecstatic expression of the soul. Take from it that significance, and you rob it of every attraction."

Sexual Junk Food

The twentieth century fulfilled this prophecy. The Victorian version of gourmet sex kept thrills from becoming cheap—the only kind we can buy in today's erotic bazaar of junk food. Temperance not only "maintains the integrity of the sexual," observed Elizabeth Blackwell in 1902, "but heightens its enjoyment, as fasting makes food more delectable." (For proof positive, just ask anyone on a diet.) Keeping the flames of desire burning was "the key to a happy marriage. And while it may seem at first to be a sacrifice, you will soon learn that it is instead a means of adding exquisite pleasure to both your lives that you were formerly strangers to."

Strange as it may seem to our oft-sated appetites, the Victorians knew how to respect and even relish deprivation. Writing to her husband in 1883 after a six-week separation, one wife dwelt on the "great wave of sweet memories and longings and the touch of clinging warm lips, and the still magnetic thrill of your warm body, and I was all lost to the present. Let us be very tender and careful of this physical bliss . . . and not abuse it, but keep it sweet and clear through the years."[8]

When sex and women were both considered precious jewels, rather than costume jewelry, it was not only possible but essential to distinguish mere appetite from passion. "The term 'passion,' it should always be remembered, necessarily implies a mental element," Elizabeth Blackwell said in 1902. "Passion rises into a higher rank than the instinct of physical impulse, because it involves the soul of man. In sexual passion this mental, moral, or emotional principle is as emphatically sex as any physical instinct." Nearly a century later, sexperts have rediscovered that, as we now put it, the brain is our most important sexual organ.

Nevertheless, many self-styled sexual advisers still uphold the twentieth-century standards that treat females as second- class citizens in the realm of the senses. They tell women who crave the crumbs of romance to let men set the menu or risk starvation. For example, the popular TV therapist Barbara DeAngelis asserts that women who want their men to make love must compensate them with more stripped-down sex. For women who don't take this carrot, DeAngelis wields an awesome stick—scary numbers on adultery and divorce.

Similarly, in their Christian marital advice guide, Tim and Beverly LaHaye warn Christian wives who are not always in an obliging mood that husbands denied a "necessary means of relief" will become "irritated." And trendy gender astronomer John Gray is on the same wavelength when advising Venus and Mars on how to navigate their crossing orbits. Since the typical male gives love to get sex while the female gives sex to get love, Gray asserts, women must be willing to dispense fast food in return for the occasional gourmet treat. No wonder he refers to this once-exalted experience as "getting it."[9]

Few women know that their ancestors celebrated more female-friendly ideals of sex and love. But some of them recognize that they're being screwed in more than one sense. When John Gray appeared on *The Oprah Winfrey Show* in June 1995, one female audience member told the good Dr. Gray that his prescription encouraged men to treat women like machines. Call it women's intuition. Even without realizing that history is on their side, women know that a male meal of fast-food sex may satisfy the body but not the soul. They deserve a long-overdue feast with all the Victorian trimmings that made intimacy a banquet to be savored course by course.

SEX ED AND ROMANCE

We have done sex to death for ourselves and our kids, many of whom are begging for the help we no longer know how to give. In a 1994 Emory University survey of 1,000 teenage girls, 82 percent said the top issue they wanted to discuss in sex education classes was how to say no without hurting a guy's feelings.[10] In fact, "sex ed" is one of the hottest battlefields in the current culture wars. But for all their differences, both liberals and conservatives advocate a modern approach that is equally sterile and narrow.

Former surgeon general Joycelyn Elders exemplified the permissive safe-sex agenda by comparing sex ed to driver's ed: "We taught [our kids] what to do in the front seat of the car, but not what to do in the backseat of the car."[11] What the Victorians once described in the transcendent language of religion has become a technical handbook for rules of the road. Sex ed as a public-health campaign, like those long waged against various diseases, is also the philosophy behind "home health parties" sponsored by Planned Parenthood for low-income women across the country. Combining the giggly atmosphere of a sleep-over with Tupperware-style demonstrations, Planned Parenthood reps dispense nonjudgmental nuts-and-bolts advice on contraceptives, lubricants, and AIDS tests while handing out token prizes like crockpots and compacts.

Some notches up the economic scale, schools such as the University of Maryland and George Washington University give their students "safe break" survival kits for spring vacations that include aspirin, sunblock, and condoms. Thus equipped, students can frolic risk-free on the beach and in bed alike. (The aspirin is presumably for the morning-after hangovers.) More parent-palatable programs in elementary and secondary schools combine contraceptive instruction and condom distribution with lessons on how to resist peer pressure—the chief reason teenage girls say they start having sex.

The sad futility and resignation felt by girls who are sexually used by boys surfaced in a *New York Times* profile of teens in city and suburban schools. The headline says it all: "For Some Youthful Courting Has Become a Game of Abuse." Guess who gives the abuse and who gets it. The article describes how the flagrant mistreatment of girlfriends has become a status-winning male bonding rite. "If you dis a girl you get respect," one adolescent male told the *Times* reporter. "Like, 'Yeah, you dissed her, you're the man, you're the man.' That's how people think."[12] As one indication of just how widely young males think this way, the massive Mall of America in Bloomington, Minnesota, recently imposed a curfew on youths unescorted by adults after a rash of rowdiness in which boys were physically harassing girls and shouting remarks like "Meat!" as they passed by.

Girls too jaded to hope for the thrill of romance, or even the charm of puppy love, have learned to accept being treated like dogs. They don't even expect their boyfriends to acknowledge them in public. "Nobody loves nobody anymore," one girl lamented. "And there's no respect, no trust."[13] I remember a teen telling me she thought courtship had something to do with being sued. Despite all the feminist progress in the professions and education, this century has left male footprints all over women's faces.

Woman's reign in the lost world of romance doesn't appear on either side's syllabus in the sex education battle, where the weapons of choice are frightening AIDS statistics and lectures on the lost opportunities produced by premature parenthood. While liberals throw lubricated condoms at confused adolescents, conservatives bombard them with the dry dust of moral instruction. What both sides neglect are the aesthetics of love. The absence of this dimension would have mystified the Victorians, who knew that beauty was essential to both morality and pleasure.

Chastity and Passion

Liberals cannot be expected to tout chastity, except on the open menu of choice. But conservatives, who like to think they control the turf of personal integrity, are too busy intimidating kids to explain how early promiscuity can ruin what suffragist Mary Livermore called "the appetite for higher pleasure."[14] ("Appetite" and "pleasure" are not exactly buzz words in the conservative lexicon of sex.) Even the feminist heroine Margaret Sanger, the midwife of the modern birth control movement, voiced her quintessentially Victorian belief in the

A Victorian woman's chastity gave her power in courtship.

power of transcendent passion. Writing in 1926, she entreated the young "to refrain from lesser sex experiences and temptations." As Mary Livermore put it, such experiences "render impossible the great drama of love of which all humans are desirous."

The Victorians were too enamored of this drama, a value they sought to instill in their children, to rely so heavily on sin, fatality, and fear to keep their kids out of each other's drawers. Today's pro-virginity apostles lend new meaning to the label Spiro Agnew gave to the media—"nattering nabobs of negativism." For example, in a lengthy newspaper ad soliciting funds, a group named Focus on the Family focused on afflictions such as syphilis, chlamydia, and pelvic inflammatory disease to discourage premarital sex. In this group's view, virginity is not a noble ideal that sweetens and spices anticipated love. It is a "necessity" propelled by studies showing that the microns of HIV can penetrate latex condoms. The only way to survive this growing epidemic is to wait until you marry an "uninfected partner."

Instead of inspiring the young with elevated sentiments of sex and marriage, we try to scare them off with dire warnings of disease and death. Still, millions of easily exploited teens are still getting pregnant by males who get it on and then take off. Those clueless young moms might not have grabbed the first ride that came down the pike if they thought a better one would come along. Instead of instructing them about toxic microns or proper condom use, let kids rediscover how their ancestors once raised the heat of passion to a level we can only envy.

If stamping a skull and crossbones over sex won't stop kids, who assume they're immortal, from doing it, let them read this letter written in 1867 by a young man to his equally chaste but eager fiancée:

> And now, love, you with the warm heart and loving eyes, whose picture I kissed last night and whose lips I so often kiss in my dreams, whose love enriches me so bountifully with . . . sweet anticipations . . . making my heart beat faster, my flesh tremble, and my brain giddy with delight. . . . Good night: a good night and a fair one to thy sleeping eyes and wearied limbs, the precursor of many bright, beautiful mornings when my kisses shall waken thee and my love shall greet thee.[15]

FORGOTTEN LESSONS

In a revived culture of romance, deferred gratification would be its own reward. But the modern sex education line, whether it comes from left field or right, is enough to make anyone with heart and soul give up on school programs and return sexual edification to the home, as many conservatives would prefer. Surprisingly, history sides against them. While our ancestors believed home should always be the primary school of the personal and the political, the sexually reticent Victorians wanted outside authorities to supplement these lessons or even to provide full instruction when parents neglected their obligations.

In 1887, Dr. Joseph Howe urged his colleagues to ensure that all their patients knew the score to promote the "health and happiness of the race" and to prevent a "ridiculous performance before the marriage was consummated." In 1902, Dr. Elizabeth Blackwell called for "sexual morality" instruction in schools, and she chastised churches and religious organizations that "are afraid or ashamed to deal with this most powerful force of our God-created human nature." In 1876, the marriage and etiquette adviser Eliza Duffey also saw such candor as the ally of adolescent virtue, and the only way to correct misinformation acquired from friends or the street: "There should be no fables of babies . . . being found under cabbage leaves."

But at home and in school, sex was never intended be taught with today's Joe Friday matter-of-fact driver's ed approach. Sex was "not proper for general or frivolous conversation," Duffey stated. Reflecting the unique and sacrosanct status of intimate relations in her day, Dr. Blackwell explained in 1902 why she assumed this subject would be treated with tender loving care, even in open debate, and why it never should be bandied as

> . . . a topic of idle gossip, of unreserved publicity, nor of cynical display. . . . Happily, in all civilized countries there is a natural reserve in relation to sexual matters which indicates the reverence with which this high social power of our human nature should be regarded. It is a sign of something wrong in education, or in the social state, when matters which concern the subject of sex are discussed with the same freedom and boldness as other matters.

The "something" that is wrong today is the corrosive incivility of relations between the sexes and the resulting infectious debasement of sex, which is proving as fatal as the diseases sex can spread. When Elizabeth Blackwell spoke of "this natural and beneficial instinct of reserve, springing from unconscious reverence" for sex, she could not envision a Parents' Weekend at elite Smith College, where guests and students were invited to enter condom relay races. Contestants tried to put five condoms on a banana without breaking it.

Similarly, at a private elementary school in New York City, a book for seven-year-olds not only discussed orgasm but compared it to the pleasure of jumping rope. The authors certainly succeeded in bringing sex down to a child's level, where it has stuck tight. Sex is just "an exchange of pleasure" like any other, as Howard and Martha Lewis described it in *The Parents' Guide to Teenage Sex and Pregnancy* (1980). Exchanging gifts, business cards, bodily fluids—it's all part of the same flat continuum in a world that sees no natural hierarchy of experience.

Such books assume that even worried parents have "no nostalgia for Victorian standards"—which are exactly what we need for adults and kids alike. Both the conservative mantra of abstinence and the liberals' sexual smorgasbord cheat young people of the "great drama" that elevates love beyond wearing a glove. One high school English teacher in a Washington, D.C., suburb discovered these starved sensibilities in his students, even among those who knew all about condoms but nothing of romance. A movie based on the work of the virgin spinster Jane Austen provided their most enlightening lesson. Teacher Patrick Welsh writes about his students' discovery that "a flavored condom is no substitute for a nosegay": "When I took my class recently to see the movie *Sense and Sensibility* (in which the touching of a female ankle is the most overtly sensuous moment), I was steeled for the hoots of my macho male students. Instead I was pleasantly surprised to find in class the next day that the boys loved the movie as much as the girls. Perhaps there is still hope for civilization."[16]

That hope depends on our desire and determination to rescue sex from the gutter of low expectations and restore it to the lofty heights of romance. To save our future, we must shed our prejudices, fears, and misconceptions of the past. Rescuing the history that it took a century to destroy won't be an easy task, or a quick one. But period books and faithful films are a good place to start. In a recent survey of 750 randomly chosen ten- to sixteen-year-olds nationwide, 62 percent said portrayals of sex in TV shows and films influenced their behavior.[7]

Spurred by populist criticism and concern over mounting welfare costs, many schools now sponsor abstinence classes. In California alone, students in an abstinence program learn practical reasons for not having sex—you can't support a child on lunch money, and condoms don't protect you from herpes, genital warts, or psychological scars. Shifting cultural winds ensured that the bipartisan welfare reform legislation enacted in 1996 allotted $250 million for such programs, along with $400 million in bonuses to states that reduce their rates of illegitimate births.

THE OVERLOOKED ADVANTAGE OF ABSTINENCE

Some enthusiastic teens are even starting virgin clubs and proudly proclaiming their status on T-shirts. Like most new ideas, this one is quite old. Starting in the 1880s many young people joined White Cross Societies and wore the badge of purity that symbolized their commitment to premarital virtue. The historian David J. Pivar noted that males who took the oath "tacitly agreed that women's moral standards were higher than men's . . . the common goal . . . implied the sanctification of womanhood."

While pregnancy and disease are strong inducements for today's kids to heed this example, many girls are rediscovering and reclaiming the power Victorian females considered their birthright. For example, a counselor at a Maryland high school reported that taking a virginity pledge boosted girls' self-esteem and gave them a greater sense of sexual control. They desperately need all they can get in the down and dirty dating-mating game that stacks the odds against them.

Sex may be instinctive, but love is largely learned, and great love is nurtured. We can either break it or make it what we will. And we had better make it a priority if we ever want family values to be more than rhetoric. All the think-tankers and politicians have forgotten that home is where the heart is. Before preventing or mending broken homes, we must first mend love's broken heart.

PART 4

HOME
SWEET HOME

14

You Can Go Home Again

What is a home these days? It's a place we go to find our "space," a mail drop where we stash our stuff, a revolving door we rush through to change our clothes and roles. The Victorian concept of home was so alien to the contemporary version that we need a different language to describe it. Home was the very heart of nineteenth-century culture, the central icon for a national creed. It was an emotional and aesthetic environment that provided the essential nutrients of family values, not just the box within which parents preached them. But it was also a physical structure whose design and decor were infused with moral significance.

THE RELIGION OF HOME

The Victorians regarded the home as a kind of sacrament that rendered the intangible tangible, through the daily rituals of dining, chores, and leisure. In fact, the Victorians often resorted to religious metaphors to describe its significance. For example, Horace Bushnell, the most famous theologian of his time, said, "Home and religion are kindred words: names both of love and reverence; home because it is the seat of religion; religion because it is the sacred element of home."[1] But it wasn't only theologians who talked this way. Julia Ward Howe enjoined her audience to "revere the religion of home," and Harriet Beecher Stowe hoped her readers would cultivate "that most sacred flame, the fire of domestic love."[2] Even this wasn't enough for the marriage adviser Henry C. Wright, who ranked the home above religion as the centerpiece of human existence. Compared to the home's "power over the organization, character and destiny of human beings," he wrote, "the Church is nothing, the State is nothing . . . government, priests and politics are nothing."

Such accolades may sound excessive or even comical to our own domestically challenged sensibilities, but they represent far more than the Victorian penchant for "flowery" language. Home was a passion

The Victorian home was considered a sanctuary, and the family, central to one's life.

you lived daily, as well as an ideal you sought to honor. To the Victorians, a life worth living required just a kind of ineffable charm, and home was the haven where it flourished in ways great and small. At a time when the marketplace was still a man's world, home provided what the physician William Alcott called "his blessed retreat from the turmoil of business." Reinvigorated by this nightly respite, he could return the next day to the business that paid the family's bills.

THE WORKINGS OF THE VICTORIAN HOME

But maintaining the home was no one-sided affair. Every family member was expected to contribute to creating this prized oasis, and every contribution was respected. Sharing the load fostered reciprocal obligations, reinforcing family ties and reverence for the home that only such joint efforts could enrich and sustain.

It is difficult to overestimate how much the nineteenth century valued the skills and hearts of the women who provided the precious refuge of home. The fifties brought us the famed television show *Queen for a Day*, but Victorian women were queens of the home every day, managing and overseeing the large and small details. Domestic manuals of the period assumed the mistress of the house could master a staggering range of tasks and topics that would now daunt any would-be "supermom." These included the basics—which are not so basic anymore—such as cooking, cleaning, showing all guests "the perfection of hospitable entertainment," and tending to her children's bodies, minds, and souls.

Women were expected to serve as the family doctor and pharmacist, who dispensed home-brewed remedies without the backup help of emergency rooms and all-night drug stores. Preserving domestic health also required a working knowledge of ventilation and heat and lighting apparatuses, plus waste disposal systems and the potentially lethal vermin that carried infectious diseases. As if her plate weren't full enough, she was the household accountant, the seamstress who made clothing, drapes, and linens, and the carpenter who crafted pictures and mirrors. And she had to pull all this together to what Catharine Beecher called a "beautiful effect by the wise disposition of color and skill in arrangement." Martha Stewart, eat your heart out.

Above all, women were the paragons of that defining Victorian virtue, thrift. Frugality was highly respected as a "feminine" accomplishment, and a wife's ability to budget, bargain, and keep her financial house in order determined her family's fate as much as her husband's paycheck. The *Ladies' Home Journal* editor Edward Bok even advocated teaching young girls this skill not only through maternal example—their chief means of all domestic education—but by giving them charge of their father's business ledger. Any Victorian homemaker worthy of the name did not buy now and pay later. She took to heart the widely read advice (and edifying example) of Dickens's immortal wastrel, Wilkens Micawber, who failed to practice what he preached to David Copperfield: "Annual income twenty pounds, annual expenditure nineteen, result happiness. Annual income twenty pounds, annual expenditure twenty pounds ought and six, result misery."

Today's thoroughly modern woman is far more apt to identify with the profligate Nora who was "imprisoned" in Ibsen's *A Doll's House*. Like the *Kramer vs. Kramer* heroine who has to leave her family in order to find herself, feminist prototype Nora is distinctly modern—that is to say, she violates every quality and ethic that principled Victorians admired. A chronic spendthrift, she secures a loan through forgery and then can't pay it off. But she shrugs off her behavior and scoffs at the obligation to square her debts with strangers.

By nineteenth-century standards, Ibsen's Nora personified unfit motherhood and domestic disaster—the doll-wife few men would have wanted or could afford, and no self-respecting woman of her time wanted to be. Yet our liberated age has lionized this narcissistic ninny who abandons her own children. (One Victorian actress refused to play the role of Nora for just that reason.) The Victorians put too much stake in the home to let a self-absorbed child act as its broker (a lesson that David Copperfield learned by sad experience).

Victorian women had so many domestic responsibilities that many had to hire help. During the 1870s, about one in eight families had at least one servant, which was more necessity than luxury in an age when muscle, not gadgets, performed most tasks. Except in the case of the rich, hired help was just that, help—not complete relief from extensive domestic responsibilities.

Although the husband's major contribution to the home was financial, even the king of the castle was expected to reciprocate the devotion of his queen, not his slave, via the dishes or the dustpan when required. Since family love and the home's intrinsic worth gave dignity to chores, whoever did them never compromised his own dignity. As Henry C. Wright explained in a chapter entitled "Home and Its Influence" in his 1855 marriage guide, *Marriage and Parentage*: "The details of domestic economy can never be repulsive to the true husband. On the contrary, to relieve the wants and cares of the wife, in any way, and help her to bear the burdens of household labor, is not to serve as a menial, but to cherish her and sustain her as a husband. However minute the service . . . it seems refined and manly."

It is whining about taking out the garbage that would have been unmanly. Pulling your weight on the home front wasn't just permissibly masculine in an age before that quality meant controlling the TV remote. It gave real substance to the love that "must ever be the one consecrating sentiment of the husband's life. This fathoms the depths of his being, and swallows up all other experiences."

More than any other, this notion that a man should pull his weight at home separated the men from the boys at a time when such distinctions were essential. The now-alien idea that scrubbing the hearth you cherished was ennobling also illuminates the gulf between the genuine Victorian home and Martha Stewart's version of what is often mistakenly assumed to be its current incarnation. In a recent speech at the National Press Club, this multimedia mogul described the crux of her business as "giving women permission to enjoy home-making."[3] The fact that they need public approval demonstrates that its status is about as low as you can go within legal limits.

In an age when irreverence is our national religion, ridicule is the sincerest form of flattery. Ms. Stewart's boundless energy and exacting standards have spawned a satirical backlash, from a parody of her magazine (entitled *Is Martha Stewart Living?*) to aprons that lower expectations to mortal levels by announcing that the wearer isn't Martha. Such reality checks are needed protection from someone who probably forges her own flatware for dinner parties after personalizing each guest's napkin with their initials. But for all Martha's magic with a glue gun, the real magic is missing. Even her finest feats lack the cohesive transcendent sense of home the Victorians conveyed through simple eloquence, unaided by soft photography or the pristine country setting that costars in her TV show. Martha once unwittingly revealed her great limitation to an interviewer: "My life is my work. My work is my life. I think about it twenty-four hours a day." The single-minded drive of this empire builder is hardly surprising, since she endured a nasty divorce, and her relationship with her only child has been described as "cordial." If something deep and vital is missing from the life she fills with a marathon schedule, it is definitely missing from her sense of home—and ours.

THE SUM OF ITS PARTS

For the Victorians, impressing visitors with time-consuming decorating projects would hardly have been considered the point. The singularly resonant power of the Victorian home, and one's membership in it whether as breadwinner or breadmaker, endowed the smallest act with shared value and respect. The everyday tasks that made up the bulk of women's work were valued because they were performed out of love for the family.

Life in the Victorian era was always considered more than the mere sum of its parts. Yet each part had meaning beyond the literal functions that still maintain, if not emotionally sustain, the modern home. Catharine Beecher, writing in *American Woman's Home,* wove this uniquely Victorian view through the once rich fabric of domestic life:

> The most minute details of household economy become elegant and refined when they are ennobled by sentiment. . . . To furnish a room is no longer a commonplace affair, shared with upholsterers and cabinetmakers; it is decorating the place where I am to meet a friend or lover. To order dinner is not merely arranging a meal with my cook, it is preparing refreshments for him whom I love.

The Victorians presumed the primacy and integration of home, as opposed to the current presumption of an atomized home, which seems to be less than the sum of its parts. We are not the first to discover that its maintenance can be tedious and taxing. Without mechanical washing machines, for example, for the Victorians the laundry alone could consume an entire day of each week. But whatever the chore, it served a grander purpose: the family and the home. (Our ancestors rarely discussed one without the other; and while we speak of mere chores, they preferred the higher implications of duties.)

Recognizing this grander purpose is an essential first step to respiritualizing the home and restoring the traditional values three quarters of Americans want to strengthen, according to polls. One 1993 *Wall Street Journal*/NBC survey concluded that the country is "vaguely searching for some old-fashioned notion of family."[4] What we long for is a lost sense of home, not just a place but a sanctuary from a world in many ways far meaner than it was a century ago. Without restoring the home to its former elevation, family values are destined to remain an airy hope tossed about by the winds.

FROM HOME TO THE WORLD

When home provided a refuge from the world, it was also the axis on which the world turned and which kept it from spinning out of control. The influential editor Sarah Josepha Hale argued in 1868, "The moral tone of a people must depend . . . upon their domestic institutions." In her autobiography, the suffragist Mary Livermore echoed these sentiments when she linked the success of her crusade for women's civic rights to their role in the domestic realm: "The real humanizing and civilizing of the world is carried forward in homes, and as the aggregate of these may be, so will the nation be." This is another Victorian lesson we have relearned through the harshest possible means, by encountering an explosion of amoral young predators raised in "homes" that parody the meaning that once inhered in this word.

In retrospect, Frances Willard, president of the Woman's Christian Temperance Union, may sound hyperbolic in her description of home as "the citadel of everything that is good and pure on earth." But the Victorians applied their superlatives to what they valued most for both its personal and public rewards. "The family home, carrying on its proper work, is no narrow circle of selfish exclusiveness," observed Dr. Elizabeth Blackwell in 1852, "but a living centre, attracting to itself and widely radiating healthy social life. Its influence is felt in intercourse with all classes."

Although home may have been the ultimate private domain, it was as omnipresent as oxygen, the one institution that bridged the realms of personal identity and social stability. Men fought wars for God and country, but even in this God-fearing age, home was the linchpin of life. As the sartorial innovator Amelia Bloomer, who popularized "bloomers," wrote during the 1850s in her women's rights journal, *The Lily*, "Without home, without the domestic relations, the love, the cares, the responsibilities which bind men's hearts to one treasury of precious things, the world would be chaos, without order, or beauty, without patriotism, or social regulation, without public or private virtue."[5]

To the Victorians, the primacy of home was accepted by men as well as women. In fact, men even viewed the home as the best barometer of a nation's strength. "In love of home, the love of country has its rise," declared Charles Dickens in *The Old Curiosity Shop*. And no country nurtured this bond more than the United States, as de Tocqueville attested in *Democracy in America*: "Whereas the European tries to escape his sorrows at home by troubling society, the American derives from his home that love of order which he carries over into affairs of state."

Today's impoverished debate over "family values" attests to how much we have lost since then. Our ancestors believed in building a house from the foundation up, not from the roof down. Neither family-friendly legislation nor cloning Martha Stewart will accomplish what needs to be done. In 1852, Dr. Blackwell warned that any country where the family was "degraded," not "cherished as the precious centre of the national welfare," was doomed to "rapid dissolution." That path led us to the place we live now, where liberals and conservatives serve up competing nostrums from workplace flextime and day care to tax-code tinkering and tougher divorce laws. We must retrace our steps and understand our missteps if we are ever to rediscover the road not taken.

15

Home Wreckers

How did our notions of home and its virtues turn so topsy-turvy? The usual suspects look depressingly familiar: historical events such as the Great War, social processes such as mass production and consumption, and technological advances like the automobile. All these historical changes had corrosive effects on domestic life, just as they did on public civility and personal intimacy. But history has a human face. The decline of Victorian ideals is the product of personal decisions as well as impersonal forces. And women themselves bear some responsibility for subverting the domestic ideals that their grandmothers held so dear. Yet like the three witches in *Macbeth*, three early-twentieth-century women were instrumental in bringing the pot to a boil: Charlotte Perkins Gilman, Lillian Gilbreth, and Christine Frederick.

HOME AS HELL

Ironically, the first oracle (and current feminist icon) Charlotte Perkins Gilman rebelled not only against her time but against the domestic ideal celebrated by her influential great-aunts Catharine Beecher and Harriet Beecher Stowe. Gilman never lost the taste of sour grapes that were a staple of her childhood diet.[1] Abandoned by her father when she was six, she and her mother had to move eighteen times in fourteen years. All she knew of solid family life came from occasional visits to cousins. "I saw how loving [it] could be," she recalled many decades later. "Here was courtesy and kindness." But such rare tender memories could not sweeten the bitter anger and resentment that forever blackened her view of the Victorian home. Her "loathing for the home limited her ability to envision how domesticity and justice for women could be compatible," wrote the historian Glenna Matthews.

A classic ideologue who despised what she could not have and did not understand, Gilman is still remembered for her 1903 book *The Home*, a diatribe against domesticity. In it, she denounced "the sanctity of home," "the omnipresent domestic ideal," and the "cult of home worship." Like a termite, she gnawed at its foundation by doing what Masters and Johnson later did to sex: reducing transcendent values to animal functions. "The beehive is as much a home as any human dwelling," she wrote. "We are merely large animals living in large boxes." Gilman's concept of home was not of a shelter that nurtured body and soul but a virtual torture chamber. "The home is the place where we suffer most," according to this sad, scarred woman. In that "hotbed of personal feeling," love (which it seems she never knew) "grows intense and often morbid."

Despite the greener pastures she had glimpsed, Gilman believed if we were all flies on the walls of Victorian American homes, rather than visitors duped by company manners, "we would see how miserable everyone is." Later feminists would echo this paranoid vision by charging that all those white picket fences hid a national epidemic of spouse and child abuse. The dysfunctional circus of TV talk shows further assures us that domestic hell is the rule, not the exception. But Gilman was far ahead of her time in spewing her fiercest contempt at the women who maintained the home with their labor and their love.

Where Elizabeth Cady Stanton said that women's duties required common sense and wisdom, and Catharine Beecher considered them as sacred and important as any man's, Gilman found them "primitive" and "savage." She labeled the Victorian wife and mother a "parasite" and a "domestic vampire" who lived and worked in a "prison" that "impedes social progress." She ardently supported the inevitable evolutionary march toward socialism, when the state would usurp all functions of the home, from caring for children to preparing meals. While women would work everywhere but the home (unless it was someone else's), all domestic tasks would be performed by hired menials or professionals. This new utopia would not only cool the dangerous emotional heat of the Victorian home, it would replace cherished but "inferior" female traditions with the latest efficient scientific methods.

Gilman's own prejudices seemed to escape examination by her superior mind, perhaps because of her own dysfunctional family background. She married a man who was, by all known accounts, loving and attentive, but she had a complete nervous breakdown soon afterward. Her convalescence in a sanitarium inspired her noted work of feminist fiction, *The Yellow Wallpaper*, which essentially blames men for the heroine's insanity. After divorcing her mate, Gilman recovered, although she continued to suffer from bouts of depression. She eventually married another man who was so incidental to her work-obsessed life that she barely bothered to mention him in her memoir. Had she been born a century later, Prozac or twelve-step programs might have tempered her rancor toward the home and family she never had. But she relished the cultural inferno she sparked with her version of progress.

HOME AS ASSEMBLY-LINE FACTORY

Gilman's cult worship of science was shared by her two sisters in crime. The most famous and least likely member of this home-wrecking trio was immortalized by her children's memoirs and the classic 1950 movie *Cheaper by the Dozen*. On the surface, Lillian Gilbreth seems worlds removed from Charlotte Perkins Gilman. This matriarch of a family of twelve children was mistress of a cheerfully bustling house she occupied with her adored husband and colleague, Frank. She appeared to have the kind of charm-infused life that inspires wistful nostalgia, down to the treasured but unreliable family car—a Pierce Arrow named Foolish Carriage. But under the skin she was as revolutionary as Gilman in her quest to run the home like an assembly line.

From 1910 to 1921, the Gilbreths conducted some of the earliest filmed time and motion studies as consulting experts for industrial plants. But they didn't stop at the factory door. So they crossed that great Victorian divide between the public and the private by using their home as the primary "school for scientific management and the elimination of wasted motions." That modern mentality needed only time and technology to obliterate domestic arts and sentiments.

With their ever-present stopwatch and their children as ready (if reluctant) guinea pigs, the Gilbreths clocked and dissected every household exertion, from making beds and washing dishes to buttoning a vest. (They found that starting at the bottom rather than the top saved three seconds.) This relentless experiment even extended to filming the removal of the children's tonsils. Individuality, however harmless, had no place in a roost ruled by seconds gained or lost. While your hair was technically yours, sheer efficiency determined how you combed it. (And we think of the Victorians as conformists.)

After Frank Gilbreth died in 1924, Lillian continued to apply industrial concepts to the home. In a 1927 book, *The Home-maker and Her Job,* she defined its ideal as a "well-run business" that could be minutely analyzed, summarized, and governed by charts and graphs. The full fruits of her labors took decades to bloom, but she was confident that the winds of change were blowing in her direction: "So many of the prejudices of an older generation are passing away; and any one who has been through modern laundries, bakeries, and preserving plants will find herself looking with suspicion on the unstandardized procedures of many a home."

HOME AS CONSUMER BASE

"Scientizing" the home was also advocated by a third home wrecker, Christine Frederick. In her 1929 magnum opus, aptly titled *Selling Mrs. Consumer,* she wrote that households should "run like a clock." During her tenure as editor of *Ladies' Home Journal*, she faithfully chipped away at the domestic vision that had been promoted by Sarah Josepha Hale during her forty years at *Godey's Ladies' Book.* An enemy of what Edith Wharton called "the art of civilized living," Frederick urged women to trade quality for quantity by standardizing each household task "so you can do it everyday in an identical manner without much mental attention." This typified the counsel dispensed

through women's magazines by the second decade of the new century. No longer was "the whole process of home-making" an "art and a profession" that required "the best qualities of heart and mind." The new religion rendered it both heartless and mindless.

No one deserves more responsibility than Christine Frederick for turning the home into a home shopping network of family demands, where women acted as the "chief purchasing agent." In *Selling Mrs. Consumer* she equated increased consumption with "the advance of civilization" and promoted the new doctrine of consumptionism as "the greatest idea America has to give the world."

In her recipe for that perfect world, business would emotionally and physically revamp the home until the latter's raison d'etre became buying from business. Frederick's lifelong mission—"the conversion of luxuries into necessities"—hinged on teaching manufacturers how to sell women an endless bill of goods, a mission she fulfilled with blazing success. Unlike Victorian domestic advisers, she believed it was impossible to underestimate the intelligence of wives and mothers. Therefore, ads aimed at them should be direct, visual, and simplistic. For example, Frederick discovered that women initially resisted buying the first generation of radios because they were as intrusively large and aesthetically displeasing as many women find today's jumbo-screen televisions. So she convinced manufacturers to design them like furniture and stress their surface appeal, not their technological sophistication.

She applied the same approach to any salable good (and she treated everything as just that). Even when peddling the staff of life, she highlighted the appetizing look of bread, not the nutritional value that once concerned Victorian cooks. Portray apparel as smart; durability be damned. Indeed, the lack of durability became a virtue rather than vice in Frederick's schema. To keep the corporate cash machine churning, she told producers to focus on developing items that would become obsolete almost as soon as they were made. Nowadays we take this planned obsolescence for granted, but it was heresy to those nurtured on the Victorian creed of thrift. Domestic frugality was no longer an accomplishment and a character-forming lesson for children but a "petty and ridiculous" practice.

Beyond the question of home economics, this represented the abdication of women as moral exemplars both in and out of the home. Like the majority of her sex, Frederick favored Prohibition, but not to protect wives and children from the abuse of drunken husbands. Always the money-minded pragmatic, she feared that earnings wasted on booze "curtails man's consumptive power," especially among the lower classes she wanted to consumerize. But it was loosening women's purse strings that mainly occupied Frederick. She mocked every expression of the old "pinching economy," like rolling tapers from newspapers to start a fire instead of purchasing matches, and using stale bread to make bread pudding, even though hard bread works best. Frederick's thriving legacy of what she blithely termed "creative waste" gifted us with myriad waste disposal and other environmental problems.

The indelible red ink Christine Frederick splashed on the household budget more than half a century ago also robbed us of our rightful inheritance—the Victorian domestic soul. When saving time became the bottom line for home as well as business, every appliance that replaced or expedited human labor became a must. Tradition fell before acquisition. Treasured family keepsakes that embodied continuity and cushioned households against the crudities and pressure tactics of the commercial world became hated hand-me-downs destined for the scrap heap.

Homemade vs. Store Bought

Frederick denounced any object that had "lasting heirloom" potential, including the signature Victorian ebony piano her mother bequeathed to her. To her mind, pianos became as dated and disposable as hats. So you traded it up and moved it out every few years, like all the other manufactured marvels you couldn't live without, and eventually couldn't live with. Replacing them extracted a financial rather than emotional investment, unless one meant the emotions that were the not-so-whimsical whims that triggered impulse buying.

Perhaps most tragically, women were told they had "better things to do" than engage in the formerly time-honored domestic arts. Frederick deemed it unforgivably passé to prepare meals from scratch instead of opening cans, or to dress your family and your rooms with the unique items you crafted rather than the cookie-cutter goods you purchased. The intricate needlework that gave such distinctive charm to the Victorian home was no source of pride or sign of family devotion, just a "petty medieval accomplishment." And petty is what the home was destined to become.

This lesson that the home is unimportant is not an easy one to unlearn, as I was to discover. Upon completing college in the late 1970s, I was gravely disappointed when my graduation gift from an aunt turned out to be not the check I expected but a set of bed linens my great-grandmother had embroidered in the 1880s for her trousseau. This seemed not only a useless relic but an insult to a newly minted careerist. I shook my head in self-pity and disgust as I imagined all the hours my ancestress wasted stitching those fussy monograms, flowers, and scrolls for some anticipated home her Prince Charming would provide and rule. If I had to keep a memento of a woman I never met, why did it have to be this utterly impractical testament to her domestic bondage? I would have preferred her faded but proud college degree. Alas, she had none.

After burying the linens in my parents' closet, I went off to graduate school with plain, wrinkle-free sheets to pursue a vision of womanhood unfettered by froufrou items I couldn't bank or list on a résumé. I forgot those linens for several years, and by the time I was obliged to reclaim them, my irritation had mellowed to indifference. Yet I toted them from house to house, ignoring them except to unpack and repack them after debating their fate with the Goodwill box. It was only gradually that I came to realize the value of those linens—beyond the escalating prices they command in antique shops. Like Mark Twain's father, who seemed to grow so wise between his son's fourteenth and twenty-first birthdays, the linens too seemed to change over the years as I began to understand why the glue binding Victorian homes and families had cracked and crumbled.

Like other girls of her day, my great-grandmother learned such a reverence for home that she began to craft the things that would warm it with her personal touch even before she had her own home. She knew her efforts would be honored, not disdained, by her family-to-be, because such efforts were almost universally practiced. Far from being quaint creations of small-town provincials, needlework provided inspiration to the most noted artists of her time. The Impressionist Gari Melchers's wife inspired him to paint *Penelope* and *Young Woman Sewing*. Mary Cassatt did a portrait of the same title, as well as *Lydia at the Tapestry Loom*. Women also stitched domestic sentiments into samplers (some now costing thousands of dollars) that were prominently displayed. "Peace to This House,"

This Currier & Ives print celebrated the feminine art of needlework, which was passed down through the generations. Handmade crafts became passé as mass-produced goods became available in the 1920s.

"God Bless Our Home," and "Home Sweet Home" were among the messages that would now prompt mostly snickers.

I finally appreciate the meaning of their art, which lies beyond mere artistry, along with the art in the linens I once found useless and now feel unworthy to use. Even without a string of degrees and a key to the executive washroom, my great-grandmother created both a place and a sense of home most of us will never know. By current standards, she may have been an imprisoned victim of sex discrimination, but her descendants are the real losers. I sometimes wonder whether she made Edith Wharton's prescribed "twelve of everything" for her trousseau, and I envy the skills I lack. I owe a much-belated apology to the woman I was never privileged to meet, except through her legacy. But it's too late to atone, as it was decades before I was born.

HOME AS HOTEL

My grandmother would never have described herself as "just a house-wife," a phrase that first appeared in the twenties, not the sixties. In the Jazz Age, the once-exalted domicile this deposed high priestess had tended was becoming more of a hotel than a home. As the historian Ellen Rothman put it, the altar where the Victorian family worshipped devolved into a "base of operations." And thanks to the latest techno-toys, it is has even become a base for spying on our nearest and dear-est. Almost any object, from planters to coffee pots, can conceal tiny cameras and recorders to catch abusive nannies, drug-using kids, and adulterous spouses. According to industry experts, business is booming.

The writing on the wall could be read without a Dick Tracy decoder decades before your average Joe started playing detective. A 1920s resi-dent of Middletown, the town studied by Helen and Robert Lynd, lamented the "physical service station" that replaced a "sacred institu-tion." Frederick Lewis Allen, who also witnessed this domestic demise, similarly described the home as " becoming less of a shrine, more of a dormitory—a place of casual shelter where one stopped overnight on the way from the restaurant and the movie theater to the office."

Allen detected mounting angst among women as they lost the satisfaction and esteem of creating life's central experience and were demoted to the status of "engineers" who managed an increasingly mechanized house. The model home was scientific and rational, not emotional and transcendent, as the houses of Gilman, Gilbreth, and Frederick became the new model. The historian Glenna Matthews notes that "efficiency had become a goal to be served for its own sake, irrespective of the emotional life of the housewife and her family, rather than a means to serve any larger purpose." Nothing before or since aspired to a larger purpose than the Victorian home, and nothing has been more devastating than its loss.

Instead of providing a haven from the depersonalized cash-based world, the home became just one more commodity. As a result, the legendary Victorian respect for its makers went straight into all those new toilets even common folk acquired. The old-time religion of the home was so weakened by the creeping corrosion of change, it was set to collapse when attacked by the first wave of feminists in the 1960s. Glenna Matthews astutely observed, "The desperate letters sent to Betty Friedan after she identified 'the problem that has no name'—that is the emptiness of many housewives' lives—testify to the damage inflicted by the twentieth-century version of domesticity."

"JUST A HOUSEWIFE"

Friedan's own experience confirmed the complete demolition of the bridge Victorian women built to the wider world by means of—not in spite of—the moral power they wielded at home. By the time she began writing for women's magazines in the 1950s, it was widely assumed that women had few social, cultural, or political interests beyond the narrow confines of shopping and housewifery.

We wrongly assume that Friedan launched the first full-scale assault on domestic work as an activity that could never compensate for the "emptiness" of women's "narrow lives." She wasn't the first, but she did up the ante by pronouncing the vocation of homemaker as "dangerous" in the extreme:

> In a sense, that is not as farfetched as its sounds, the women who "adjust" as housewives, who grow up wanting to be "just a housewife," are in as much danger as the millions who walked to their own death in the concentration camps—and the millions more who refused to believe that the concentration camps existed.

In fact, there is an uncanny uncomfortable insight into why a woman can so easily lose her sense of self as a housewife in certain psychological observations made of the behavior of prisoners in Nazi concentration camps. In these settings, purposely contrived for the dehumanization of man, the prisoners literally became "walking corpses."

Reading this statement with the benefit of over thirty years of hindsight, we might wonder whether it was Friedan who completely lost her senses. Even if we allow for her anger and hyperbole, her judgments reflected a half century of misguided reforms that transformed queen bees into drones. This proud inheritor of Charlotte Perkins Gilman's legacy believed the sole route to dignity was a distinctly masculine one paved with paychecks. The new working woman's free time—as if there would be any—belonged not to hearth, kin, or self but to volunteering for the correct political causes. Indeed, in Friedan's revolutionary plan, women would breeze through domestic tasks, since any "eight-year-old" could handle the "trivia of housewifery." This presumably included raising children—who now often raise themselves.

By the time *The Feminine Mystique* fired its shot heard round the world in 1963, even Friedan's natural opponents were lobbing grenades at the same Swiss-cheese target. That very year, *Playboy* ran a scathing satirical piece that also portrayed the housewife as an idle parasite:

> Tired of the Rat Race?
>> Fed up with Job Routine?
>> Well, then . . . how would you like to make $8,000, $20,000—as much as $50,000 and more—working at home in your Spare Time? No selling! No commuting! No time clocks to punch.
>> BE YOUR OWN BOSS!
>> Yes, an Assured Lifetime income can be yours now, in an easy, low-pressure, part-time job that will permit you to spend most of each and every day as you please.[2]

These days Gloria Steinem complains that traditional women's work, which nearly all women do, was demeaned during her hardscrabble childhood in East Toledo, Ohio, and during her years at elite

Smith College. She still attributes this problem, and most others, to the "patriarchal rule," existing from time immemorial, that crosses class lines. Aside from having herself helped nurture this denigration of homemaking, she overlooks the fact that in the "patriarchal" Victorian era, the work now demeaned was highly esteemed.[3]

Despite Steinem's call to compensate domestic labor like any other paid occupation, which Victorian women would find insulting, even hints of the emotions once connected to that labor remain favorite cans to kick among feminists. Susan Faludi rails at the "domestic sentimentality" featured in publications such as the hugely successful *Victoria* magazine. She denounces "cocooning" among adult women as a return to the "gestational stage," but fails to notice that the modern cocoon is a flimsy excuse for one. However, movement matriarch Betty Friedan admits encountering many professional women who crave a taste of this forbidden lifestyle. They now ask themselves, she reports in *The Second Stage,* "What do you do about life, children, men, loneliness, companionship, the need to have a real home—things no one thought about when we were so obsessed with liberating ourselves?"

Yet the contempt for traditional domestic skills is still so ingrained that it passes for conventional wisdom, especially among female higher achievers—until they discover they don't know it all. One acquaintance, a supremely self-assured financial executive, decided she would make her daughter's Halloween costume because "any idiot could," including her mother, who sewed on a machine, and her grandmother, who learned to sew without one. After ruining a mountain of fabric and her flawless manicure, she was forced to contribute to the yearly $1.5 billion Halloween business by purchasing the kind of flimsy but overpriced costume every other kid had. Admitting a rare defeat and a new respect for a skill she once mocked, she pronounced herself the "real idiot."

THE MYTH OF THE FIFTIES HOME

The spiritual and substantive stripping of the twentieth-century home explains why the vague sentimental longings of baby boomers are misdirected if they settle for 1950s nostalgia (where liberals rightly charge that the family values of many conservatives are stuck). The hard truth is that the 1950s home was no longer "the" institution but only "an" institution. It no longer thrived on the wisdom, dedication, and moral inspiration of women whose immeasurable worth was valued on its own terms. Instead, it was based on the crass number crunching of the rat race. The Victorian home was a world and a century apart from what a *New York Times* critic wrongly but all too typically described as a myth "no different in essence from the saccharine family-oriented American television fare of the 1950s."

While we may have loved Lucy, she was a domestic dodo whose home and marriage routinely survived in spite of her efforts, not because of them. We laughed at Lucy Ricardo's wacky hijinks more than we laughed with her; that was the point. Although many security-hungry boomers and their parents fondly recall her antics, and the straightman TV housewives like June Cleaver and Margaret Anderson, nothing about them radiates the combination of strength, solidity, and spirituality of the nineteenth-century home and the women who defined it.

THE IDEAL HOME

The gap between such women's expectations and experiences and our own allows cynics to dismiss the claim that Victorian home life was the good life. In a recent review of a museum exhibition of Currier & Ives prints, the *New York Times* ridiculed these once wildly popular prints as "kitsch," "idealized," and "impossibly uncomplicated" views of the past."[4] The reviewer simply can't understand that the Victorians bought these pictures by the millions not only because they saw themselves in such scenes but because those endearing prints honored their sentiments of what a true home should be. As one domestic adviser wrote in the 1850s:

> To the Victorians, domesticity seemed as instinctive as breathing, because their first allegiance was the home— creating it, perfecting it, revering it, and, above all, instilling its spirit in the next generation. Since women largely dispatched this duty, home was called "the empire of the mother." Motherhood lost its deepest meaning and its most exalted domain when we lost the Victorian sense of home.

Throw Momma from the Train

One of the most enduring images of the Victorian era is of the revered mother, whether in famous paintings by artists such as Mary Cassatt, Gari Melchers, and Francis Coates or in popular songs. Mother's Day is a Victorian invention. Anna Jarvis, a teacher who was very close to her mother and cared for her all her life, decided upon her mother's death in 1908 to lobby for an official day honoring all mothers. In 1914 Congress passed a resolution requesting that the president proclaim just such a holiday, and on May 9, 1914, Americans first observed Mother's Day; they have observed it on the second Sunday in May ever since.

In the Victorian era, mothers had a moral authority that was respected not only in the home but also in the public domain. To build this "empire of the mother," as the historian Mary P. Ryan called it in her book by that name, the Victorians didn't begin at the beginning. They began *before* the beginning, at the prenatal stage. Their great respect for motherhood conferred both dignity and privacy on pregnancy. *Household*, a popular magazine of the era, declared, "A modest woman does not publish her sacred secret."[1] While the desire to share one's happiest impending event with the world is certainly understandable, by making pregnancy and childbirth such a public affair we have unwittingly destroyed the very specialness of this experience we so want to celebrate.

PUBLIC PREGNANCY

Once a Victorian woman began to "show," she abstained from parties and other celebrations, opting instead to quietly entertain family members and select friends at home. The Boston socialite and art collector Isabella Stewart Gardner recalled taking carriage rides while swathed in strategically placed blankets that her husband lovingly arranged. But no one dared rub her stomach as if it were Aladdin's magic lamp. The women of her time understood that discretion, not exhibitionism, inspired general respect for their "condition." You don't get that by breastfeeding in public, or suing for the right to do so.

Just as promiscuous women have turned all women into targets of insults and assaults, expectant exhibitionists make all pregnant women the subjects and objects of often unwelcome personal comments and presumptuous pawing. While no one would ask today's pregnant woman to withdraw behind her parlor doors (especially if she needs a paycheck), there is a gulf of lost discretion and respect between a discreet carriage ride and a spectacle swaggering across a beach in a bikini. Fecundity, like attitude, is now in-your-face, whether or not you welcome its presence. Demi Moore puts it on the cover of *Vanity Fair*, while former CBS correspondent Connie Chung launches a publicity effort to advertise her desire to become a mother. And of course, there is the ever-tiresome Madonna, who considered taking out a personal ad for someone interested in "the fatherhood gig."

Childbirth as a Public Party

Women who are not celebrities unfortunately can be just as crass. These days brag books of sonogram pictures are passed around at offices and parties like vacation snapshots. Strangers, including reluctant males, are encouraged to feel the baby move. And when the blessed event does occur, the entire town is invited to attend, as if birth were a barn raising. Dad was the first required addition to the delivery. Then came the video camera, so the birth could be shown postpartum. I have heard audiences compare and review these movies like regular theater fare. All that's missing is popcorn.

As birth has become a more public event we have seen an increasing number of "homey" birthing suites in hospitals and birthing centers across the country, which accommodate parties of family, friends, and coworkers. Sometimes these gatherings literally are parties. During one typical fete at the Elizabeth Seton Childbirth Center in Manhattan, Mom breastfed her bundle of joy to the sounds of mariachi music while five guests feasted on takeout.

Siblings frequently witness the arrival of their family's latest addition, although experts are divided on the wisdom of exposing youngsters, even toddlers, to a potentially damaging trauma. Advocates, who naturally believe that nothing natural can be bad, stress the unique opportunity for siblings to bond with the baby, and claim it is especially important for "little girls to see how wonderful giving birth can be."[2]

Coach Dad

What does it mean to treat this momentous event like a football tailgate picnic, complete with coach, fans, and food? It's no picnic, at least for some women, according to a recent firsthand account by the *Washington Post* contributor Elizabeth Chang. In her opinion,

> . . . when you stop and think about it, the idea of having a coach in the delivery room is really absurd, so completely off-target that people who conjured it up must have been male. . . . A woman in labor already has several coaches: She's got a team of nurses telling her to "breathe, bear down, harder" along with a doctor barely stopping by once every few hours to say coachlike things as "Not there yet" or "That's not very productive pushing."

Chang maintains that men often forget the mother's tribulations and focus instead on their own discomfort. "In fact, men are eager to talk about the pain they endured during childbirth. A favorite topic of conversation is how hard their wives squeezed their hands." Those poor babies. Our ancestors could have predicted Chang's most devastating assertion about turning childbirth into a macho game. "The perhaps not-so-surprising result is that men have begun to treat childbirth like sports, complete with training, statistics, and competition that somehow entirely avoids the mind-blowing point: the emergence of a new life."[3]

PREGNANCY AS A SPECIAL, PRIVATE TIME

The Victorians believed birth made every baby's family "akin to all humanity." But acknowledging this kinship did not entail debasing it with casual locker-room chatter or the naked proclamations of expectant mothers that make them grist for the mills of standup comics who try to get belly laughs out of belly jokes. Many women cringe at these sordid doings staged at their expense, yet they repress their objections for fear of being labeled repressed.

There is far more at stake than questions of sexual frankness or our cultural compulsion to wallow in the nitty gritty of human biology, which the Victorians civilized and we trivialize. Feminists have long insisted that pregnancy is just another physical condition, like hives, as motherhood is just another "role" we play in our varied acting careers. This means macho moms don't slow down, despite swollen ankles or morning sickness that may last all day.

This mentality, not just the cold corporate bottom line of the health insurance industry, surely contributes to the epidemic of drive-through deliveries. Horror stories abound of hospitals that, until recent legislation stopped them, tossed out mothers as little as two hours after birth. As a result, infants not under the observation of hospital staff sometimes developed potentially fatal ailments. In pressing for remedial legislation, Ralph Nader accused insurance companies of devaluing women and children. This assessment is accurate but sadly incomplete. And neither liberals nor conservatives have a clue about how to re-value this experience. For all their recent hand-wringing over broken families, illegitimacy, and delinquent kids, most conservatives fail to connect them to the denigration of motherhood and home.

THE HAND THAT ROCKS
THE CRADLE RULES THE WORLD

To the Victorians, a woman did not simply have a child. As one writer phrased it, "She is adding another and equally essential constituent to the home. Indeed, she is helping, as in no other way so efficiently she can help, to build a home." This home was not her prison, as *The Feminine Mystique* would have it, but her bridge to the outside world. The moral influence mothers wielded in their empire both demanded and legitimized its reach to a wider arena. When Frances Willard, the president of the Woman's Christian Temperance Union, told all women to make the world more homelike—and in so doing protect their homes—the Victorians knew this was no crusade to hang lace curtains in Congress. Willard's agenda, which was shared by many other female activists, included not just Prohibition but suffrage, public sanitation, prison and school reform, and the elimination of child labor and prostitution.

Willard's use of home as a rallying cry was more than a savvy choice of a concept that women understood. It demonstrates both the reverence and the clout that home commanded in every quarter a century ago. The historian Mary Ryan notes: "The home was only the imperial center, the mother country, from which women launched their vast social influence." Because the Victorian home had this "broader, sweeter, grander significance," she writes, mothers were considered a nation's builders, not its menials.

Sarah Josepha Hale specifically traced a country's "prosperity and greatness" to Mother's "character and conduct," intangibles that can't be measured like the GNP. Lydia Maria Child described her "empire of the heart" as the "domain of moral affection" distinct from man's commercial world but the "co-equal sovereignty of intellect, taste, and social refinement."[4] Catharine Beecher felt that it was the mothers of America "in whose hands rest the real destinies of the republic." As with any sovereign, everything she said and did affected her subjects in small but potent ways we no longer recognize or value. William Alcott wrote in 1837:

> She does not take a step which does not educate herself,
> her husband, or others. So surely as she lifts a finger, or
> utters a word, or gives a direction, or casts an approving or

disapproving look, that modifies the feelings, or the conduct, or the health, of those around her, so surely does she
become their educator—the former of their character for
time and eternity.

Today's clueless conservatives tell Mom to just chuck the job
and raise the kids, without first restoring her to her proper premier
place. Without this bridge to the past, mothers who choose that full-
time occupation become family serfs instead of a precious national
resource. Their dominion over an institution that shapes all others
entitles them to a voice in the world. Nor should stepping beyond
their threshold ever diminish the admiration for what they achieve in
the home. Lucy Stone's husband, Henry Blackwell, paid tribute to
suffragists when he said, "Never have I known more affectionate
wives, more tender mothers, more accomplished housekeepers, more
satisfied husbands and children, more refined and happy homes" than
among these women's dominions.[5]

The Authority of Motherhood

Creating those refined and happy homes was a confidence-boosting
source of pride that Victorian women relished. In contrast to modern
feminists, the Victorians believed they were effective reformers
because of their domesticity, not in spite of it. For all its practical
demands, home, and especially motherhood, was not a burden to be
relieved or banished. On the contrary, to activists like Elizabeth Cady
Stanton, motherhood was an ennobling experience, "an added power
and development of some of the most tender sentiments of the
human heart and not a limitation."[6]

The magazine editor Sarah Josepha Hale lived this fusion of
maternity and reform. Among her many public activities, Hale was
instrumental in establishing Vassar College and preserving George
Washington's home at Mount Vernon. A devoted mother of five, she
wrote with as much frequency and ease—but without apologies—on
knitting infants' socks as she did on raising funds for medical mission-
aries, promoting physical fitness, public playgrounds, improved labor
conditions, and higher education for girls.

Because the importance of homemaking and motherhood were
constantly reaffirmed in print and pulpit, women could apply their

insights and integrity to the gravest issues of the day. For example, the historian Glenna Matthews notes that Harriet Beecher Stowe "used the moral authority of the housewife to justify speaking out against slavery. . . . The political impact of *Uncle Tom's Cabin,* filled as it was with domestic imagery, demonstrated how the influence of home on the world could manifest itself."

Now moms have the moral authority to speak on little more than diaper rash. I learned this lesson uncomfortably up close and personal while dining with a wealthy Republican party activist and his wife, who had quit her job to raise their children. He fancied himself a living paragon of family values, and preached accordingly to those who wished to listen and to those who didn't. Yet when his wife dared to voice her opinions on a political issue he was discussing, he instantly interrupted. "No one cares what you think," he snapped. "You're nothing but a housewife from Connecticut who rides horses and takes her kids to tennis lessons." (This woman also does volunteer work for several educational projects that benefit inner-city kids.)

What happened to motherhood to allow the merchant princes of contemporary conservatism to toss bombs of contempt at the symbol venerated by the Romantic poet Samuel Taylor Coleridge as "the holiest thing alive." Contrary to the myth cherished by those who blame the insidious sixties for all social ailments, Betty Friedan was not the first to whack maternity like a child a piñata.

DETHRONING MOM

The chronic home hater Charlotte Perkins Gilman, whom we met earlier, fired the opening shot against maternity in 1903. Six decades before Betty Friedan portrayed American mothers as mental midgets who "infantalized" and "dehumanized" their kids, her patron saint accused Victorian women of raising a "huge and growing crop of idiots, imbeciles, cripples, defectives, and degenerates, the vicious, and the criminal . . . the vast mass of slow-minded, prejudiced, ordinary people who clog the wheels of progress." Gilman declared that motherhood was just a "brute instinct" no higher than any other of "nature's processes of reproduction." She saw posterity as doomed by "untaught mothers," programmed to "repeat the mistakes of their more ignorant ancestors," whom she likened to a "dog turning three times before he lies down on a carpet." And Gilman was by no means all talk. She walked the talk by giving her young daughter to her ex-husband and his second wife to raise, in an early form of day-care dumping. The woman who called her own mother "cold" froze out her child until she was a self-sufficient adult.[7]

In her own day, Gilman was a lone voice crying in the wilderness. By the 1920s, though, her swan song for motherhood was becoming a siren's song for a new generation. Analyzing popular literature of the period, Glenna Matthews found a growing chorus of Freudian "scientific" child-care experts who warned against "excessive motherly affection." Some, like the pioneer behavioralist John B. Watson, even questioned "whether there should be individual homes for children—or even whether children should know their parents." Making the most of the bad situation—the still lingering home—the new high priests of parenthood told America's mothers to mistrust their once revered instincts and adopt in their place the severely structured schedules and habits cultivated by "scientific" laboratories. This was the Jazz Age version of test-tube babies.

By 1927, one worried nostalgic wrote in *Ladies' Home Journal*, "'Mother, Home, and Heaven!' used to form the pious three. Now the Home is more of an exception than a rule; Mother is cast down from her pinnacle; and a good many people are trying to take away Heaven." Three years later, Dr. Abraham Myerson echoed these dying sentiments in another woman's magazine. Noting the "devaluation of motherhood," he yearned for the days when "Freud had not yet corroded the delight of the infant's attachment to the mother nor the mother's joy in the child, and [John B.] Watson had not yet destroyed the self-esteem of the mother by making her worse than worthless in her own eyes."

Even female voting power could not salvage all the moss Gilman's rolling stone had flattened. Indeed, historians cite the crippled authority of home and motherhood for women's failure to become a formidable political bloc after finally winning the suffrage battle in 1920. When the Nobel Prize–winning author Pearl Buck returned from ultramisogynist China, she was shocked to find the once-honored female sphere "despised" in her native land. "Women's influence is almost totally lacking in the centers of American life," she lamented in 1941. Unlike the powerful suffragette, she said, the modern housewife "putters about on the fringes of her world which really goes on without her." Even within her own domain, "she is no longer the spiritual and moral influence she was once to man and child."[8]

It was only a single generation—and an even shorter psychic stretch—to *The Feminine Mystique's* demonization of Mom that continues to the present day. Our ambiguity about the role of motherhood is most evident in our struggle to define a "working mom." Potomac Mills, a Virginia mega-mall that is one of the state's top tourist attractions, recently sponsored a tribute to "working women." In TV ads inviting nominations for admired achievers, viewers had to be told that full-time moms were eligible because they too "work." Barbara Bush did not fare even that well when she was asked to give the commencement speech at Wellesley College in 1990. About 150 students objected to the then First Lady as an unsuitable role model for aspiring professional women because she did not work outside the home for a salary.

If women collude in this mental matricide, how can we expect any better from men? And how do we save our nation's troubled children, whom everyone agrees are in crisis, if the truly challenging job of raising them must be justified with every breath?

SUPERMOMS AND JUST-A-MOM'S

Stay-at-home moms often feel compelled to defend themselves by reciting every nanny and day-care horror story they know, then assuring you they are pursuing a second masters degree in their spare time in order to reenter the work force with added credentials and earning power. Without the cushioning self-esteem of a career plan, their absence from the "real world" seems wasted, because they can't take it to the bank. In the 1989 movie *Parenthood*, a woman whose youngest child is about to start school laments, "Everybody's asking me when I'm going back to work, like I'm supposed to." Though she had a job before she had kids, "I'm better at this. I'm good at it," she says, laughing nervously. But no matter how good she is, "People make me feel embarrassed, like I don't have goals."

Even that old barn burner Betty Friedan expressed belated concern about the defensive and diminished status of mothers. In *The Second Stage*, her 1981 reassessment of feminism's impact, she described many women as bitter, confused, and depleted by "female machismo" and the constant strain of juggling the competing demands of work and family—"the blind spot in feminism." Acknowledging that motherhood was "more important than we wanted to admit," she urged gender cooperation rather than conflict, more male responsibility for domestic tasks, and congressionally mandated corporate policies like parental leave. Without them, women must continue to split like atoms between their jobs, their homes, and Friedan's obligatory commitment to political change. But neither Congress nor the Fortune 500 can stretch the hours in a day. And the superwoman Frankenstein that Ms. Friedan helped create still suffers from the same fatigue, "brittle disappointment," and "disillusionment" that she recognized the second time around.

Women have been told they can do anything; now they feel they must do everything. If they don't, all too often nothing gets done. Small wonder that mail-order catalogs sell caps and shirts declaring "I am woman. I am invincible. I am tired." Not exactly the image the Helen Reddy song was intended to convey.

The news is not that women are too tired to roar but that they're even conscious. In dual-income families, a recent survey found that women did over 80 percent of the shopping and cooking and 70 percent of all child-care activities. In *The Overworked American*, the sociologist Juliet Schor observed that our national time crunch is particularly acute and harmful for double-duty moms. And in a survey by the Families and Work Institute, 40 percent of women said it was hard to get up each morning and face another day at work, and 42 percent described themselves as "used up" by the end of the day.[9] Women who work outside the home often find that in trying to do it all, something ends up getting shortchanged. Too often it is the children.

Scholars warn of a "parenting deficit" that cheats children of their childhoods, with predictable consequences—drugs, alcohol, academic problems, and teen suicide. Couples don't fare much better than their offspring, says Schor. "Growing numbers of husbands and wives are like ships passing in the night, working sequential schedules to manage their child care." No wonder so many of those battered and leaky vessels are sinking.

Beleaguered moms and dads are trying to shrink this growing deficit by becoming "virtual parents" through pagers, fax machines, cellular phones, and voice mail that were once used strictly for business but are now sold by companies that exploit parental guilt. In a *U.S. News & World Report* article titled "Fax Me a Bedtime Story," Beth Brophy cited some heart-tugging examples. In the Motorola brochure "Paging All Families," little Billy contacts Mom when he gets a tummy ache so she can drop whatever she's doing to fetch him.[10] Pager or no pager, can most working mothers just bolt from the office when Billy calls?

RETHINKING PRIORITIES

Many moms want to stay home to raise their kids in spite of a cultural code that denies social status and self-esteem to women who lack a brilliant career, yet they feel they must earn a salary to make ends meet. In a recent survey, a majority of working mothers polled said they must work to support their families. A Yankelovich poll found that a clear majority (56 percent) would quit their jobs if they didn't need the money. This represents a steady rise from 30 percent over the past two decades.[11]

Whether such data seem enlightening or obvious, they fail to explore a sensitive and neglected issue—the meaning of need versus choice. The historian Stephanie Coontz observed that married women first entered the workforce in substantial numbers during the 1950s. Essentials like rent and food did not spark this exodus from the prefab hearth. Rather, as motherhood was "divested . . . of any larger social and political meaning" that empowered Victorian women, and the home lost its spiritual and physical preeminence, we increasingly stuffed our houses with luxuries that became necessities.

Obviously, some women must work to keep their children fed. But for others, feeding the constantly ballooning appetite for goodies is a diet of choice—one often made without sufficient information or deliberation. Many women forego the decision and dash back to work soon after giving birth. Either the added expense of a child seems to

automatically demand two paychecks, or else the loss of a professional identity and status is unthinkable. Some women willing to pay
that hefty price are astonished to learn they can remain solvent on
their husband's income. These are the women who ruthlessly reassess
all their previously unquestioned material priorities, which the arrival
of children often reshuffles. Can they live without the apparent
essentials they once took for granted? Some say yes.

After scrutinizing the family budget, a former bank vice-presi-
dent I know traded her coveted corner office for a stroller. It wasn't
easy to sacrifice her exotic vacations, upscale restaurant meals, and
designer clothes, not to mention her hard-won title. But they could
not compete with raising her child. "The more you have, the more
you spend," she observed six months after her career change. "The
more you buy, the more you think you need. Now I just say no. That's
the kind of power I never had before." Creativity became a new
necessity; she even learned to cook in the kitchen that she once used
mainly to store and reheat doggy bags. And she discovered that
coupon clipping did not dent her dignity. Another woman who quit
her job to stay home learned to save up for luxuries such as a satellite
dish because, as she says, "I look at life differently now. I've learned
things like that are not the God-given right I thought they were."

The race to keep up with the Joneses (or Madison Avenue's
image of them) has reached breakneck speed, costing health, sanity,
marriages, and the precious maternal time the Victorians valued far
above frills. Instead, we spend $4 billion a year just on baby products
that are a "must" for competitive parents who parade their bedecked
offspring like show dogs. Yet not all women enjoy earning the cash to
buy such things. In one recent survey of 3,000 women, only 31 percent reported getting great personal satisfaction from their work, and
38 percent wanted more opportunities to work at home.[12]

A WORKABLE NUCLEAR-FAMILY MODEL

Even after all these years of gender warring, both sexes express surprising agreement on their preferred concept of home. According to
an international Gallup poll of 1,000 adults in twenty-two countries,
47 percent of American men polled and 49 percent of American
women describe the ideal domestic arrangement as one where dad

brings home the bacon and Mom fries it up in the pan, rather than burning the candle at both ends. Of all those surveyed, Americans were among the greatest fans of the traditional family.

Even if men's wages and a family's downsized demands allowed mothers to do that job full time, however, they would still be left scrounging for social validation and self-respect. Neither hubby's megasalary nor generous tax credits can restore child-rearing to what the unmarried Susan B. Anthony called "the highest and holiest function of the physical organism." Though she often had to pick up the slack for sister activists who put maternal duties above their causes, she did not deny the unrivaled importance of training the next generation for the world she labored to change.[13]

Victorian priorities were reversed by those who presumed to continue the mission started by suffragists, yet failed to fill their shoes. Despite their conflicting emotional effect on ordinary women, feminists have scored undeniable and dramatic triumphs in transforming media images and cultural prescriptions for gauging female worth. But for all their rhetoric of freedom and choice, the feminist mentality used its muscle to narrow choice by delegitimizing the old division of labor between Mom and Dad. They redefined success in monetary and masculine terms, and grossly distorted the history of a "woman's place."

The eminent progressive historian Carl Degler, in *At Odds*, says that in the middle-class Victorian family, "The typical husband . . . was hardly the patriarchal father who gave little recognition to his wife. By definition, the companionate marriage placed limits on the power of the husband." Neither was he the nonentity of the Simpsons' cartoon world, where father knows squat. If we want fathers to be more than sperm and paycheck donors, we need to carefully select who sits at one head of the table. The conservative flavor of the current men's and fatherhood movements smacks of *Father Knows Best*. But is the likes of Jim Anderson the best we can do? If his factual counterparts were so esteemed, effective, and manly in America's alleged golden age, why did their authority melt down so quickly?

The Victorian Papa

Robert Young's paternal archetype may seem Herculean compared with Tim Allen's ineffectual character on *Home Improvement*. But he pales beside the real leading man who inspired *Life with Father*. In both content and style, the actor William Powell's portrayal of Clarence Day, Sr., was remarkably faithful to Clarence Jr.'s famous book. One of the movie's early scenes finds the well-polished clan assembled around an equally well-dressed breakfast table. From where we sit, it already seems like another planet. It would have been unthinkable for Mr. Day to exchange mumbled greetings with his kids or bury himself behind a newspaper—a gross violation of Victorian dining decorum and familial respect.

Papa Day extensively questions his sons about every detail of their lives, from one child's reluctance to eat his oatmeal to violin and baseball practice and the welfare of a finger injured from hugging an unfriendly cat. This is an intensely involved and interested parent accustomed to commensurate responses, not rolled eyes or a generalized grunt. The tenor of the family's conversation shows such queries to be an integral part of daily life. While the children might privately dissent from their father's opinions and admonitions (especially concerning oatmeal), they expected them and respected the concern behind them. They clearly loved their father, but they also revered him as much as the home he defined.

Jim Anderson may have dispensed useful advice, à la Ann Landers, but this mellow marshmallow was hardly the inspirational presence who embodied the meaning of parenthood and home with his words and his bearing. Jim was an unthreatening coaxer, a guidepost on the road of life that points in the right direction. Clarence Day, Sr., was an awesome and dignified traffic cop who enforced the rules of the road. Like that oatmeal his son disliked, he stuck to your ribs through the years. And this potent effect was neither a fluke nor a rarity in his time. Teddy Roosevelt's relations said that he always tried to imagine what his late father would do before making a decision, even during his presidential tenure. Can you picture a middle-aged Bud Anderson doing the same with a comfortable old shoe like Jim?

Victorian fathers could be personal heroes; contemporary fathers are dads. Like every facet of the Victorian home, parents provided the subterranean roots that helped their children to grow. And while the father of old might seem a bit stiff, like the horsehair sofa that scratched young Teddy Roosevelt's legs, he was hardly all work and no play. "It is not only the father's duty, but it should also be his pleasure to look after his own children," said an 1897 marital guide for husbands. Victorian men may not have roughhoused with their children, although some memoirs recall piggyback rides and blindman's bluff. But men were expected to participate in games, read to their children, and put them to bed—all expressions of "the true father spirit." This was indispensable to the meaning of paternity and manhood, not a lesson harried mothers verbally beat into self-absorbed couch potatoes, golfaholics, or robots in gray flannel suits.

Victorian fathers played an important role in their children's education and development.

The cold cash–based relationships that have gradually evolved since Pop first handed Junior dough for a date and the keys to the family jalopy would have appalled the Victorians, even though their child-rearing practices were intensely mother centered. "Despite the differences between men's and women's natures, the pleasures and satisfactions of parenthood are as great to the father as the mother," wrote Rev. Sylvanus Stall. Dr. Elizabeth Blackwell noted that when a newborn is laid in its father's arms, "the man awakens fully to the wonder and infinite tenderness of paternity." If Mama had her instincts, Papa did as well, and the two were expected to blend rather than clash in rearing their children. The suffragist Mary Livermore fondly remembered this joint rule in her childhood home, and the prayer her father offered at every evening meal: "Bless the united heads of this family."

The Wholeness of the Victorian Family

Despite this surprisingly modern message, the Victorian view of parenthood sharply diverged from ours in its unbreachable bond to the sacraments of marriage and home. We like to believe couples can split or remain nominally paired and still be good parents, while warring with or ignoring each other. Even after a savage divorce, we (hopefully) continue to love our children, despite the hated source of half their genes. In contrast, Victorian parents loved their offspring as extensions of their mutual love. Like sex, domestic sentiments, and the countless other links that made nineteenth-century culture a seamless web instead of a patchwork quilt, the romantic love that sired parental love was its essence; they were not paired in a marriage of convenience.

Children were "love's tokens" or "pledges of love," rather than another must-have on one's wish list. In a letter to his wife, Nathaniel Hawthorne described a heart that "yearns, and throbs, and burns with a hot fire, for thee, and for the children that have grown out of our love." These sentiments were echoed by ordinary parents of the period. One woman referred to her child as a "tie to both our hearts" in a letter to her husband. Another man told his undoubtedly gratified spouse, "You are my life Darling, and I cannot look upon our baby, except through you. My love for him does not arise from consanguinity alone, roots deepest in the soil of the love I bear my wife."[14]

KEEPING THE ROMANTIC FIRES BURNING

Such effusive emotions demonstrate what the Victorians called "keeping your courtship in marriage." Both were expected to endure in an era that thrived on high expectations. Romantic love provided the bricks and mortar of the home that enabled the raising of solid, civilized children. "The presence of one man and one woman, who have mutually chosen each other out of all the world . . . are the common centre of the circle of home," wrote Dr. E. H. Ruddock in 1899. "They make its earliest constituent, and its prime and essential condition. Without this, there may be much that is charming and bright, but there is no home. . . . It is a power so enduring and sacred that death itself cannot quite cancel it."

Not only did such deeply valued home-binding sentiments survive the grave, they infused daily domestic life in ways we can scarcely recall, even less, recapture. But there is no better place to learn them than at the Victorian dinner table, which fed both body and soul.

17

Soul Food

Perhaps the most flagrant (and certainly the most fragrant!) contrast between the Victorian home and our own is the frequency and quality of family meals. For evidence of this we need look no further than the shrinking modern dining room and its transformation into an office or walk-in closet. The architectural designer and critic Roger K. Lewis wrote in a column called "Let's Put Real Dining Rooms Back on the Table" that "the contemporary American family meal is often little more than grazing in the kitchen, a ritual of search and retrieval quite different from sitting around a dinner table. Eating has become an adjunct to doing other things: watching television, talking on the phone, reading newspapers or sitting in front of a computer."[1]

THE DINING RITUAL

Lewis predicts that if this once crucial space continues to contract, like the portion sizes of "lite" foods, it will soon be extinct. But we have lost far more than square footage since the nightly ritual Clarence Day, Jr., recalled from his youth: "Every evening from six to seven o'clock, while Father and Mother were having their dinner, this dining room became as sacred a scene, in my eyes, as a high court or shrine. . . . I sometimes leaned over the banisters in the narrow hall outside, looking down in through the doorway."

On his seventh birthday Clarence was "promoted" from the basement kitchen, where he ate with his younger siblings, to the sanctum where his parents took their meals. This generational division was typical at dinner. Sharing it with adults in its proper setting was considered a privilege earned with age and civilized behavior. Like the first teen in the house to obtain a driver's permit—now the prime symbol of domestic liberation—Day reveled instead in the tighter domestic integration of his newfound status. "I strutted around in the nursery beforehand, with my hands thrust into my pockets, saying good-bye to my brothers, who, as I condescendingly explained to them, were still little boys."

The religious aura of dining in Victorian times extended to the symbolism of popular Gothic-style sideboards that resembled altars. But the reverenced meal was a daily affair instead of a special rite to be displayed and then mothballed like holiday decorations. Just as civility was not reserved for guests, the everyday family table rated the same care and attention to detail demanded by lavish parties, which were a recipe for disaster without the right ingredients. Whatever the event, with or without servants, every meal deserved to be treated as a special event. Even simple family dinners were treated with the same formality of meals prepared for company.

Guests were always treated to the best service and food your budget would allow. The notion of potluck would have stunned the Victorians, who placed reflective "butlers' balls" on sideboards so servants could see subtle signals from the master or mistress without interrupting their work by looking over their shoulder or staring at guests. Even families who couldn't afford their own Jeeves expected and received far more than leftover aesthetics at their daily meals. Every meal was served on the obligatory white tablecloth, be it plain oilcloth or the finest damask. Both were respectable and equally respectful of domestic sensibilities. In this hallowed arena, it was the thought, not the cash, that counted.

Leisurely family meals were so important that they merited the special space now often occupied by multimedia entertainment centers. The hours we spend with a remote control or a mouse our ancestors devoted to dining together two to four times a day. Even if

In the Victorian home, the dining room, not the multimedia center, was the central focus. The formality of the room echoed the formality of the family ritual of dining together. In this picture from 1897, a family is gathered for a birthday party.

clashing schedules precluded sharing lunch and afternoon tea, breakfast and dinner were a must. Long before dietitians preached the importance of a good breakfast to physical development, job productivity, and weight control, the Victorians realized that how they broke their fast could make or break their day. Because cookbooks of the era assumed their readers understood the crucial link between meals and school or work performance, they mentioned this link only in passing and focused instead on suggested menus that today's food police could almost love. These usually included modest portions of fresh fruit, whole grain cereal like oatmeal, eggs, and bread items such as waffles, biscuits, or toast. Today six in ten children fix their own breakfast—if they get any—which is more likely to run to high-sugar superhero cereals than a measured medley of the major food groups.

What Was on the Table

While we may think our shortened menus have spared us pounds of that stereotypical Victorian plumpness, just the opposite has occurred. According to researchers at Tufts University School of Medicine, just 15 percent of the population was obese in 1900, compared to 33 percent today. Diamond Jim Brady and Edward VII notwithstanding, most adults refrained from compulsive raids on the cookie jar. In the modern era, we have grown fat not on the fat of the land but by becoming potato chip–consuming couch potatoes, paying for overpriced convenience foods with calories as well as cash. Despite our image of multi-dish Victorian meals that would take more time to describe than we take to eat, the typical family dinner was a three- or four-course affair that included soup, meat, vegetables, a starch, and some dessert like pie or pudding— not an endless gravy train of evening snacks and fast-food "meals."

Our ancestors used meals to nourish both body and spirit, right down to the elegant flowers that graced every proper table. As the *Ladies' Home Journal* proclaimed in 1894, "Elegant serving is the soul of living." Even in winter, "accomplished ladies" of any means could force bulbs indoors and create attractive arrangements to complement meals—another lost domestic art. In his famous turn-of-the-century forays through New York's slums, Jacob Riis found blooming bits of beauty in window boxes, just as his memorable photos reveal china and linen neatly displayed in the glass cupboard of a one-room hovel. Even the fiercest destitution could not kill the home sensibility that Victorians considered a religion. No one had to tell them to stop and smell the roses, even if they were only daisies.

Civilized Dining

Like sex and etiquette, the dos and don'ts of Victorian dining were considered a mark of triumphal evolution over man's primal roots. The McMeals that we gobble like slaughtered prey in our cars, offices, and on sidewalks prove that man can devolve as well. (At least the lower orders have fresh kill.) "Animals eat; only man dines," declared cookbook author Isabella Beeton. And the way he dined revealed nothing less than a country's history and its destiny:

> Dining is the privilege of civilization. The rank which a
> people occupy in the grand scale may be measured by

their way of taking their meals, as well as by their way of treating their women. The nation which knows how to dine has learnt the leading lesson of progress. It implies both the will and the skill to reduce to order, and surround with idealisms and graces, the more material conditions of human existence; and wherever that will and skill exist, life cannot be wholly ignoble.

Like the web of civility, the quality and aesthetics of family meals shaped the individual's temperament as well as the nation's.

Our "new age" discovery of the mind-body connection was sheer common sense in an era when the world was viewed as a tightly woven whole, not a motley mess of fraying threads. A century before we gratefully goldplated the bank accounts of Eastern gurus who showed us the light, the educator and cookbook author Mary B. Welch noted without fanfare, "One of the weightiest influences which determine the life of the individual is the nature of the food he eats." Improper nutrition "undermines both intellectual force and physical vigor, and, as upon the combination of these two depends the advancement of the world in any direction, religious, social, polit-ical, or commercial, some notion can be gained of the responsibility of those who prepare food."

We tend to ignore this responsibility except when contaminated supermarket products are recalled during the media scare of the week. Yet even in the throes of terror, we assume that preparing appealing and healthy meals at home requires little more than a minute to spare and a microwave. We respect the paid hamburger flipper more than the uncompensated domestic cook, unless she becomes Mrs. Fields. Many gadget-laden yuppies with drop-dead kitchens have turned into amateur chefs. But showing off the wares of a high-status hobby to friends on weekends as you show off your tennis backhand hardly qualifies as nourishing the home spirit or the family's health.

DINING AS A SHARED FAMILY EXPERIENCE

On the rare occasion when families sit down together for a meal today, the experience is often spiritually barren, aesthetically disinfected, picked clean of the cherished moments and memories that defined and anchored our ancestors' lives. Family meals once provided children with essential nutrients for their character, not just their constitution. Everyone, but especially the young, dined for improvement. Meals had a social, intellectual, and religious element, and children learned daily lessons in these areas as they participated in and listened to dinner table conversations.

Victorian children didn't buy their meals from a vending machine or a mall food court. They earned them through doing their part, and by being part of something that transcended the food on their plates. "Every child should have some specific duty to the progress of the meal," noted Mary Welch in her cookbook, which was typical in dispensing general advice along with recipes. "They will early come to enjoy and be proud of the perfect smoothness of all the routines of a well-ordered table."

Family meals were intended to teach children both obedience to parental authority and the selflessness of assisting younger siblings. Along with the basic table manners and conversational habits they would carry beyond the home, they learned to appreciate and emulate the efforts of a meal well prepared and presented in a clean and pleasant atmosphere, which they were obliged to reflect in their conduct and personal appearance. All this took time and work, but the Victorians knew there was no free lunch. You always get what you pay for, and we've paid plenty for living on the cheap.

In a half-baked nod to the importance of breaking bread together, a TV public service ad announces, "If you want better kids, you've got to be better parents." This announcer pleads for one family dinner a week at the kitchen table, which is shown poignantly surrounded by empty chairs. The family-first Victorians would gasp at this thin-as-gruel formula for bonding, and would wonder whether adults who require such instruction should be anyone's parents. They knew that children's habits were formed by habitual contact with parents, not by sporadic meetings. If kids got the Sunday Christian treatment, vice was certain to outrun virtue in the formative years and thereafter.

Contrast the meal-time experience of an average working mom today, Lori Lucas, a car-repair shop manager from Shrewsbury, Missouri, who was recently profiled in *Time* magazine. She is determined to prepare dinner every evening for her year-old son and his live-in father figure, but a photo of the actual event shows the limits of her good intentions. Instead of sitting at the table, she is crawling under her son's chair to retrieve the food he spilled. Her significant other, clad in a cap and T-shirt covered with advertisements, seems completely oblivious to both of them. Their meals are more or less homemade, yet the table is a littered mess of plastic wrappers, condiment jars, and soda bottles, a fitting complement to Dad's billboard attire.[2]

While this rushed, middle-class family technically satisfies the quality-time mantra, it is hard for the viewer to detect the seeds, no less the fruit, of the home spirit that was mother's milk to the Victorians. Such poor proxies lose something fundamental in translation, leaving a hole in the soul that can never be filled.

Our bottom-line society has sacrificed the very intangibles we grope for—the immeasurable "otherness" of aura and aesthetics that former generations revered. They understood why frills like crisp table linens, flowers, and sprigs of parsley were not frivolous, and how the sensibilities children learned, or failed to learn, at meals could steer a nation's fate. Without the living cultural memory of that intensely domestic past, we are left trying to spice a stew that "needs something" we cannot name because it has become so foreign to our modern palate.

I sampled a small vicarious taste of this "something" through a ninetyish lady I met at a retirement home I visited twenty years ago. As a child, she asked her father why he always changed his collar and cuffs (which used to be separate from shirts) when he came home from work, even if they weren't dirty. This was the prescribed custom of the time, but her father also explained why it was no empty formality: Wearing a collar and cuffs as fresh and white as the dining-room tablecloth was, first, a mark of respect to her mother and the food she carefully prepared on a modest budget. Many years later, that elderly lady I met wondered whether her own grandchildren would have divorced so quickly if they had experienced family dinners that fed not only the body but the soul.

THE BEGINNING OF CONVENIENCE FOODS

The Victorians' shared repasts, and the skills that produced them, were a distant memory to most Americans by the time Hillary Clinton declared her disdain for staying home to bake cookies. The contemporary palate, along with family meals, was doomed to gradual canned standardization by modern marvels such as the birth in 1916 of Piggly Wiggly, the first self-service grocery chain. Commercial sliced bread, whose nutritional value was processed to a pasty death, appeared in 1928. (So much for what Catharine Beecher called the "divine principle of beauty" in creating the staff of life; the Jazz Age literally traded wheat for chaff.) During that same decade, Clarence Birdseye introduced prepackaged frozen food. These antiseptically sealed blocks taught the public to detach vegetables from their natural roots in every sense of the term.

Another pivotal first of that era—the franchised drive-in restaurant—arrived with the automobile in the guise of the White Castle. It was just a matter of time (thirty years, to be exact) until McDonald's made food fit for a clown. Wherever people went, they could be assured of finding the exact same hamburger bun (three and one half inches) and a total preparation time of fifty seconds for their burger, shake, and fries. Countless younger siblings like KFC and Wendy's put our meals in Styrofoam and cardboard, instead of on the dining-room table, and turned the most ethnically diverse country on earth into one of culinary accidental tourists.

The home economics movement, which started early in this century and came to symbolize the dreaded domesticity of the fifties, was instrumental in destroying the Victorians' craft traditions and cultural admiration for the women who practiced them. Comparing the Middletown of the 1890s and the 1920s, Robert Lynd noted a decline in the quality of food preparation, "one of woman's chief glories." As a local butcher told him, "The modern housewife has lost the art of cooking. She buys cuts of meat that are easily and quickly cooked, whereas in the nineties her mother bought big chunks of meat and cut them and used them in various ways. Folks want to eat in a hurry and get out in the car."

By the twenties, the hours women once lavished on unique and memorable dishes were spent instead on congested roads and the task of chauffeuring offspring to a burgeoning smorgasbord of sports, hobbies, and other activities. After all this obligatory driving, which still drives Mom crazy, she had a stiff back and frayed nerves but no gratifying masterpiece to show for her efforts. External activities for both kids and adults cut so severely into mealtimes that one father told Robert Lynd, "A fellow has to make a date with his family to see them."

A second comestible casualty of this decade was the ritual Sabbath dinner for the extended family. Putting extra leaves in the table to showcase the "great Sunday roast" and to accommodate relatives and close friends was becoming obsolete. These are the kin we now "know" via yearly Christmas cards. Social life was increasingly becoming family-free. Thus did Middletown's, and every other town's, grand feasts of old contract into "quick bites."

In Christine Frederick's 1929 book *Selling Mrs. Consumer*, she pronounced elaborate cooking from scratch as "a social accomplishment of the dark eras before the auto, the movie, the radio, and other inventions came to provide more interests." While deriding Victorian cookery as "conspicuous consumption," Frederick worked for food manufacturers such as General Mills designing labels, recipe booklets, and enticing advertisements. These taught benighted women how to substitute "scientifically correct" canned soups and other packaged products for "inferior" homemade fare. Such blandishments also undermined the authority of lessons learned at mother's knee, making everyone, especially women, distrustful of their own tastebuds and vulnerable to corporate manipulation and deception.

Even Betty Crocker was a crock. An ad man for a flour-milling company that eventually became Gold Medal invented this fictional sage in 1921 to answer letters from customers seeking baking advice. But of course, Betty's bottom line was peddling the goods. By the time she earned a face in 1936, the male executives of food conglomerates had substantially rewritten the menu American women once controlled. These thriving kings of heat-and-serve ransacked not only the larder but also the aesthetics of the family meal. In her bittersweet 1933 memoir, Edith Wharton pined for the lost household arts, which she described as ". . . a most important and honourable part of the ancient curriculum of house-keeping . . . swept aside by the 'monstrous regiment' of the emancipated young women taught by their elders to despise the kitchen and the linen room, and to substitute the acquiring of University degrees for the more complex art of civilized living."

Mercifully, the soul-starved Wharton had departed from that brave new world by 1940, when Emily Post started to lecture her countrymen on the declining manners she traced to the prevalence of dirty tablecloths and diners who ate in their undershirts or curlers. Gone was the dining room "shrine" of Clarence Day, Jr.'s boyhood. But such slovenly clothes increasingly fit the fare. Our military victory in World War II was a crushing defeat for our tastebuds and the Victorian concept of family meals. Along with aluminum siding and tail-fin cars, the public was avalanched with processed foods. Many, including the infamous Spam, were adapted from rations developed for GI Joe, who had more pressing priorities than fine dining. But what was our excuse?

TV Dinners and Wonder Bread

In 1952, America met the mother of microwave meals in the first frozen TV dinner of turkey, cornbread, potatoes, and peas. Eating à la tube, which got top billing, became the order of the day that many conservatives now hold so dear. Ralph Kramden and Lucy Ricardo supplied the conversation while mute munchers ingested the crusty contents of compartmentalized trays that were eerily reminiscent of those shown in prison chow lines from 1930s gangster movies. As the individual TV table began competing with the communal table, even "shared" meals ceased to be truly shared, since each family member could choose his own poison.

Ads for Wonder Bread—the signature sandwich bookends of baby boomer adolescence—now pursue this target audience with carefree images of its lost youth. That polka-dotted plastic era not only taught us the "wonder" of bread that tore like tissue paper, it reached what the historian Glenna Matthews calls "the nadir of American cookery." "This was the heyday of prepared foods and the cream-of-mushroom soup school of cuisine where the cook could pour a can of this product over anything that was not a dessert and create a culinary treat according to the standards of the day."

Matthews's review of women's magazines from this period found that most recommended meals were mere blends of manufactured goods. Typical recipes from *Ladies' Home Journal* contained frozen vegetables, and salmon, potatoes, and pears—all as canned as the TV laugh tracks that became another staple of prefabricated mass consumption. Matthews notes that by 1960, the "creativity" of a once esteemed and highly personalized craft "consisted in combining a pudding mix with a cake mix." After the Second World War, "The level of skill involved in cooking—no doubt that area of housework with the most potential for inspiring job satisfaction—declined to an all-time low."

Those of us who had some living link to our Victorian-era relations witnessed this sad decline and its implications for the gradual fraying of family life. When I was a child, my grandmother had a kitchen that seemed a wonderland of simmering soups, fresh-baked scents, and carefully selected produce waiting to be transformed by her magic hands. She measured ingredients by instinct instead of using the scientifically precise cups and scales that always remind me of high school chemistry class. Everything she made drew acclaim (or least satisfied sighs) from her husband and children, no matter how often she served a dish.

Although she dutifully taught her daughters to cook, their efforts never approached her art, and they knew it. By the time they grew up between the wars, cooking was just another household task. Most of their meals were dependable but forgettable. Although they sometimes ventured my grandmother's sauces and breads, the factory foods that never dared darken her shelves were right at home on theirs. They did preserve many of her recipes on the three-by-five index cards she never needed. But their own eat-and-run kids never voiced a whisper of the appreciation she had rightly earned.

Instant Meals

Today there is a booming market of dinner kits that give the illusion you're cooking without reading a recipe, slicing, dicing, or measuring any ingredients. Even processed spices and herbs are now combined into single containers to spare you the trouble of unscrewing more than one bottle. With manufacturers determining the balance of garlic powder and paprika, forget finesse. We are fooling only our deadened palates and the souls we have robbed of food's sentimental meaning when we forfeit our cultural history. Researchers at Chicago's Smell and Taste Treatment and Research Foundation found that for those born before 1930, fond images of youth were triggered by the aroma of freshly baked goods, especially bread. In contrast, later generations grow nostalgic from the scent of Cocoa Puffs and SweeTarts.

Ironically, bread machines represent the only real growth area in the "home baking" industry. While sales of raw ingredients such as flour are dropping like ruined soufflés, "no- bake" desserts have become bestsellers. "Today, many people think the term 'baking by scratch' means opening a box of mix," concluded a *New York Times* reporter who recently profiled this phenomenon. Those willing to turn on the oven need only water the mix like a plant—something a trained chimp could do.

Studies show women now spend on average a scant quarter hour "preparing" dinner. This meal was once the bread and butter of domestic life. It embodied high esteem for a distinctly feminine craft, the continuity of the generations that had bequeathed their precious culinary legacy, the nourishing of family bonds, and a deep sense of all that home implied. It is this loss that enables us to apply the bastardized label "meals" to fortified candy bars and canned drinks.

The twentieth century surrendered the power of home traditions to the almighty god of convenience—the main reason American adults visit fast-food restaurants an average of six times a month. (Perhaps the accumulated hours spent waiting in their not-so-fast lines could be applied to some home cooking worthy of the name.) Not only do we increasingly "dine" out or carry out, we are now eating solo on wheels. Vehicular techno-wonders like the jumbo cup holder have mutated into lap trays for motorists. Nine dollars buys you five separate sections to hold beverages, food, and utensils. The standard money-back guarantee does not include the promise you will taste what you eat, nor does it reimburse you for staining your clothes and upholstery.

The National Restaurant Association estimates that Americans spend forty-four cents of every food dollar for edibles (or inedibles) prepared outside the home. The attractions of that "special sauce" notwithstanding, working women don't have time to cook anymore, and no one has filled their shoes or their aprons. We may well ask whether we have lost more than the welcoming scent of some delicacy simmering on the stove after battling like gladiators through rush-hour traffic?

DEPERSONALIZED FOOD

A harried professional woman I know whose mother recently died confided that she still missed the comforting smell of the soup her mom used to create from scratch. It made her feel special because it could be had only at home for love, not for money. With no time to cook such intricate dishes, she lamented, "I have no smells to leave my children."

We have traded the intangible but irreplaceable sentiments of home for hollow "McMemories." Like burgers, shakes, and fries, their immortal incarnation can be purchased from the official McDonald's Collectibles Club. For $39.95 you can own a three-and-one-half inch "authentic replica" of the first McDonald's franchise, which opened in 1955. Ever since then, claims the ad for this "hand-painted" model, "McDonald's has been a beloved part of the American scene—the place where good food, fun and family come together." If this whets your appetite for more, you are invited to view additional memorabilia at the McDonald's Museum in Des Plaines, Illinois.

Popular Victorian sculptures also enshrined food and family—if not what we consider "fun." But they portrayed parents and children gathered together, not the golden calf of the Golden Arches. That is the crucial difference between bona fide memories and McMemories. The first is warm, filling, and sustaining. Its pretender has the staying power of a Chinese meal that leaves us emotionally starved. Those raised on this meager diet are destined to confuse quality food with whatever commands hefty prices in restaurants. But not even the wealthiest gourmands can buy a substitute for the home fare they have missed. Like those who yearn for great romance, they'll always sense that something vital is missing from their lives, even if they can't define it. Another acquaintance of mine said she had come to realize that the parsley her mother used to garnish the meal on the family china "meant something more than a small green sprig." But she can't articulate its meaning.

The need for this personalized "something" is increasingly being catered to by professionals who perform every domestic chore, from ferrying the kids to sports events and purchasing their birthday presents to decorating their rooms and even arranging family photos in albums. And while Grandma is probably touring the country in her RV, new moms pay a substitute to give them a crash course in breast-feeding, bathing, baby rocking, and the lost maternal wisdom of the ages. As an added service (and expense), these surrogates will even prepare a home-cooked meal, whose origin is part of someone else's home.

Can families survive if these functions are narrowed like geneti-cally altered plants and livestock, stripped of the skills, frills, quirks, and traditions, however small, that indelibly stamp our character?

The anthropologist David Murray worries that reducing the unique, defining aspects of family life to "sterile, rational transactions with strangers" teaches children that even the most intimate service is a matter of mere dollars and cents. (Of course, the same applies to prostitution.) Even for those women who still cook for their families, cooking has become little more than just another hassle, another chore best dealt with quickly and efficiently.

The Lost Art of Home Cooking

In contrast to today's back-of-the-box cooks, Victorian women needed smarts to separate the wheat from the chaff because adulterated foods were rampant in their time. As it did other domestic duties, their culture respected their culinary talents, giving them a source of self-esteem women lack today. Victorian cast-iron stoves, which were fed by wood or coal, had mercurial temperature ranges that demanded human vigilance and judgment. With the bells and whis-tles of progress came contempt. Glenna Matthews notes that by the 1920s, "experts" who assumed that home cooks had the wits of ado-lescents advocated the quickie processed foods that a budding indus-try hawked for an age of "compressed living." Two decades earlier, Fannie Farmer had warned that cooking would descend to "mere drudgery if one does not put heart and soul into the work."[3] Both were compressed into extinction by this new brand of living.

The Victorian mistress of the house was expected to master the art and science of cookery, to have a thorough working knowledge of herbs, spices, meats, fruits, breads, and vegetables. Without pack-aged foods, refrigerators, preservatives, or a counter cluttered with time-saving appliances, the Victorian home cook had to employ far more elbow grease, planning, and imagination than modern-day homemakers do. Yet however much drudgery the work could involve, they understood that their work was extremely important for the health and well-being of the family and, by extension, the world.

In contrast, the extent of contemporary gastronomic illiteracy today is attested to by the success of cookbooks with titles like *The Complete Idiot's Guide to Cookery* and *Cooking for Dummies.* The culinary historian Karen Hess notes disdainfully, "In the [nineteenth] century, the books were written by cooks for cooks. In the [twentieth] century, mainstream cookbooks were written by dummies for dummies."[4] Describing the proliferation of "dysfunctional cooks" as the kitchen equivalent of "Why Johnny can't read," cookbook author Elaine Corn complains that only "conversations with waiters" keep a substantial part of the population from starving. Weinraub concluded that since so many baby boomers grew up eating canned soups, frozen veggies, and TV dinners, "today's books are aimed at an audience that often hasn't learned to cook at home, and doesn't come equipped with treasured family recipe books."[5]

Kitchen-dummy syndrome is not just a prescription for heartburn or a lifetime sentence of leftovers. It is poison to the psyche. The holistic Victorian view of food traced the influence of the table far beyond the dining room. Sour stomachs produced sour tempers, and coarse food was thought to produce coarse natures.

The intangible effects of what and how we eat were noted in a recent *New York Times* article on the decline of baking. One of the few women interviewed who continues this fading tradition struggled to describe the psychological impact of homemade bread:

> If I serve some of my banana or pumpkin bread at the meeting, people seem to interact better and tend to be more relaxed. It helps to stimulate dialogue and bring out the best in people, maybe because they connect it with images of family and home.

Future generations may experience these images only via history or virtual reality unless we revamp our agenda. Even Betty Friedan, writing in *The Second Stage,* asks, "Shouldn't [homemaking] be valued somehow? And what about the rest—arranging the flowers, baking the cookies? It makes life more pleasant, surely, even if it's not necessary or paid for. What would life be like if no one did that work?"

It is a question many of us have already answered, and our conclusion is that we have definitely lost a great deal along the way. It is no wonder that interest in Victoriana is increasing, as we try to buy and decorate and read our way back to a sense of artful living that has escaped our grasp. Yet a few well-laced doilies and a Jane Austen video-fest offer us only a tiny glimpse of the well-ordered, harmonious lives the Victorians lead. To truly regain their sense of grace, we must look, as they did, at the larger picture. We must, like the era's greatest sleuth, Sherlock Holmes, look carefully at the details if we are to reconstruct the whole.

PART 5

LOST ARTS AND FORGOTTEN RITUALS

18

The Art of Living

We live in an age where we document all of our customs in as much detail as we can, through high-tech gadgets that allow us to capture every Kodak moment, from birth to the after-the-funeral beer bash. For all our endless fascination with recording our modern rituals, however, we are intrigued by Victorian customs because they are so very different from our own. Moreover, they baffle us. Why such attention to time-consuming detail? Why such morbid displays when a loved one died? How quaint their wholesome parlor games and croquet matches seem to us now. But for the Victorians, who lived in a holistic and integrated world, there was great meaning and even great love behind many of these rituals and ephemera that we dismiss as curious relics of a bygone era.

MODERN HOLIDAY CELEBRATIONS

We are most aware of our forgotten customs at holidays, when we long for an old-fashioned celebration that emphasizes God, family, and love over want lists, office parties, and social obligations. Although ornate Victorian holidays required extra effort and preparation, they were natural extensions of what Isabella Beeton called the "ceremonials for common days" that "joyfully united families, adding beauty, grace, and charm to life." Our holidays are anything but, as we struggle to compensate—via added obligations, aggravation, and maxed-out credit card balances—for the patchwork daily "ceremonials" that impoverish our lives throughout the rest of the year. We trim our Christmas trees with reproductions of Victorian ornaments and deck our holiday mantels with a picturesque "Dickens village" that includes steepled churches. We put out the extra effort to do it all, but no matter how much we spend, we can't achieve the feeling of that old-fashioned Christmas/Easter/Passover we seek.

In contrast to the past, modern holidays are more stressful than special precisely because they require not just the time but the domestic skills we lack. Some experts claim that such stress, combined with alcohol, contributes to increased spouse and child abuse during the "ho-ho-ho" season. In addition, frayed family ties mean we never develop the facility and patience to peacefully coexist with difficult relations. As a result, the "shock" of occasional forced family togetherness unleashes endless backbiting, bickering, and complaints about long lines to use the bathroom.

Ceremonies that were once de rigueur for holiday feasts are increasingly shunned. A national 1995 survey commissioned by Lenox China found that over one third of all families planned to serve the Thanksgiving meal in their kitchen instead of the dining room. Kitchens allow even special celebrations a casual air, and they are far less threatening to a culture that has lost the art of dining and views any hint of formality as a hanging offense. But as those sensibilities disintegrate, like Miss Havisham's wedding dress, we forfeit the beauty, grace, and charm that drive us to period movies, where we get a tantalizing whiff of the bounty we cannot taste.

Even as we recognize that such holidays as Thanksgiving, Christmas, and Passover afford us rare opportunities to convene the gasping patient we call family under an oxygen tent, we frequently subcontract to strangers the unique and unifying rituals that gave holiday spirit its meaning. Hired Santa's helpers thrive in the Washington, D.C., area and other regions populated by upscale working couples with more money than time to spend. These all-purpose elves will write your season's greetings cards and select the perfect personal gifts for your friends and relatives, whom they've never met.

This is a true Christmas miracle; I'm still struggling to find acceptable presents for people I've known forever. Even when we take the pains to choose presents for our nearest and dearest, instead of using hired hands or resorting to increasingly popular gift certificates, just how thoughtful can these gifts be when at least a third of all shopping is done the week before Christmas?

If your bank balance is sufficiently merry, all your holiday decorations will be erected and dismantled by a service hired for the purpose. (No more nasty pine needles to pick out of the carpet.) And a feast will be prepared as big as your budget—not your culinary skills—will allow. One upscale catering service reports that requests for complete holiday meals doubled every year between 1990 and 1993, at prices that can surpass $100 for just two people. For some harried consumers who want to have it all, painless soup to nuts won't do at any price. A growing trend in the catering industry called "speed scratch" does all the hard, heavy prep work while allowing buyers to pretend they created the "vittles." These gourmet shops and services offer fully stuffed and roasted turkeys that need only reheating.

Many women realize how their cheated families pay with more than cash when the aura and accoutrements of holidays are ordered like takeout pizza. Indeed, if holiday fare can be so casually obtained, it is no big deal—what is these days?—to schedule or reschedule the meal around football games. This macho madness would have stunned Victorian males, for whom being a man meant actually practicing the family values we preach. They also took pride in presiding over the dinner table and demonstrating the art of carving the turkey or goose as expertly as it was prepared.

Among fifty pairs of mothers and daughters interviewed for a recent *New York Times* article on declining domestic holiday traditions was a grandmother who remarked wistfully, "The rich close relationships my family enjoys took hours and hours to develop." While she admires her daughter's professional achievements, "I worry that the demands on her time may be detrimental to the next generation." One baby boomer mom recalled her parents and siblings constructing an entire miniature village beneath their Christmas tree, an experience her kids will never share. "I don't have the time," she lamented. "I take my children to the mall. So what will they remember?"

"I'm not giving my children the same memories," said another rushed but candid mother who had abandoned all the elaborate Christmas baking that once lovingly linked the generations. "I feel real bad about that." Others assuage their guilt with mail-order remedies designed for just this purpose, like the prefab, prebaked gingerbread house kits that families can assemble with the aid of enclosed instructions. Even if the finished product looks Christmas-card perfect, it is just another cookie-cutter version of those made from every other kit.

VICTORIAN HOLIDAYS

Whether your tax bracket is Bloomies or Wal-Mart, the memory of freshly baked homemade gingerbread or challah cannot be catered or ordered by phone, fax, or Internet. This is why even wealthy Victorians made their own decorations, gingerbread, and other treats filled with symbolism as well as taste. The goal back then was not look-at-me razzle-dazzle but a rich, if simple, experience to share.

The Victorians' Christmas preparations began right after Thanksgiving, and not by running to the mall. Fruitcakes (light and dark) were first on the agenda because they required time to age—though not into the fossilized teeth-cracking versions we love to hate. Making plum pudding was another prized tradition. Every family member took turns stirring it from east to west to commemorate the journey of the Three Kings. The circles represented eternity while the pudding's spherical shape signified the family's connection to the wider world. The heavy symbolism of this dessert was leavened by the hope of getting a slice containing a penny or a silver charm, both omens of good luck.

Rather than purchasing holiday decorations by the box, the Victorians made theirs from bits of yarn, lace, ribbon, and fancy papers everyone saved throughout the year for just that special purpose. This moneyless moral Christmas club emphasized the venerated virtue of thrift; we might call it recycling. It also made holiday celebrations a slowly savored mutual treat, not a shock suddenly sprung on us, like those first gray hairs we spot in the mirror. Children learned to appreciate both the beauty of nature and the value of home by helping to adorn the house with wreaths and garlands of assorted evergreens, leaves, and pine cones they had gathered. They took particular pride in making Christmas tree trimmings such as ropes of cranberries and popcorn, crocheted snowflakes, cotton batting figures, and cornucopias—the ornate tasseled cone-shaped ornaments that were filled with assorted nuts and sweets.

Holidays of long ago involved more active creation than passive consumption. The former instilled treasured memories often recounted in written recollections of that era. Passive consumption taught us to discard the effortless expected booty we received because the novelty wore thin so quickly. Thus Victorian youngsters usually made gifts for their parents and siblings—a muffler for Father, a sachet or pin cushion for Mother, dolls or doll clothes for girls, carved blocks and soldiers for boys. Why were all these time- and thought-consuming rituals so essential to the Christmas spirit? The editor Sarah Josepha Hale answered this question with one of her own in 1868: "Are not these enjoyments the bread of life and the wine of love that strengthen the best energies of the soul that give beauty and enjoyment to our homes?"

PARLOR GAMES AND OTHER VICTORIAN RECREATION

This enriching soul food also nourished family recreation throughout the year. We run to our separate televisions after dinner, but the Victorians gathered in the parlor to read to each other and play word or board games based on literary classics and Bible stories. Religious images were especially popular for inexpensive jigsaw puzzles, another joint activity that promoted patience. While both have fallen from favor since then, I recently saw an ad for a company that turns the photo of your choice into a "personalized puzzle" for sixty-plus dollars. The ad featured an attractive couple with three young kids. But rather than emphasize the potential for togetherness, this item was hawked as a "conversation piece" for your coffee table. Like coffee-table books, the pleasure it provides is measured by the number of your friends it impresses.

Almost every Victorian parlor had a piano to accompany frequent family sing-alongs. This prized possession was considered a necessity rather than a luxury, and plain or secondhand models were affordably priced. Music could be shared by all, even the tone-deaf, and it was considered morally uplifting. All children, especially girls, were encouraged to master the piano, but pleasure was more important then perfection. Although Clarence Day, Sr.'s renditions of Beethoven and Bach were "limited," according to his son, his feeling for music was "deeply rooted. . . . It gave him a sense of well-being."

Because singing together was a favorite form of home recreation for the Victorians, many homes had a piano and most young ladies could play and sing. Note the gentleman standing by to turn pages and assist the lady in any way she needed.

Like most women of her time, Mrs. Day also did her musical best. "We often heard her sweet voice gently singing old songs of an evening. If she forgot parts here or there, she swiftly improvised something that would let the air float along without breaking the spell." The off-key female songbird at family gatherings later became a figure of derision to a cynical century that devalued traditional notions of feminine accomplishment and domestic skills. Like the savory smells of Victorian meals, we have lost the endearing sounds that once made homes not just a place but a state of mind.

Family time also provided cleverly instructive outlets for sibling rivalry, while cultivating the love of learning we wish our kids would acquire. Victorian children competed with each other to memorize and recite passages from Shakespeare and the classics. In his autobiography, the journalist Hutchins Hapgood called this exercise "the chief civilizing influence of childhood." Private theatricals were another favorite pastime. Mark Twain's family and neighbors often dramatized scenes from his novels. Performances could be simple and spontaneous or involve extensive preparation and homemade costumes.

In tableaux vivants the actors staged a famous painting, statue, or story, while onlookers tried to guess its name. Edith Wharton immortalized this form of entertainment in *The House of Mirth*, where Lily Bart represented Joshua Reynolds's portrait of Mrs. Lloyd. "It was as though she had stepped, not out of, but into, Reynolds' canvas, banishing the phantom of his dead beauty by the beams of her living grace."

Fun in our gluttonous age is merchandise-dependent, but the roots of this syndrome predated our addiction to the tube. The authors of *Middletown* noted that by the 1920s, the rich range of shared home entertainments had severely declined. Dancing to recorded music that divided the generations, as opposed to music you made and all enjoyed, became the major domestic amusement— when families weren't going their separate ways. And increasingly, they were. Living meant living it up, which demanded cash and a car. As one person interviewed by the Lynds observed, "It almost seems as though family members simply couldn't wait to get out of the house and away from one another."

We have been deserting the hearth ever since, despite the proliferating video toys that feed us processed leisure while starving the creative "mental vision" Edith Wharton so poignantly described. Even when we technically nest together, like strangers in a hotel, no one is really home. Instead we surf solo on the waves of cable television channels or the World Wide Web. We need to disentangle ourselves if we are ever to go home again.

We have cut away at the ties that bind us not just to each other but to the very rhythms of life itself. We surrounded ourselves with creature comforts and entertainments in order to fend off the hard realities that we try to wish away. This is nowhere more evident than in our inability to deal with death.

A TIME TO MOURN

In an age when we can't stop talking about sex and our appetite for personal revelations seems boundless, the subject of death is taboo. One ultrasensitive town in Colorado replaced its DEAD END street signs with NO OUTLET signs because the former were considered too macabre. In abridging the classic novel *Little Women*, a book publisher eliminated a section that dealt with heaven in the context of Beth's death. According to the abridger, Laurie Lawlor, today's ten- and eleven-year-olds have "too little life experience" to accept the "very Victorian concept" that Beth's family believes she is "well at last."[1]

The squirming silence that greets the topic of death not only denies an undeniable reality, it also deprives us of the acceptable ways Victorians had to publicly express their grief or offer comfort to the grieving. Without clear etiquette guideposts to follow, we are confused about what to say when people die, how to express sympathy without giving offense, and whether to visit the family or leave them alone.

Most people would say good riddance to Victorian mourning rituals—the dull black crepe worn by female survivors, the family's withdrawal from social activities, and the various death mementos they made. Contemporary historians label these customs grotesque, macabre, grim, creepy, and necrophiliac. Our own method of "dealing" with death—going on, keeping active, jumping back into the swing of life—is much healthier. Or is it?

The "stifling" Victorian formality that so many scorn prevented such awkward situations, as it was intended to do. Ten days after the funeral, friends and acquaintances left their personal calling cards with a handwritten note of condolence at the "mourning house." When its residents wanted to begin receiving guests, they sent out their own black-bordered cards as a signal people should come. Discussing the loss with the bereaved might be tearful, but it was natural and expected. And no one's face turned red.

Today, the voices of self-expression turn suddenly mute in the face of life's final challenge. We struggle just to select some mass-market sympathy card to express our condolences. But you'll have to search high and low for cards that dare to mention death. Hallmark executives report that the word makes us uncomfortable. And since funerals are also discomforting (not to mention inconvenient), attendance is steadily shrinking, according to funeral directors. Some who do attend come as they are without apology, if basic black doesn't suit them. After all, the departed won't notice.

The Victorians would have found our casual response to the death of a loved one as appalling as we find their formal rituals. Widows wore black for the prescribed two years, only gradually adopting "colors" as they passed through three phases of mourning. (Because the typical male business suit was black, Victorian widowers wore armbands.) A widow's entertainment agenda was limited to quiet gatherings of family and friends. If she partied hard before the mourning period ended, she was considered a disgrace and a disrespectful spouse.

Though such limitations may look excessive to modern eyes, they expressed a central tenet of the Victorians' social code: Respect was the heart of civilized life; it did not stop beating at death's door. Queen Victoria, the queen of mourning, wore "widow's weeds" for her forty remaining years after her adored Albert's premature death. This deeply romantic response to one of history's great romances would now be called dangerously dysfunctional, if not deranged. We would press mopey Victoria to get a makeover and take a singles' cruise. Had she outlived the age that bears her name by only a few years, etiquette books would have told her that such extended grief was sheer "self-pity." By then, broken hearts were passé.

In his bestseller, *Listening to Prozac*, the psychiatrist Peter Kramer documents the successful use of antidepressants to treat (mostly female) patients suffering from prolonged bereavement. Then he wisely asks a culturally loaded question: What is prolonged? These days the answer is beyond one year, according to most experts. But is this calculation of the mourning a dead spouse merits any less arbitrary or intrinsically healthier than the Victorian rule of two years (or a lifetime, if needed)?

And is forgetting a past love too slowly any healthier than forgetting too quickly? For decades after the death of his young fiancée, Washington Irving could not bear to hear her name mentioned, and even thirty years after her death, he was so upset by the accidental discovery of some of her embroidery work that he was unable to speak. Though he never awoke from his grief, it nourished the talent that gave posterity Rip Van Winkle.

An example of a Victorian-era memorial picture, which incorporates the hair of the deceased.

Mementos of the Dead

Where we would clean house of any depressing reminders of the dead, the Victorians memoralized them with a variety of personal objects that were treasured and proudly displayed. These living mementos included mourning portraits, embroidered pictures, and custom-made rings and lockets and jewelry woven from the hair of the dead.

The most morbid type of memento to modern eyes is also the most sentimental. While we barely blink when body parts fly across our movie screens, I've observed many visitors at museums and antique shows gasp openly at the necklaces, earrings, men's watch chains, and women's bracelets woven from the hair of the dead. The Victorians made and wore these intimate objects as symbolic links to their loved ones in the hereafter. Hair art also expressed affection among the living. Sweethearts often exchanged locks of their hair, and hair wreaths and floral bouquets created from the mingled strands of family members were common ornaments in the parlor—where funerals were held. A century ago, death came into the household, instead of being shunted into sterile hospital wards. There was no denial of death's role in the cycle of life when it was so much a part of people's everyday experience.

The Victorian way of mourning helped people cope with grief in an age of high infant mortality, when the average life span was less than two thirds of our own. Science and technology have bought us time, but they have yet to make us immortal. While many of us outlive our ancestors, we live without the rituals and trappings that sweetened their sadness, and made leaving this world or being left behind a little easier.

The Victorian Cemetery

The transcendent meaning that elevates life beyond ashes and dust derives from our ability to forge the connections that the Victorians saw. Those who make them will feel inspired and elevated, rather than alienated or repelled, by visits to Victorian graveyards. Far from being reminiscent of creepy Charles Addams cartoons, they are peaceful havens whose monuments and headstones speak a silent language all Victorians understood. Here eternal souls symbolically rest in urns or in the cradling hands of angels. Crowns promise future

Victorians, accepting that death is a natural part of life, often went on picnics in cemeteries, which were beautifully landscaped parks for the dead and the living. The Victorians saw themselves, their ancestors, and the physical beauty around them as creations of the same divine grand plan.

glory, while oak and ivy leaves affirm religious faith. So many infants' graves are marked by empty cradles or lambs of innocence, but their sadness too is an enriching part of this walk through the not-so-distant past.

A distraught woman recently wrote to Ann Landers for advice on how to derail her sister's "morbid" wedding plans. The bride-to-be wanted all her guests to join her at the cemetery after leaving the church so she could lay her bouquet on her father's grave. Ann said the bride could she do as she pleased, but nixed taking the guests as "a downer." My heart ached for that misunderstood bride who wished to honor the father she had lost twenty-one years before. The point of her lovely gesture was to demonstrate connections the Victorians would have instantly understood. This wedding-day visit to a grave fuses the past and the future, the love for a lost parent and the love for a new spouse.[2]

VICTORIAN CLOTHING

Weddings, of course, bring out the Victorian in many of us. Young women don romantic Victorian gowns for their special day and rent restored Victorian mansions for their receptions. Brides—and grooms—find comfort in the old rituals of something borrowed, something blue, and the flowing, lacy dresses from the previous century capture a sense of old-fashioned romance while they drape beautifully across the female figure.

The line of such gowns was not lost on the Victorians, but their clothing styles were not inspired by such shallow aims as showing off one's figure or one's money. A woman who adorned herself in a beautiful gown was sending a message to her friends, family, and neighbors, which was not about her taste so much as about her state of mind, and her respect for others.

In the modern era, our problematic relationship with clothing reflects a contradiction of contemporary sensibilities—we use our clothes to express ourselves, but we balk if others use them to judge the self we choose to express.

The Victorians, however, were untroubled by such contradictions. Their consensus on morals and manners extended to the meaning of the wrappings in which they chose to show themselves. As Mary Eliza Haweis, author of *The Art of Beauty*, explained in 1878, "Dress bears the same relation to the body as speech does to the brain; and therefore dress may be called the speech of the body."

Like its vocal counterpart, dress could either bolster or batter civility. Appropriate dress was no mere personal preference but a social obligation, said Eliza Duffey, "a duty . . . we owe to others because we have no right to put our friends to the blush by untidiness or uncouthness." Indifferent or slovenly appearance was considered selfish contempt; dishabille was considered a sign of moral laxity. Now it is considered fashionable, which explains why many churches must post signs barring visitors in shorts, halter tops, or other revealing garments. Even many high-end restaurants have abandoned the tie-and-jacket rule for fear of losing patrons. In some cases their sartorial standards have sunk to the point of admitting any bipeds who still wear socks and shoes. Can entreaties to use utensils be far behind?

Transcendent Clothing

Like all aspects of Victorian life, clothing was invested with a significance that was more than material. It had a transcendent quality, which had an elevating and even refining influence on the wearers and those with whom they came in contact. Everyone was obliged, within their means, to contribute to this aura rather than debase it, because to be slovenly was considered an affront to the feelings of other people. Compare this to the gruesome trend in the fashion industry of "heroin chic": Magazine spreads celebrate the ugliness of heroin addiction and feature pale, thin, drugged-out-looking models slumped on the floor. If we are outraged by the dangerous message this sends to youth, we should remember that, as Michael Gross, the author of *Model*, explained in *The Washington Post*, "Fashion is amoral. Fashion doesn't care what messages it is sending out as long as the message sells frocks." Presumably, this amorality also applies to the people who create these reckless images.

In our search for comfort we sneer at the impracticality of clothing from an era we see as hopelessly restrictive. True, men wore stiff and starched shirt fronts, while some whale-boned women wore up to thirty-seven pounds of clothing, with nineteen pounds suspended from the waist alone. It should be said, however, that corsets were quite controversial in their day, and, Hollywood movie images notwithstanding, many women of the era rejected them. Any modern smugness toward Victorian dress should also be tempered by our fondness for Wonderbras that are as tight as any corset, and the masochistic decades-long devotion to spiky high heels—our version of Chinese foot binding. Fashion demands its due in every age and many seem more than willing to pay the price, which explains why after decades of being relegated to the darkest corner of the lingerie department, girdles and foundation undergarments have come back in vogue.

We also dismiss Victorian dress as too conformist: all those women in long dresses and men in black top hats and tails. It is ironic that in the modern age we claim to value dress as a vehicle of self-expression while sporting designer logos or on everything from underwear to luggage and company brand names on T-shirts and hats. What is more conformist than this "body advertising," which the Victorians relegated to men who were paid to wear placards in public places?

At least the sartorial conformity the Victorians practiced balanced rhyme and reason. They were attuned to how clothing "fit" different surroundings and occasions—a lost sensibility.

The Victorian ideal in dress was to look modest, not ostentatious or dowdy, and clothes suited the activity and surroundings.

The Victorians admired utility in clothing as in design, but they also valued form as much as function. In 1880 William Morris stated his "golden rule" for all types of artistic expression: "Have nothing . . . that you do not know to be useful, or believe to be beautiful." A century later the tawdry and the crude are equally at home in discount outlets and pricey boutiques. The runways of New York and Paris have recently featured shirtless suits and dog collars for men, as well as entire outfits of "S and M" leather straps for women. Not many consumers will be attracted by such self-conscious emblems of sexual perversion. But today's designers do their best to debase rather than elevate everyday life. Their fin-de-siècle creative spirit manifests itself in styles that combine what one news report calls "cheesy fabrics, loathsome colors and obnoxious patterns." They are modeled by spindly, hollow-eyed runway walkers and made fashionable by customers like the actress Uma Thurman.

Brooks Brothers and Lands End–type clothing is more typical garb for mainstream America. Neither shocking nor seductive, these clothes are simply bland. But whether we practice exhibitionism or a clothes-in-the-crowd philosophy by what we wear or bare, we have lost all sense of personal appearance as a source of social uplift, signifying self-respect and facilitating mutual respect. The Victorians, however, were very conscious of both functions of dress. In the succinct but potent words of Sarah Josepha Hale, "Dress is both a cause and consequence of civilized life." The idea that clothes could have a civilizing or higher moral power became one of many discarded Victorian "pretensions." Where *Godey's Lady's Book* melded a philosophy of dress and life, the burgeoning fashion magazines of the twenties, fed by advertising dollars from the new cosmetics industry, sold women on a perfectly polished surface as their highest goal.

Now such polish is reserved by most for only the most formal occasions. Flying in an airplane has become so commonplace that many make themselves comfortable and dress in cutoffs, flip-flops and tank tops. Recently, a new disincentive to poolside lounging appeared when a 300-pound woman announced on *The Montel Williams Show* that she wears bikinis because they make her feel good. No word on how her fellow bathers feel.

Now, earnest reformers can do little more than complain, and "serious" discussions of fashion are confined to a narrow clique of sanctified designers and their wannabes. Yet a century ago, the style and meaning of clothes occupied eminent critics of architecture, art, and life. The English philosopher John Ruskin wrote of "true nobleness in dress," while the poet and playwright Oscar Wilde asserted that reforming dress was more important than reforming religion. (Like all the best Wildean mots, this comment was at once facetious and deeply serious.)

Constantly changing fashions used to provide endless fodder for serious debate. The swinging-cage crinoline was denounced as a "monstrous caricature that vexed the artistic eye" or was praised as a "visual charm." The bustle was deemed both a "contorting rigidity" and a "delightful invention." Some praised the "sweeping dignity" of trains, and Tissot's painting *The Stairs* celebrated the flowing beauty of a tea gown. Others denounced trains as "dirt catchers." (Sensible ladies compromised by wearing their trains indoors.) Of course, the incessantly controversial corset "murdered the muscles," even as it "lent the grace of curves to figures lacking the fullness of rounded outlines."

Critics would verbally duel to the death on this subject because the Victorians thought of dress not just as a badge of individual expression but as a collective experience that could help civilize society and elevate the quality of life. By contrast, the solipsistic function of modern self-expressive dress was epitomized for me by a twenty-something man clad in a bright yellow sweatshirt that proclaimed in bold black letters, "Me, Myself and I." At least it wasn't obscene.

We will never again fuss with twenty-button gloves, even though it is just these nuances of Victorian life that charm us in the telling. We may scoff at the antique notion of clothing as an "index and prologue to character" that could ennoble or degrade the nation, but to recapture the sense of community we all claim to want, we need to view community spirit as more than prodding people to vote or do volunteer work. We must rediscover the commonsense wisdom that recognizes how individual appearance subtly colors the aura of our goals and behavior.

The value of this lesson has prompted a growing number of schools, especially those in the inner city, to adopt traditional uniforms and restrict oversized jewelry, gang colors, and other items that feed conflict and distract clothes-conscious kids from their education. Not only have disciplinary problems declined as a result of these reforms, student performance has improved, and the general environment is more controlled. A year after schools in Long Beach, California, mandated uniforms, officials reported a 50 percent decrease in incidents of students fighting, a 36 percent drop in overall student crime, and 32 percent fewer suspensions. In a national survey of secondary school principals, 70 percent favored uniforms. Even President Clinton cast his vote for them in his State of the Union Address.[3] All across the political spectrum, people are beginning to recognize what the Victorians knew: Clothes, like reading and writing, are potent tools of civility.

Social obligation does not demand bankrupting ourselves to mimic the Victorian wardrobe that included a specified outfit for every occasion and hour of the day, but we need to raise our clothing consciousness. Eventually, we might even aspire to a graceful life again, to wear something simple or grand that is worthy of art for the ages. But first we must establish shared standards for acceptable dress, like those we are trying to develop for civility and education. The indispensable foundation of that wardrobe is not a navy blazer or a little black dress, but a sense of respect.

Even more than Victorian elegance and charm, we have lost what might be called the Victorians' environmental fashion sensitivity—how people complemented and completed their surroundings with what they wore and how they wore it. The contrast is perhaps most obvious when twentieth-century sensibilities come into physical contact with nineteenth-century environments. On a recent architectural tour through restored Southern plantations, I joined parades of tourists clad mostly in shorts and T-shirts or jogging suits, tramping through those meticulously crafted treasures. Only the unpaid volunteers leading the tours seemed to harmonize with the homes, even though they wore modern attire, not period costumes. Although they were friendly and gracious, the occasional tight-lipped look betrayed their opinions of their rumpled charges. One docent cast an apologetic glance at the portrait of an antebellum matron before politely giving a gum-snapping, spandexed visitor directions to the nearest McDonald's.

Any attempt to reform the "no-rules" rule of our inflexibly informal dress code will undoubtedly be criticized as snobbish and undemocratic. We prefer to practice the reverse snobbery of dressing as low as we can go. In contrast, the Victorians' attentive care to dress and manners was profoundly democratic. Because it asks more of us than we usually ask of ourselves, civility is always more demanding than self-indulgence. Appearance was never a substitute for virtue; etiquette advisers often warned that image could be deceptive. But as one who held such sentiments said, it gave an "additional lustre to real merit." We need to rediscover the importance of aesthetics so that civility can shine again.

19

Art and Soul

The Victorians' sense of aesthetics reached beyond their person to their surroundings, encompassing their buildings, their public spaces, and the people who inhabited them. They understood that they were a part of their fellow humans' environment, and they believed that all people, of all classes, were entitled to surroundings that were uplifting and inspiring.

Of course, regardless of how it resonates symbolically, a house is first of all a physical structure designed for a very practical purpose. But the inhabitants of a Victorianl-era house understood how physical forms could shape our spiritual as well as our material existence. When the great English philosopher John Ruskin wrote, "There is religion in everything around us," he did not expect people to sing hosannas to their carpets or drapes. Yet as a man of his time he naturally presumed the home environment shaped the moods, the minds, and the hearts of its occupants.

ART, AESTHETICS, AND THE HOME

Across the Atlantic, Sarah Josepha Hale spoke of the "perpetual influence [which] emanates from [the home] upon those who see it and those who inhabit it." Many other architects, designers, and household advisers extensively discussed and debated what we dismissively label "bric-a-brac" or "stuff." The celebrated critic A. J. Downing explained that next to worshipping God, all "beautiful forms" of furniture, paintings, and sculptures "most tend to purify our hearts and our lives." Such purification cannot be obtained at starving artists sales of paintings held at a hotel by the airport.

Where we see mere objects on our floors, walls, and tables, our ancestors saw "the chief nourishers in life's feast." "It is no trifling matter," asserted Clarence Cook in his 1881 book *The House Beautiful*, "whether we hang poor pictures on our walls or good ones, whether we select a fine cast or a second-rate one. We might almost as well say it makes no difference whether the people we live with are first-rate or second-rate."

Designer extraordinaire William Morris reflected the domestic religion of his day when he observed in an 1882 lecture: "It helps the

The free-flowing flowers in this early William Morris wallpaper design ("Fruit," 1864) are a product of Morris's belief that nature is the basis of good art—and good art is the basis of a moral society. Morris was no elitist; his designs were often found in middle-class homes.

healthiness both of body and soul to live among beautiful things." In this view, physical objects were never just "things." Like his hero John Ruskin, who compared the social responsibilities of artists to those of preachers, Morris believed all forms of art had a distinctly ethical dimension and a grander purpose than the selfishness of self-expression. That is why he judged "any decoration futile if it does not remind you of something beyond itself, craftsmanship involving not only the mastery of technique, but the evocation of spiritual qualities of breadth, imagination, and order." In short, Victorian art imitated Victorian life!

Like so many other aspirations of Morris's era, this was a tall order that seems to have stretched beyond our reach. Yet he fulfilled it so brilliantly that his designs endure a century after his death. Believing, as many of his contemporaries did, that home decorations should unite the useful and the beautiful, Morris created his signature natural motifs of leaves, fruits, flowers, animals, and birds, which flowed through his wallpapers and fabrics. This prolific genius also created highly collectible and much copied furnishings, tapestries, stained glass, carpets, and even richly ornamented books based on medieval printing techniques. Morris was far more than a Victorian Ralph Lauren; he had grander ambitions than merely beautifying the home with his designs. Indeed, can we imagine contemporary aesthetic tastemakers also writing poetry or political essays, as Morris did?

Collectors of Victoriana eagerly buy Morris's products and those of his contemporaries, but many are oblivious to their deeper intent and value for the home. Morris's ideas about the importance of aesthetics were echoed by nondesigners as well. Although the dynamo crusader Jane Addams never believed that art alone could cure poverty or an impoverished spirit, when she opened Hull House in 1889, she decorated the settlement house—not with Elvis-on-velvet equivalents but with European artistic treasures that would spiritually nurture its inhabitants. Addams knew that even the most far-reaching reform legislation wouldn't nurture the cultivated citizen that a healthy democracy required.

Ordinary Victorians owned reproductions from Renaissance masters, especially those with religious themes, like Raphael's numerous Madonnas and Tintoretto's *Last Judgment*. They also favored morality plays on canvas, including the series done by Tissot and

William Powell Frith. In five paintings executed in 1887 collectively titled "The Road to Ruin," Frith unfolds the story of a young gentleman's downfall through gambling. Nothing curbs his dissipation, and a few years later his family is shown reduced from solid domestic comfort to drab, modest lodgings. Finally we see the gambler distraught and alone in a dingy garret, with a pistol that bespeaks his impending doom.

Such paintings may now seem insufferably self-righteous, yet at the time they instilled and reinforced core values through the constancy of aesthetics. Are the sporadic and futile lectures we give our kids to counter the "values" of pop music and trash TV more effective?

Even those unable to afford the cheapest prints had attractive options for creating a home that provided inspiration and education. Beauty, like civility, was not exclusive but democratic. For especially pinched purses, advisers extolled the art of nature. Simple flowers, said the legendary Rev. Henry Ward Beecher, "appeal to the power within us which spiritualizes matter." Andrew Weil, author of the bestselling book *8 Weeks to Optimum Health*, is simply revisiting our Victorian past when he recommends keeping fresh flowers in one's home to nurture the spirit.

NATURE AND THE HOME

The ever resourceful Catharine Beecher offered several ideas for making botanical displays. Her directions were much less complex and costly than Martha Stewart's. She suggested training ivy over curtain brackets crafted of common pine, or making hanging baskets and wall pockets from empty coconut shells. Filling this indoor grotto with plants, rocks, minerals, and shells created a "magical, charming effect" that would teach children "to enjoy the beautiful, silent miracles of nature."

The Victorians enjoyed tending their own outdoor gardens as well. In Dwight Blarney's 1901 painting *Hollyhock Garden,* family members lavish care on the colorful bounty surrounding their cottage. This simple scene illustrates family values that relied not on shallow platitudes or politics but on a deep and enduring network of small acts with grand meanings, of home as a place in the world and a place in the heart.

Am I reading too much into the image of a little shared mulching? Not if you think like the Victorians. For example, complementing the overtly moralistic paintings just described were subtle yet sublimely spiritual landscapes, like those of the Hudson River School. Its founder, Thomas Cole, regarded nature as a direct divine manifestation "fraught with high and holy meaning." Cole hoped his art would

Kindred Spirits by Asher Brown Drand, 1849, is an example of the popular Hudson River School of painting. The Victorians liked to bring the spiritually uplifting influence of nature into their homes through art.

give "your souls . . . a sweet foretaste of heaven."[1] Sadly, the assessment of Cole's art has turned it into kitsch while aesthetically impoverished consumers can now buy their self-described "glimpse of heaven" in the just-invented Window-lite: a backlit plastic window designed by the Bio-Brite Company to cheer windowless rooms and office cubicles. All you need is a picture hanger, an electric outlet, and a minimum of $150 to get a surrogate view of an English garden, a golf course, or a Hawaiian beach. (Studies, which have replaced common sense, show that people are happier, more efficient, and recover from surgery faster when they can look at nature instead of walls.)

When beauty was still taken from reality, and not concocted by Bio-Brite, it was expected to provide moral inspiration and seed the imagination, especially in the formative years. As we devalued the importance of home and its aesthetics, we did the same to the women who were responsible for all the little details that enriched and beautified family life. Before the Jazz Age threw those priorities into the shredder, home was considered the place where people were happiest, and therefore home decorations were of great importance (This importance also applied to those who did the adorning.) Now home is the trifle, and our happiest hours are more likely passed at the mall or on the golf course.

SHOCK ART AND THE TRIUMPH OF UGLINESS

In 1882 William Morris warned that "the extinction of the love of beauty and imagination would prove to be the extinction of civilization." The twentieth century proved him a prophet. I needn't recount the ugly triumph of Dada, Surrealism, and all the other motley modernists who lit the fuse of the current raging conflict between two camps of artists and critics—the outrageous and the outraged. The former was epitomized to its full in-your-face effect by a 1993 exhibit at the Whitney Museum in New York City. Interpreting gnawed cubes of chocolate and lard, and photos of hookers, gangs, and transvestites, curator Lisa Phillips proudly called them "crude, tawdry, and lacking finish. It deliberately renounces success and power in favor of the degraded and dysfunctional."[2]

Such anti-art fairly begs for indignation, especially if your tax dollars help foot the bill. It is easy for conservatives to lambaste the

National Endowment for the Arts when it awards grants to "performance artists" who smear their nude bodies with food, or to bargain-basement provocateurs who proffer portraits of a crucifix suspended in urine. The sensibilities of average Americans are probably just as offended by all this as they were by the Pentagon's purchase of $640 toilet seats. But even on this no-lose issue, the conservatives' hold on the high ground is shaky, because they lack the ennobling vision of art that made it a fundamental Victorian family value. It is pointless to rail at a Serrano or Mapplethorpe unless you extol a Titian or a Thomas Cole.

Do conservatives advocate art education or mercilessly slash it from school budgets? Do they orchestrate voluntary efforts to democratize access to art by bringing it directly to disadvantaged people (or vice versa), as Jane Addams did? For all their rhetoric, do they even discuss ways to enrich the lives of the ghetto-bound poor whose behavior they rail against? Do they fill their own homes with inspiring prints and paintings, and take their kids to museums to teach them the religion of art? Or is their religion limited to finger-wagging forbiddens and telepreachers who use God as the ultimate marketing tool?

ART FOR ALL CITIZENS

True to their distinctly modern brand of nostalgia, many conservatives view historic art (not to mention history) through the myopic lens of the Jazz Age. Their opponents have given up on convincing them of the intrinsic value of art. NEA Chairwoman Jane Alexander and her allies push the value of museums and concerts as economic stimuli, a virtue to which free marketeers can relate.

By the 1920s the disheartened authors of *Middletown* noted that even educated people had ceased regarding art as "a thing of unusual merit." They used it instead "almost entirely as furniture," which had also lost its aesthetic and symbolic meaning. Art became mere decoration, and decoration was all about show, not substance. In her 1930 work entitled *Personality of a House*, Emily Post counseled women to choose household goods that would enhance their own appearance by matching their eyes and hair. You tailored your "setting" like a wardrobe, and damn the rest of the family if their features clashed with yours. Another adviser of the 1920s, quoted in *American Home Life 1880–1930*, pronounced every room just "the background of the people who live in it, " as if we were comic-strip figures inhabiting backgrounds.

Since our domestic investment today is chiefly financial, whatever hints at an earlier sense of home is derided as deceptively nostalgic. For example, the writer Holly Bruback, in a *New York Times* article on "Mail-Order America," criticized the L. L. Bean catalog for selling a romanticized image of an earlier age in its pitch for sampler quilts and crewel-stiched sweaters. Those who sneer at Victorian aesthetics might ponder the metaphor to be found in the fate of the 1950s Tupperware collection at New York's Museum of Modern Art. Not only are its "museum-quality" plastic bowls disintegrating into shapeless blobs, but they began to smell so rank that they had to be encased. Thus far all salvage operations have failed to preserve the miracle material that was supposed to last forever, or the foam and Naugahyde furniture that made the fifties home an aesthetic chamber of horrors. In commenting on their quality, a candid curator finally admitted, "The fact is they weren't so great in the first place." (Better late than never.)

RECAPTURING ENVIRONMENTAL AESTHETICS

This obsessively sensual age is finally beginning to rediscover its senses. Many people swear by aromatherapy to alter their moods with an alphabet of fragrant oils. And retailers, convinced of scents' merchandising power, are piping them into their stores. Researchers at institutions like Johns Hopkins University have found that music influences how much and how quickly we eat, and colors affect everything from casual purchasing decisions to suicide rates. Beauty products in bright containers sell faster than those wrapped in brown. A prison in New York reduced aggressive behavior among inmates just by painting its common rooms pink. And when a bridge spanning England's Thames River went from black to a calming blue, fewer people jumped to their deaths.

If you need more proof that aesthetics is the diet of the soul— that there is more to our environment than saving trees—consider the Chinese practice of feng shui. The art of arranging interiors to enhance creativity, harmony, luck, and prosperity has gone from New Age to mainstream. Several major corporations, such as Motorola, utilized its principles to design office layouts. Individuals also hire feng shui consultants instead of standard decorators. These people are searching for more than coordinated pillows and drapes, even those that match their complexions. Satisfied clients say their homes not only feel more orderly and peaceful but also have changed how their residents interact with the world. At last we can reclaim this Victorian legacy, even if we had to go by way of China to find it.

Aesthetics of Exterior Architecture

The deep significance our own ancestors vested in a house's decor also applied to its exterior. Because we view architecture as mere style, Oliver Smith may sound completely off the walls he constructed when he wrote in 1852 that, "Nothing has more to do with morals, the civilization, the refinement of a nation than its prevailing architecture." Just as manners were a hallmark of morality, architecture was its face.

Even if twentieth-century Americans had preserved instead of trashed the Victorian aesthetic religion, not to mention its art of living, America, of course, would not be Shangri-la. But it would be a safer, saner, more civilized place, unblemished by an epidemic of eyesores from Levittown to erector-set office towers with windows that don't open. (Mobile ones might tempt their prisoners to jump.) We attack our growing laundry list of social problems with money, legislation, and technical fixes, while ignoring what Calvert Vaux called our abused and deadened senses.

Vaux collaborated with Frederick Law Olmsted in gifting this country with some of its greatest parks, including New York's Central Park. But the wisdom of this landscape artist stretched far beyond the garden gate. He understood that if we are what we eat, drink, and smoke, we are also the buildings we inhabit. "Good architecture," he wrote in 1857,

> must spring up in any society where there is a love of truth
> and nature, and a generally diffused spirit of politeness in
> the ordinary habits of thought. Wherever, on the other hand,
> there is a widespread carelessness as to the development of
> the refined and gentle perceptive faculties, there inevitably
> must be a monotonously deficient standard of existence and
> a very paltry architecture as a necessary consequence.

This park at Saratoga, New York, captures the Olmsted aesthetic with landscaping that encourages casual walking and intermingling.

We can imagine what conclusions he would draw from our concrete-slab, near-windowless buildings.

Although the Victorians did not believe design alone determined the state of a nation's civility or morality, that century of subtlety understood how beauty—or its absence—affected attitudes and behavior. This recognition made it natural and essential for prominent members of the clergy like Timothy Dwight to preach on the moral effects of architecture, something it is hard for us to imagine a man of the cloth concerning himself with today.

A house was considered to have a nearly mystical, potent impact on its residents and their neighbors. As one midcentury architect put it,

> No man . . . could live the life in a well-proportioned and truly beautiful dwelling that he would in a mud shanty or rude log cabin. Certain elevating influences would steal into him unawares . . . that would lift his life above its otherwise lower level. . . . And so, too, the power of the tasteful is seen very often in the influence which a single dwelling will exert upon almost all in the neighborhood.

THE URBAN BEAUTIFICATION MOVEMENT

Given the Victorians' strong ethos regarding environment, it is no surprise that starting in the mid–nineteenth century, a variety of reformers, urban planners, and artists united to combat the blight of factory pollution, ugly billboards, and carelessly discarded trash. They were part of what historians term the "city beautiful" movement, although it wasn't limited to cities. But for the aesthetically minded Victorians, purging the unsightly and the toxic was a mere first step. Because they assumed the visual shaped a country's ethics and civic spirit, that country needed more than breathable air. It needed broad boulevards adorned with flowers, trees, and shrubs, and it got them.

Above all, reformers thought, we needed public parks. Like his partner, Calvert Vaux, Frederick Law Olmsted claimed the elevating powers of nature had "a harmonizing and refining influence . . . favorable to courtesy, self-control, and temperance," especially in cities, where they were scarce. He also hoped bucolic settings where rich and poor could mingle would reduce class conflict. Until his death in 1903, Olmsted applied his theories to creating parks around the continent, from Brooklyn and Boston to Buffalo, Chicago, and Montreal. By then the nation boasted more than two thousand "improvement societies" in small towns and cities.

The World's Fair of 1893 accelerated this beautification movement. A coalition of the century's artistic giants transformed six hundred acres of Chicago swampland into the White City, a palatial extravaganza of classical, French, and Italian Renaissance buildings and fountains. Because the Victorians so richly mined what the architect Daniel Burnham called the "social possibilities of municipal architecture," many of our most inspired and inspiring public buildings, with their equally impressive interiors, were begun or completed during this era. It gave us some of Washington, D.C.'s greatest monuments and institutions, such as the Library of Congress, the Lincoln Memorial, and the Museum of Natural History.

Recovering Our Environmental Aesthetic
Does this mean our most promising prescription for urban ailments is to give our sterile modern cities a massive architectural makeover? Financially strapped municipal budgets guarantee that will remain a fantasy. Yet in our quest to control crime and our slip-sliding quality

of life, we have already borrowed bits and pieces of the past to save our future. Increasingly, cities and neighborhoods are implementing policies based on Victorian atmospherics, unaware of their origin or age. For example, the sociologists James Q. Wilson and George Kelling are often credited with coining the "broken-window theory" of crime and urban decay. In essence it states that ignoring small infractions, like the breaking of a window that stays broken, can propel a snowball of similar offenses that eventually devastates an area physically and morally. As vandalism spreads, residents become apathetic and withdraw from public places. Once predators see that no one is in charge, drug dealers, gangs, and assorted thugs claim the turf.

The "innovative" notion that minor crimes trigger progressively larger ones harks back to the holistic Victorian philosophy we have seen applied in many other contexts. The fashionably "novel" idea that reversing physical negligence and destruction reduces crime is pure old-fashioned aesthetically flavored common sense. It worked then and it works now. New York City has been especially aggressive in targeting the petty "quality-of-life" violations it once ignored, such as graffiti, ear-splitting boom boxes, subway turnstile jumpers, panhandling, and urinating in public. Gone are the infamous squeegee men, who cleaned the windshields of cars stopped at red lights, then extorted money from intimidated drivers. The crime rate in the city has plummeted, and, not surprisingly, police discovered that many of those arrested for misdemeanors were wanted felons or had links to them.

MORE THAN MEETS THE EYE

The Victorians were convinced that even the most trifling incivility laid a cobblestone on the road to crime and social chaos. This steadfast certainty may now seem puzzling when viewed against the constantly shifting background of Victorian architectural trends. How could our ancestors preach a religion of beauty when its standards kept changing? The answer is that beneath the contrasting complexions of restrained Federal houses and exuberant Queen Annes is a shared foundation. The substance of buildings transcended style, and structures spoke a language the Victorians understood, just as they understood the language of flowers. Consider two major architectural movements—Greek Revival and Gothic Revival.

Greek Revival

People usually describe the Greek Revival, which had its heyday from 1820 to 1860, as embodying imposing, grand, formal architecture, along the lines of Margaret Mitchell's fictitious Tara. Our ancestors would probably second those comments, but they also actively envisioned the ancient Greek roots of the democratic ideals their young nation cherished and won through the Revolutionary War (which some could still remember). They also sympathized with the recent Greek struggle for independence from the Turks. The Victorians were familiar with all three orders of the Greek Revival's signature columns (Doric, Ionic, Corinthian), and the culturally diverse races that developed them.

Gothic Revival

The "passionless repose" of Greek Rival's simple rational lines suited public buildings, as A. J. Downing pointed out, but was inappropriate for homes. Domestic architecture, he said, "should be less rigidly scientific, and it should exhibit more of the freedom of play of feeling of everyday life. . . . There must be nooks and crannies about it, where

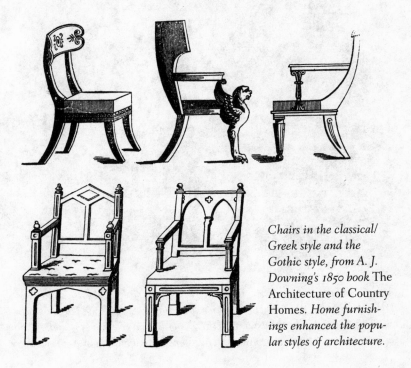

Chairs in the classical/ Greek style and the Gothic style, from A. J. Downing's 1850 book The Architecture of Country Homes. *Home furnishings enhanced the popular styles of architecture.*

one would love to linger . . . cosy rooms where all domestic fireside joys are invited to dwell."

Borrowing designs, history, and folklore from medieval Europe, especially England, Downing became the most eloquent apostle of Gothic Revival houses. In contrast to the flat, predictably balanced proportions that characterize the classical, Gothic was proudly quixotic. It emphasized asymmetrical facades, irregular placement of doors and windows, clustered chimneys, and steep gabled roofs. Other typical features included wooden or iron tracery, gingerbread scrollwork, and soaring towers.

This was a picturesque and contagious style suited to free spirits. Washington Irving revamped his sober seventeenth-century Dutch farmhouse until it seemed to its owner "all made up of gable ends and as full of angles and corners as an old cocked hat." The finest Gothic dwellings were sheer enchantments, passports to another place and time.

An example of a cottage in the Gothic Revival style, designed by Alexander Jackson Davis, featured in A. J. Downing's guide to country homes. Downing noted that "the character expressed by the exterior of this design is that of a man or family of domestic tastes, but with strong aspirations after something higher than social pleasures."

A Proper, Yet Affordable, Home

Downing believed that a "proper house" had to satisfy "all the rational desires of the senses, the affections, and the intellect." Yet his books also extensively discussed practical subjects such as lathing, heating, window sashes, and the thickness of floor boards. When he hit the bottom line—money—he paid equal attention to those who had it and those who had to scrimp. He printed plans for both sumptuous villas and modest "working men's cottages" of three to four rooms. Because the democratic spirit of Victorian manners led straight to the hearth, many house pattern books were published for those of limited means.

Downing assured the readers who took his few books through more than twenty editions that "the peculiar charm of a cottage is as great as that of a villa." And he made good on his promise. A generation before William Morris, he advocated melding "the useful and the beautiful." He showed how even a tight budget could stretch to the "charm of bay windows, gabled and bracketed roofs, beckoning porches and vine-covered trellises." What now seem like frills were then considered essentials. Downing wrote, "There is no building, however simple, to which either good forms or something of an agreeable expression may not be given." Of course, he never saw tract housing.

THE SOUL OF ARCHITECTURE IS DESTROYED

Victorian architecture was not just structure and style but an encounter with the soul. That is why Downing argued that every house must have "something in its aspect which the heart can fasten upon and become attached to, as naturally as the ivy attached itself to the antique wall, preserving its memories from decay." Nathaniel Hawthorne called that something "moral charm." Across the Atlantic, Goethe described it as "frozen music."

The guns of World War I forever silenced that song. When form became function, architecture lost its charm, its sentiment, its soul—and we lost a large chunk of ours. The budding blight of the anti-Victorian International Style had none, except to its elitist advocates. Replacing aesthetic inspiration and high aspirations were cold glass and concrete towers, along with the minimalist philosophy that less was more. And we got more and more of less and less, until the unprecedented building boom after World War II gave us American homes that were, as described in Malvina Reynolds's song "Little Boxes," "little boxes made of ticky tacky . . . little boxes all the same."

Goethe's "frozen music" became a screeching monotony that stretched from cheap Cape Cods to ostentatious but cheesy tract mansions. Now we had living rooms with built-in TV's that could be financed on a mortgage like other appliances. As Dolores Hayden pointed out in *Redesigning the American Dream,* this new ideal of living centered on "the bright, beady eye of the baby-sitting machine [which] reassured both children and adults that the scant physical community of the mass-produced sacred huts was redeemed by the magical electronic community created by national television."

Material Comforts Dominate

In the postwar period, homeowners began to have higher expectations for material household comforts and conveniences. Gradually, any remaining expectations of home as a source of morally elevating beauty and binding emotional fulfillment disappeared. The 1948 film *Mr. Blandings Builds His Dream House* made light of this change. In it, Cary Grant struggles endlessly to satisfy his family's suburban dream of private baths and separate rooms for the children without going bankrupt. Confronted with a growing list of such demands, the frustrated architect declares that the Blandings don't want a house so much as "a series of little bungalows." This was a fitting metaphor for family togetherness in its touted golden age.

Such domestic sentiments—or the lack of them—still thrive unquestioned, as I recently learned while touring the sole surviving Victorian mansion in a neighborhood of glossy new undistinguished office buildings. When the guide identified a bright spacious room as the one the family's two daughters occupied until they left to marry, a shocked woman gasped. "Those poor girls," she said to her sympathetic husband. "With all the rooms in this place [over thirty], imagine making them share one." What now seems like child abuse was a widely practiced custom that made the house a home, not a series of little bungalows.

In his 1993 book *The Geography of Nowhere,* James Howard Kunstler dissected the process that morphed the transcendent Victorian home into a "spiritual deformity" during those delusive "happy days" of the fifties:

> You could name a housing development Forest Knoll Acres, even if there was no forest and no knoll, and the customers would line up with their checkbooks open. Americans ... had more meaningful relationships with movie stars and characters on daytime television shows than they did with members of their own families. They didn't care if things were real or not, if ideas were truthful. In fact, they preferred fantasy. They preferred lies. And the biggest lie of all was that the place they lived was home.

The structure and spirit of the buildings Nathaniel Hawthorne and his era admired for their "moral charm" were bulldozed, along with the virgin countryside, by magicians who produced instant pre-fab wastelands. Few mourned the demise of those heirlooms. The glories of historic architecture were despised for the very details and artistry that distinguished them. Many older houses were abandoned and left to rot, while Charles Addams cartoons and the movie *Psycho* made the Victorian home the emblem of the macabre.

Those houses that survived amid the frosty gleam of new developments were ridiculed by neighbors who practiced the national religion of contempt for old things, including their owners. With skyrocketing property values, decaying old mansions became a last resort for those financially strapped yet desperate to escape city crowds and crowded quarters. In the 1960s comedy *Please Don't Eat the Daisies*, Doris Day jokes that she and her hubby had to buy an aged white elephant in Connecticut because they "couldn't afford anything smaller."

GETTING BACK TO THE ENVIRONMENTAL AESTHETIC

Luckily, the tide began to turn before the juggernaut of modern sprawl completely buried the beauty of the past. A few enlightened souls simply saw homes that merited saving, while aesthetic rebels like Kunstler championed a larger and nearly lost cause to revive the moribund legacy I have described. In typically Victorian vein he writes, "Americans wonder why their houses lack charm. . . . Charm is dependent on connectedness, on continuities, on the relation of one thing to another." Similarly, Robert Wilson of the National Trust for Historic Preservation criticized contemporary public buildings for being "utterly charmless, utterly lacking the capacity to inspire," a quality once deemed essential to civility and community participation:

> Our civic leaders who are responsible for our public spaces seem clueless as they inflict artistic atrocities on us. The prestigious hundred-thousand-dollar Pritzker Prize, awarded by architects to their peers, recently went to a home with a windowless wall made entirely of reinforced concrete. Similarly, a prizewinning "park" in a middle class area of Queens, New York, exemplifies "design excellence," according to the American Institute of Architects. Unfortunately, those who encounter it daily see only a concrete slab studded with oddly shaped steel benches, sparse greenery, and garish lights. The locals pronounced it a "strip park" and a setting "generated from a computer."

So hostile is this latter environment to its original intent of providing recreation and promoting community ties that it is frequently used as a dump for shabby furniture and garbage. The residents have done everything but firebomb what they thought would be "a traditional park with old-fashioned benches, gardens, and lots of shade." The benefits of such a park are more than aesthetic: Researchers who measured the effects of foliage and open vistas on commuters found they had better respiration, blood pressure, and heart rates than those who battled roads hedged by billboards and strip malls, a legacy of the 1950s.

Of course the Victorians relied on aesthetic intuition, not environmental psychologists, to tell them that beauty matters. For example, it was the Victorians who began New York City's Fresh Air Fund. Following the common sense of his age, Frederick Law Olmsted believed exposure to nature brought "tranquility and rest to the mind." This observation was recently certified by an official Justice Department report that concluded our deserts of high-rise slums breed crime, fear, and demoralization.

In the twentieth century, place has become mere space filled by corporate brands of houses that offer no home to the senses or the soul. Meanwhile, growing numbers of tourists flock to our nation's living museums of historic architecture, from Charleston, South Carolina, to Saratoga Springs, New York. Can you imagine tourists a hundred years from now spending their time and money to visit the buildings our age leaves behind—if they're still standing?

Rediscovering the Beauty of Older Buildings

Happily, some people are recovering our long-lost environmental aesthetic. At the University of California at Berkeley, a school better known for protests than for drawing-room behavior, the chapter of Sigma Phi fraternity occupies an Edwardian-era Arts and Crafts mansion in a neighborhood laid out by Frederick Law Olmsted. In this shingled Gothic-style delight, not just toga parties but even putting tacks on the walls are verboten. The same goes for all the other college pigsty habits that could mar the delicate friezes painted on Belgian linen, the original amber glass lighting fixtures, or the rare Burmese teak and Honduran mahogany trim. (Before any party, the walls at Sigma Phi are covered temporarily with protective particle board.)

The fraternity members are not only obliged to respect the house (a lesson few kids learn at home), but every week each must contribute some serious elbow grease. Students polish the paneling and carefully scrape through multiple layers of paint to find the original wallpapers. Moreover, they don't mind the labor or the time spent raising the hefty sums that renovation requires. Although those interviewed by *The New York Times* struggled to articulate how they are affected by the house, they are certain they are so affected. One called its craftsmanship "an epiphany." So potent is its aura that at a dinner where new members were introduced, the others snapped their fingers instead of applauding because, as the fraternity's president noted, "It's quieter."

If architecture can coax such remarkable behavior from Berkeley frat boys, controlling crime seems like a walk in an Olmsted park—but only if you think like a Victorian. We often do, even if we don't know it. When James Howard Kunstler asked visitors why they came to stroll through historic Woodstock, Vermont, most fumbled for words before settling on some version of enjoying its "old-fashioned feeling." Kunstler notes gloomily that these tourists were "members of a culture that had long ceased to value place except as a sales gimmick, and they had no vocabulary with which to think about it."

Happily, our gut response to architectural treasure troves like Woodstock reveals the spark of our forgotten aesthetic conscience— a lost concept that is ripe for recovery. As A. J. Downing said, "The Beautiful is an original instinct of the sentiment of our nature. It is worship, by the heart, of a higher perfection manifested in material forms . . . an instinct as strong as for life itself." Similarly, in her 1889 work *The Art of Decoration*, the English author Mary Haweis called the "eye for form" a "birthright."

We forgot how to "see" when function buried form. But its light was dormant, not dead. We are searching for that transcendent experience of place that enriches both body and soul. This is why people increasingly crave what Kunstler calls the "organic wholeness" of historic towns, with their "everyday attention to details, of intimate care for things intimately used."

Neotraditional Buildings and Communities

There are signs of revival of the Victorian aesthetic so memorably summarized by Winston Churchill: "We shape our buildings, then they shape us." Innovative architect Andres Duany and his partner-wife Elizabeth Plater-Zyberk are designing neotraditional communities explicitly modeled on nineteenth-century designs. Following their commercial and critical success in Florida's Seaside and Maryland's Kentlands, they have designed and built 135 such projects throughout the world, and their vision has inspired many others.

Exactly how do these new-old places differ from typical suburbs? Gone is the signature sprawl of isolated office, retail, and residential pods linked only by the almighty automobile. King car has been toppled, and its throne—the garage—moved from the front of the house to the rear, where the Victorians once erected their carriage houses. Residents are encouraged to use their legs, not their wheels, on tree-lined streets that lead to nearby jobs, schools, shops, and restaurants, where you actually stop and eat rather than drive through. Such conveniences not only reduce traffic, pollution, highway construction, and its accompanying destruction of the natural landscape, but also those eternal commutes that steal time people once devoted to family, socializing and civic activities.

Unlike vehicular solitude, walking promotes human contact. When the social scientist Philip Langdon interviewed residents of Kentlands and other neotraditional towns, he found "a different, more neighborly, social life" compared to that in standard developments. "If you're out doing yard work, everyone stops and chats," one Kentlands homeowner told him. "After a big snowfall, we helped each other shoveling the driveways and all had chili afterward. There's more of a sense of community than anywhere else we've lived."

In these communities, designs that promote "we" instead of "me" extend to public space as well. Land usually devoured by vast parking lots is used for playgrounds, parks, or village greens. Commercial buildings have the human scale of those they are meant to serve, not the intimidating presence of looming corporate towers and cavernous malls. In neotraditional towns, the tallest structures are usually city halls, civic centers, and churches that have a shared public function and anchor the community in their purpose and appearance. A century ago, soaring church steeples, the highest points in even the largest cities, were points of orientation for those who had lost their souls or just their way. Today's skyscrapers thrust far above them, yet fail to reach their heights.

Residents of these new old-fashioned towns are inspired to mingle because the buildings around them, whether public or private, mingle comfortably without seeming crowded. There are no remote islands ringed by asphalt or acres of lawn that tell passersby to keep their distance. All structures are set near the street, connecting them physically, aesthetically, and symbolically with each other and the people who have a stake in what they represent. Homes feature front porches rather than isolating backyard decks or the barbecue pits where 1950s males in chef hats and aprons expressed their dwindling sense of masculinity by charring burgers and steaks. Porch life was a Victorian institution. What could be more inviting or pedestrian-friendly than the visual delight of its flowering baskets and roomy white wicker chairs that were made for sipping tea or homemade lemonade sweetened by casual chatter and the lull of a gently creaking rocker? Porches subtly mediate the zone between the house and the street; they also permit discreet vigilance of local children and any sign of potential crime.

It took us almost a century to see the light. But porches are just the frosting on the architectural cake of neotraditional towns. Even expensive modern suburbs assault our senses and our sense of direction with their relentless monotony. Locating "individual" houses can be a logistical nightmare. Consider the contrast in getting directions to a house in a typical tract development with doing so in the old neighborhoods we now copy. How could you possibly miss the Queen Anne with the square turret and the tri-colored fish-scale roof? Yet how could you help but miss the third house on the left, distinguished only by its red shutters—until the neighbor paints his red?

Like their ancestors, neotraditional towns have a refreshing variety of historic styles that harmonize without sacrificing the uniqueness that is the essence of Victorian charm. You can see it and feel it wherever the past is preserved, from Rhinebeck, New York, to Savannah, Georgia. Richmond's majestic Monument Avenue, America's Champs Elysées, is a feast of Romanesque, Tudor, Colonial, and Greek Revival mansions, while in the tiny jewel of Lexington, Virginia, more modest but equally striking Southern raised cottages share the shady streets with classic Queen Annes and compact Gothic fantasies worthy of Sir Walter Scott.

This diversity is more than skin-deep. Like the genuine communities that inspired their aesthetics, the neotraditional heirs have revived zoning codes that encourage a residential mix of age and income groups. Instead of the typical suburban ghetto, where a fairly narrow span of prices attracts families in a single tax bracket, the assortment of detached houses, row houses, and apartments, some above garages and shops, offers a broad selection of accommodations to everyone from singles and families to seniors and empty-nesters ready to shed extra space. Naturally size and cost will vary. Yet even the cheapest homes feature details that complement their more extravagant neighbors. In true Victorian spirit, there are no architectural also-rans and afterthoughts.

Charleston, South Carolina's mayor, Joseph Riley, believes "there is no reason for government ever to build something that is not beautiful." So the city cooperated with developers to build houses that break the standard high-rise ghetto mold—and hopefully its mentality—by echoing the porches, materials, and rooflines of the city's historic homes.

Domestic beauty was a core Victorian family value because it solidified families and communities, which we are desperately trying to patch together with social policies and rhetoric. These efforts will continue to miss the target until we realize that home is at the heart of this matter. For our ancestors, the home was a national religion with a very practical creed. As A. J. Downing wrote in 1850, "Home's moral influence . . . is more powerful than any mere oral teachings of virtue and morality. . . . The mere sentiment of home, with its thousand associations, has, like a strong anchor, saved many a man from shipwrecks in the storms of life."

As we drift about, seeking the security our grandparents and great-grandparents took for granted, we must put aside our shortsighted, narrow views that reduce homes to houses and art to mere decoration. We must reclaim our public space and public art for all the people, even as we reclaim our lost sense of home, family, romance, and civility. We are the most forward-looking nation on earth, but it is time for us to look back in order to move ahead. The greatest hope for our future lies in our past.

Conclusion:
Back to the Future?

Eighty-nine percent of Americans say civility is a serious national problem, yet 99 percent claim their own behavior is civil. To pursue the ideal we need to get real. Change, like charity, begins at home. Having your cake and eating it too is a childish delusion that lures us to the hot stove where we keep getting burned. As comedian Joan Rivers says, "Grow up!" We can't cut taxes and balance the national budget while we gorge on government goodies. We won't find charm in a world that shrieks at a thrusting post-Elvis pelvis. We can't build solid families in emotionally hollow homes. We can't make true love while the sexes are making war. And we can't have a civilized society that celebrates "attitude," self-expression, and self-obsession, while brushing off blame like dandruff.

The qualities our culture calls healthy are personal and social poison. How do we detox? By reversing course a hundred years and switching the labels on our virtues and vices. We've done it before. Smoking used to be glamorized; now it is stigmatized. (Every ration kit the U.S. Government issued to troops during World War II contained the cigarettes that have now become federal public enemy number one.) We no longer shrug when someone drives under the influence of alcohol, thanks to the efforts of Mothers Against Drunk Driving.

Let's stop laying back, and straighten up physically, morally, and verbally. Let's get used to the sound of words like "genteel." If we respect all words as potential weapons, we might actually cultivate the art of language again. Free speech is never free; someone always pays a price. Victorian reticence—self-censorship—is no pathology but the bedrock of civility. Let's stop blowing all those noisy horns. In a civilized society people have a stake in each other; let's live that way, instead of driving stakes through each other's hearts. A cohesive code of civility is still the best internal V-chip for kids and the adults who act like kids. Let's start saving others' faces, rather than getting into them, whatever our mood or circumstances. Like the law, true civility is a constant, not a random I-feel-like-it act of kindness. If a social obligation is treated like a crap shoot, someone is bound to get shot.

In the 1800s everyday courtesies saved not just bloodshed but time, money, and general misery as well. Ralph Waldo Emerson said life was never too short for civility, and life was a lot shorter back then. Yet even Emerson could not have imagined how much time, money, and grief civility could save. Endless lawsuits and costly sensitivity training sessions that aggravate sexual, racial, and ethnic divisions, to name just a few. Let's replace narrow concepts that selectively discriminate, like politically "correct" and "incorrect," with more inclusive and equitable terms, such as "rude" and "polite." But semantics alone won't do the job. We must become as outraged by violations of civility as we are by racist or sexist acts and expressions. This would diffuse hostility while broadening and strengthening everyone's civil rights.

We must also apply appropriate punishments to civil wrongs. Legislative efforts and lawsuits should only be used as a last resort. The notorious Victorian frozen silence effectively tied loose tongues prone to crude or insensitive comments. It still works wonders with dirty jokes if the audience, male and female—or rather gentlemen and ladies—unites in its reaction. This is precisely why an established set of manners is essential. We have learned the hard way what happens when we improvise.

More serious offenses demanded fitting penalties, and the Victorians had them. Those committing ethical or criminal violations were ostracized socially and professionally by respectable folk. The effectiveness of this measure rested on several extinct assumptions we must revive. In the past, people had reputations to lose. Every community and class, not just the bluest bloods, followed a powerful moral code instead of a mercurial mishmash of laws. This culture of character—the backbone of civility—"counted" every day in every way, not just for a government-sanctioned "Character Counts" week or when some celebrity-studded interest group decides to make it their cause of the month.

This century turned "character" into a synonym for "odd," "eccentric," or "peculiar" and a reference to actors who didn't play romantic leads. The meat of Victorian character and morality—hard work, frugality, sobriety, nonbrutal honesty, sexual decency, civic participation, self-sacrifice, and self-restraint—got charred beyond recognition when the Jazz Age turned happiness on its head, making it self-centered instead of centered on others. We've been tinkering with the recipe for happiness ever since. Each dish may have seemed palatable when fresh, but they have all given us indigestion.

We have finally begun to nibble at the Victorians' table, without knowing where we are. But we won't find the healing nourishment we need unless everyone gets equal treatment by our unwritten laws, as well as our written ones. For example, the latest trend in crime control pushes the "new" idea of shame. Using mandated signs and newspaper advertisements, judges are stamping updated scarlet letters on the likes of men who solicit prostitutes, drunk drivers, and deadbeat dads. But should we brand only those who can't afford a wily lawyer to spare them such humiliation? We must stigmatize and ostracize across the board, without playing political favorites. If conservatives condemn rap music for demeaning women, they should also tune out Rush Limbaugh until he cleans up his act. If we fine Dennis Rodman for his outrageous behavior on the basketball court, corporate America should stop rewarding him with lucrative offers for product endorsements, and consumers should stop buying whatever he is hawking.

What happens when former Clinton adviser and confidant Dick Morris lets his prostitute listen to private calls with his boss? He is forced to resign, but that blow is substantially softened with presidential sympathy, a fat book contract, and continued access to journalists eager for a good sound bite. When pinstriped executives are guilty of sexual harassment, drum them out of their jobs and their country clubs. As we've seen in recent media scandals, lowly army drill sergeants are promptly court-martialed when their hormones run amok.

Our kids have seen enough double standards. We must teach them level Victorian values as our ancestors would, with a positive spin. Another simplistic "Just say no" campaign won't work because it lacks direction. Speak the snappy lingo kids understand—hypocrisy is commendable, not expendable; uptight is all right; discreet is neat; act fine, not like swine; the Golden Rule is cool.

To make these lessons stick, kids must see their parents faithfully practice what they preach. Parents must be exemplars, not pals with open checkbooks. Of course, popular culture should bolster, not sabotage, their efforts. Here the creative possibilities are as endless as the benefits all of us can reap. Imagine the sports superstars kids idolize bowing to their opponents like Victorian gents, instead of showing them up by showboating after making a slam dunk or scoring a touchdown. That would be a victory for everyone, no matter who won the game.

Recent celebrity "milk mustache" ads actually increased milk consumption. This same approach could promote basic courtesy, a nutrient essential to our social health. No matter how little else they wear, many Hollywood stars never fail to don their AIDS awareness pins. A similar pin might raise civility consciousness, and it needs raising. Let's borrow some of the star power poured into public-service campaigns to make sex safe, and keep kids safe from drugs, booze, and tobacco. Restoring civility requires the high-profile moral force of such crusades. Like secondhand smoke, the lack of that core Victorian value pollutes everyone's air.

Plugs for designated drivers have become a staple of prime-time shows. The TV elite could do as much for civility if it would just get over its anti-elitist bias that consistently portrays bad manners as good. We cannot afford any more Roseannes in fact or the fiction that so easily colors it. With or without a laugh track, the low-class ass as a national role model is no laughing matter.

The nineteenth century was civil because the Victorians lived up to solid standards. They did not go slumming for fashions, morals, or the manners that embodied mutual respect and self-respect. Instead of downscale chic, there was nearly universal pride in acting like ladies and gentlemen. Yet even as they raised the ceiling instead of lowering the floor, the Victorians invited everyone along. Contrary to the stereotype, manners were not elitist but inclusive and democratic. Every person was entitled to courtesy and fairness, not the intimate details of others' lives. It is time to exchange that entitlement for one we can use, not abuse.

Like the constitutional rights that are free to all Americans, manners were meant to unify the classes, creeds, and colors. The chaotic WASP-phobic cultural diversity we practice breeds a divisive reverse snobbery that costs us plenty. Its only standard is conveniently two-faced. We selectively condemn other countries for rituals like public flogging, animal sacrifice, bought adolescent brides, and dowry murders. Yet at home we selectively justify some of the worst attitudes and practices of historically victimized groups as their cultural best. This form of compensation is really toxic discrimination. Yes, we must acknowledge our legacy of shamefully exploiting minorities and the poor. But we can't continue to allow past sins to excuse destructive self-indulgence. Ultimately, we sink or swim together.

The Victorians understood that the more diverse a nation, the more it needs a binding code of civility. This is a common language of comportment that lets us talk to, not past, each other. Without these rules of the road, the most aggressive call the shots, and the most vulnerable get hit. This is especially important to women. Beginning in the Jazz Age, the progressive march of "liberation" succeeded in making the world safe only for those women who act like the dregs of men, and are treated in kind. Ironically, we have debased and masculinized the world even as we emasculated males.

The twentieth century's brand of equality did not expand women's rights; it took with one hand and gave with the other. We should protect, celebrate, and extend the greater educational and job opportunities that a limited segment of women now enjoy. But we must also recognize that all women have lost the fundamental rights of personal safety and respect that the Victorians took for granted. Rape, violence, harassment—every way women are mistreated—cannot be blamed on patriarchy or biology. The problem isn't men but modern men, the culture that tolerates misogynist behavior, and the women who collude in their own degradation. They will never re-empower themselves with laws, rhetoric, or karate courses but only by raising their minds, their morals, and expectations to Victorian heights, and demanding that men meet them. Likewise, men should redefine themselves in Victorian terms. This "new" masculinity is measured by honor, restraint and self-control, and by how well (not how badly) men treat women. Above all, those who act macho instead of manly must be shunned, not admired, by other men.

Rather than subordinating women, this resurrected chivalry will shield them from verbal, emotional, and physical beatings. A positive means of demonstrating manhood is a realistic and long-overdue recognition of the facts of life—namely, men are still top dogs when it comes to money, sex, and raw muscle. To thrive or even survive, women need old-fashioned equalizers, the sort that encourage a man to give up his seat on a bus (if not a lifeboat). Ask women, especially pregnant ones, if they consider this gesture insulting. A woman could decline any chivalrous offer—politely. She would reinforce general civility and avoid being a "spoiler" for those women who would welcome a taste of the treatment their great-grandmothers routinely savored. This may be sexist, but it's a healthy sexism, much like the good cholesterol that protects the heart from bad cholesterol's artery-clogging fat. We don't need a survey to tell us which type of man most women would rather encounter in a dark alley.

Perhaps when women are once again valued for their "otherness," men will feel free to reclaim the "feminine" side of manhood. Victorian men took pride in being sensitive to others' feelings and the fine points of romance. Love was not a "woman thing" that men grudgingly gave or pretended to give in order to score. It was a unisex ideal, publicly prized but privatized to protect it from degrading exhibitionist displays. A century ago manly men were intensely sentimental. They effusively opened their hearts to their heart's desire, whom they treated like gold, not dirt. They lived for love, visibly suffered lovesickness, and sometimes died of it. Men gave all to love, because it made them feel like men.

The Victorians' holistic vision of life also applied to sex and love. You loved and were loved with the body, mind, and soul, not in bits and pieces. For real men and women, sex was no casual hit-and-run game of techniques and gadgets but a banquet that satisfied "the appetite for higher pleasures." Even the elusive great lay we pursue was no substitute for grand passion. The Victorians made a religion of love. We need to get religion again to connect us to ourselves, to each other, and to the hopes and aspirations that keep us striving instead of settling for second best. This is the one true religion that can fill our empty hearts and restore our ailing homes.

Family values need that home to flourish, as plants need nourishing soil. Our homes and the women who make them must once again have the dignity they deserve. What makes a home? The very intangibles we have shrugged off and cut corners on until we bled dry the very essence of the Victorian home. Those "little niceties"—the frills, the rituals, even the chores—gave the home a deeply emotional sense of place, not just a label or an address. It can't be restored by the tax cuts touted by conservatives, liberal calls for expanded day care, or Martha Stewart's how-to kits.

We have learned the hard way that home is more than another institution, as parenthood is more than a role. It was the sovereign solidity of the Victorian home that strengthened and linked individuals, communities, and the country. The twentieth century tried and failed to trade that strength and the effort it entails for the easy mass consumption that stuffed the home with material goods while stripping its soul.

Financial prosperity alone cannot create or sustain healthy homes or sound nations. Despite our booming stock market and low unemployment, we still face severe social problems born and bred in the homes lacking Victorian sentiments that were enriching beyond measure. We need a new-old way to judge our standard of living and the one we want our children to enjoy. There is nothing wrong with wanting to give them more than what we have, or what our parents gave us, if "more" means more than trendy sneakers, a blue-chip education, or bible-thumping family values lectures. Instead we should try to give our kids the ideal and the reality of a loved and loving home, however modest. This is a precious life-giving gift, and one they can pass on to their own children.

Consider this book not an end but a hopeful beginning. And there is hope. Several months ago I received a thank-you note for a gift I sent to a member of Generation X. As if her uncommon courtesy weren't sufficiently shocking, her monogrammed off-white paper would meet even Edith Wharton's standards. Real success will come the day we notice such gestures by their absence, not their presence. That progress won't be gauged by declining rates of crime, divorce, or out-of-wedlock births. These will naturally follow when we fully reclaim the legacy we have started borrowing piecemeal.

Yes, we can go home again, and not just to the hearth but to the art of love, and the art of civilized living. We have a lot of broken windows to fix, and there are long-rotting timbers beneath our shaky foundation. But history has given us the tools to do this job. All we need is the courage to use them.

No, our world won't be perfect. But courtesy will be common. Love will be our favorite four-letter word. And home will be sweet once again. People will be more sentimental than cynical. Beauty and grace will be noble pursuits that are real, not impossible ideals. We can get there from here. Ralph Waldo Emerson said, "A healthy discontent is the first step to progress." We are already plenty discontented. Now we must take the second step and open our eyes as wide as we can to a different way of seeing.

NOTES

Introduction
1. *The Washington Post*, May 23, 1994.

Chapter 1: "The Age of Impudence"
1. Henry James, Sr., in a letter that was part of a series of articles in 1889 in the *New York Tribune* that was a running dialogue on free love and marriage sponsored by Horace Greeley.
2. Daniel Patrick Moynihan, "Defining Deviancy Down," *American Scholar*, Winter 1993.

Chapter 2: "Buy Now, Pay Later"
1. Gerry Hirshey, "Happy [ ] Day to You," *New York Times Magazine*, July 2, 1995, p. 20.
2. Justin Blum, "Conventioneers Gather to Bare Witness to the Joys of Nudism," *Washington Post*, July 23, 1994, p. B84.
3. Dr. Arthur Caliandro, pastor of the Marble Collegiate Church, quoted in Todd S. Purdum, "Trump Pledge: In This Plaza, I Thee Wed," *New York Times*, December 18, 1993, p. 1, col. 2.
4. *ABC News* report, "In the Name of God," broadcast March 16, 1995.
5. Neal Smelser quoted in Laura Sessions Stepp, "A Full Head of Self-Esteem: Praising Kids and Putting Stars on Their Work Isn't Enough," *Washington Post*, February 21, 1995, p. D5.
6. Roy Baumeister quoted in Richard Morin, "Unconventional Wisdom," *Washington Post*, February 11, 1996.
7. Barbara DeFoe Whitehead, "Dan Quayle Was Right," *Atlantic Monthly*, April 1993.

Chapter 3: "Alone in the Toy Store"
1. "Family Almanac" column, *Washington Post*, February 24, 1994.
2. T. J. Ellinwood, *Henry Ward Beecher: Autobiographical Reminiscences*, published in 1898.
3. Gary Cross, "Too Many Toys," *New York Times*, November 24, 1995.
4. Roger Rosenblatt, "Teaching Johnny to Be Good," *New York Times*, April 30, 1995.

5. Meg Schneider, *Washington Post,* August 21, 1995.
6. Eliot, "Democracy and Manners."

Chapter 4: "Portrait of a Lady"

1. "Let's Get Real About Feminism," roundtable discussion by multiple authors, *Ms.* magazine, September–October 1993.
2. Henry James, Sr., in a letter that was part of a series of articles in 1889 in the *New York Tribune* that was a running dialogue on free love and marriage, sponsored by Horace Greeley.
3. William Raspberry, *Washington Post,* November 24, 1993.

Chapter 5: "Men II Boyz"

1. Korn/Ferry International and UCLA Graduate School of Management, *Decade of the Executive Woman,* 1993.
2. According to the American Medical Association, two million women are battered each year.
3. A scary 1994 survey commissioned by *Esquire* magazine found that a majority of college males would commit rape if they could get away with it. Results of poll published in *Esquire,* February 1994. The Justice Department estimates that 160,000 rapes occurred in 1993.
4. Margaret Bonilla, "Cultural Assault—What Feminists Are Doing to Rape Ought to Be a Crime," *Policy Review,* Fall 1993.
5. Elizabeth Pleck, "Wifebeating in the Nineteenth Century," *Victimology Journal* 4 (1979).
6. John Ruskin quoted in Duffey, *Ladies' and Gentlemen's Complete Etiquette.*
7. Marilyn Goldstein, "Dell Labs Shows It Still Doesn't Get It," *Newsday,* September 25, 1995.
8. Evelyn Nieves, "Despite Acquittal, Woman Vows to Press on in Rape Trial." *New York Times,* March 27, 1996.
9. *NBC News,* October 10, 1995.
10. Ralph Reed quoted in Richard Berke, "Politicians Woo Christian Group," *New York Times,* September 9, 1995.
11. James Warren, "Lugar Looks Back on a Campaign that Never Caught Fire," *Chicago Tribune,* March 10, 1996.
12. Admiral Richard Macke quoted in Mary Jordan, "In Okinawa's Whisper Alley," *Washington Post,* November 23, 1995.
13. See Frank Rich, "I Got You, Babe," *New York Times,* May 25, 1996.
14. Leef Smith, "In Suburbs, Concern Grows Over Girls' Criminal Activity," *Washington Post,* October 30, 1995.
15. Judge Jane Delbridge quoted in "In Suburbs, Concern Grows Over Girls' Criminal Activity," *Washington Post,* October 30, 1995.

16. Judge Joanne F. Alper quoted in Leef Smith, "In Suburbs, Concern Grows Over Girls' Criminal Activity," *Washington Post, Ibid.*

Chapter 6: "The Benevolence of Manners"
1. Ralph Waldo Emerson quoted in Eliot, "Democracy and Manners."
2. As cited in Stein and Baxter, eds., *Grace Dodge: Her Life and Work.*
3. Duffey, *Ladies' and Gentlemen's Complete Etiquette.*
4. Ward McAllister quoted in Wechter, *Saga of American Society.*
5. Sir Walter Scott quoted in Duffey, *Ladies' and Gentlemen's Complete Etiquette.*
6. Raoul Julia quoted in the *New York Times*, November 1, 1991 (obituary).
7. Judy Mann, "New World Daughters," *Washington Post*, February 26, 1995.
8. Duffey, *Ladies' and Gentlemen's Complete Etiquette.*
9. John Coulter, *The Hatless Man* (1901), cited in Sarah Kortum, *The New Century Perfect Speaker* (New York: Viking, 1995).
10. Maude C. Cooke, cited in Arthur Martine, *Martine's Hand-book of Etiquette and Guide to True Politeness*, published in 1866.
11. *Standard Book on Politeness, Good Behavior and Social Etiquette*, cited in John Coulter, *The Hatless Man*, published in 1901.
12. Thomas Nelson Page, "On the Decay of Manners," *Century Magazine* 110 (April 1911).
13. Lord Chesterfield quoted in Root, *Lord Chesterfield: Letters.*
14. Eliot, "Democracy and Manners."
15. Frances Murphy quoted in Marc Fisher, "Million Man March: Behind the Scenes, the Women Count," *Washington Post*, October 14, 1995.

Chapter 7: "Keeping a Civil Tongue"
1. DeNeen Brown, "It's About Respect, Say Students Who Curse Teachers," *Washington Post*, April 18, 1993.
2. Ronald F. Federici quoted in DeNeen Brown, "It's About Respect, Say Students Who Curse Teachers," *Washington Post, Ibid.*
3. Madeline Kane quoted in Don Oldenburg, "Great Expectations," *Washington Post*, April 4, 1995.
4. Results of poll of 1,000 women age 18 to 25 commissioned by *Esquire* and reported in the February 1994 issue.
5. Stephen Dobyns quoted in Francine Prose, "Bad Behavior," *New York Times*, November 26, 1995.
6. *Wall Street Journal*, July 17, 1995.

Chapter 8: "Hypocrisy, Democracy, and Diversity"
1. Maureen Dowd's column, *New York Times*, October 25, 1996.
2. Evan Thomas, "Hurray for Hypocrisy," *Newsweek*, January 29, 1996.

3. Megan Rosenfield, *Washington Post,* July 20, 1995. Rosenfield got the story from Carolyn Curry's book *Divided Lives: The Public and Private Struggles of Three Accomplished Women.*
4. Rap musician quoted in *Washington Post,* August 15, 1993.
5. Mme Mitterand quoted in *Washington Post,* February 29, 1996.
6. William Raspberry, *Washington Post,* September 30, 1994.
7. Kareem Abdul-Jabbar, speaking on CBS's *60 Minutes,* broadcast November 26, 1995.
8. Patrick Welsh (high school teacher), *Washington Post,* March 3, 1996.
9. George W. Cornell, *Washington Post* (AP), March 13, 1993.
10. John Carmozy, "The TV Column," *Washington Post,* February 4, 1994.
11. Ralph Waldo Emerson quoted in Duffey, *Ladies' and Gentlemen's Complete Etiquette.*
12. Cortland Malloy, *Washington Post,* September 17, 1994.
13. Eliot, "Democracy and Manners."

Chapter 9: "Babes in Toyland"

1. Henry James, Sr., in a letter that was part of a series of articles in 1889 in the *New York Tribune* that was a running dialogue on free love and marriage, sponsored by Horace Greeley.
2. Celia Barbour, "Looking at Pictures" (Op-Ed), *New York Times,* April 23, 1994.
3. *New York Times,* June 14, 1995.
4. Results of poll of 1,000 women age 18 to 25 commissioned by *Esquire* and reported in the February 1994 issue.
5. Lonnae Parker, "The Body of Her Work," *Washington Post,* September 5, 1995.
6. Tailhook information from the February 1993 Department of Defense report "Events at the 35th Annual Tailhook Symposium."
7. Naomi Wolf quoted in Tad Friend, "Yes," *Esquire,* February 1994.
8. This story recounted by Deryck Cooke in a booklet written to accompany a 1969 Decca recording of "The Ring of the Nibelungs" by the Vienna Philharmonic Orchestra.

Chapter 10: "When Life Was Foreplay"

1. Henry James, Sr., in a letter that was part of a series of articles in 1889 in the *New York Tribune* that was a running dialogue on free love and marriage, sponsored by Horace Greeley.
2. All quotations of Dr. Elizabeth Blackwell in this chapter are from Blackwell, *Essays in Medical Sociology.*

3. Quoted in D'Emilo and Freedman, *Intimate Matters*.
4. Beatrix Potter quoted in Gay, *Tender Passion*.
5. Quoted in Gay, *Education of the Senses*.
6. Both letters quoted in Rothman, *Hands and Hearts*.
7. Lystra, *Searching the Heart*.
8. *Good Behavior for Young Gentlemen* cited in Lystra, *Searching the Heart*.
9. Tad Friend, "Yes," *Esquire*, February 1994.
10. University of Chicago poll discussed in Barbara Vobejda, "Survey Finds Most Adults Sexually Staid," *Washington Post*, October 7, 1994.
11. Results of poll of 1,000 women age 18 to 25 commissioned by *Esquire* and reported in the February 1994 issue.

Chapter 11: "Backseat Follies"
1. Ernest Groves quoted in Seidman, *Romantic Longings*.
2. *Forbes* magazine, cited in Bailey, *From the Front Porch to the Back Seat*.
3. Bailey, *From the Front Porch to the Back Seat*.
4. Lynd and Lynd, *Middletown*.
5. Cited in Bailey, *From the Front Porch to the Back Seat*.
6. Lynd and Lynd, *Middletown*.
7. Bailey, *From the Front Porch to the Back Seat*.
8. Betty Friedan, *The Feminine Mystique*.

Chapter 12: "The Religion of Romance"
1. Tracy Thompson, "Unhitched But Hardly Independent: Having No Husband Complicates Escape From Welfare," *Washington Post*, May 13, 1995.
2. *Washington Post*, May 23, 1995.
3. Austin Dickinson quoted in Longsworth, *Austin and Mabel*.
4. Quoted in Lystra, *Searching the Heart*.
5. Ford Madox Ford, *The Good Soldier* (1915).
6. Andrew Delbanco, review of *The Age of Innocence*, *New Republic*, October 25, 1993.
7. John Ruskin quoted in Duffey, *Relations of the Sexes*.
8. Longsworth, *Austin and Mabel*.
9. Wechter, *Love Letters of Mark Twain*.
10. *Washington Post*, October 6, 1996.
11. Wheeler, *Loving Warriors*.

Chapter 13: "Wives and Lovers"
1. Quoted in Rothman, *Hands and Hearts*.
2. Hartman and Banner, *Clio's Consciousness Raised*.

3. An 1898 report by the Physicians' Club of Chicago, cited in Reed, *From Private Vice to Public Virtue.*
4. Ann Landers's column, July 17, 1996.
5. Dr. Charles Knowlton, *Fruits of Philosophy.*
6. *Washington Post,* January 12, 1994, p A10.
7. Sears, *The Sex Radicals.*
8. Quoted in Lystra, *Searching the Heart.*
9. John Gray, speaking on *The Oprah Winfrey Show,* June 13, 1995.
10. Marion Howard, professor of obstetrics and gynecology at Emory University, *Washington Post,* May 1, 1994.
11. Former surgeon general Joycelyn Elders quoted in William Raspberry's column in *The Washington Post,* September 8, 1993. Raspberry noted that Elders said this in a video presented to the National Council on Children.
12. "For Some Youthful Courting Has Become a Game of Abuse," *New York Times,* July 11, 1993.
13. Karl Vick, "Mall and Order in Minnesota," *Washington Post,* September 18, 1996.
14. Livermore, *Story of My Life.*
15. Letter quoted in Lystra, *Searching the Heart.*
16. Patrick Welsh, *Washington Post,* April 28, 1996.
17. *Washington Post,* February 27, 1995. The poll was conducted by the polling firm Fairbank, Maslin Maulin & Associates.

Chapter 14: "You *Can* Go Home Again"

1. Horace Bushnell, cited in Matthews, *"Just a Housewife."*
2. Julia Ward Howe and Harriet Beecher Stowe quoted in Mary Durant, "The Devoted Beecher Sisters: Guardians of Home and Family," *Victoria,* April 1993.
3. All material on Martha Stewart from Annie Grower and Ann Gerhart, "The Reliable Source," *Washington Post,* November 13, 1996.
4. Survey cited in *St. Petersberg* (Florida) *Times* (Scripps Howard News Service), October 4, 1993.
5. Amelia Bloomer quoted in Ryan, *Empire of the Mother.*

Chapter 15: "Home Wreckers"

1. Material on Charlotte Perkins Gilman from Matthews, *"Just a Housewife."*
2. *Playboy* ad for homemaker position cited in Matthews, *"Just a Housewife."*
3. Gloria Steinem's views on traditional women's work from Steinem, *Revolution from Within* and *Moving Beyond Words.*
4. Holland Cotter, *New York Times,* July 14, 1996.

Chapter 16: "Throw Momma from the Train"

1. Quote from *Household* cited in Mildred Jailer-Chamberlain, "The Highest Calling," *Victorian Decorating and Lifestyle,* October–November 1994.
2. Lena Williams, "The New Birthday Party," *New York Times,* October 17, 1996, on the Elizabeth Seton Childbirth Center and children watching their siblings being born.
3. Elizabeth Chang, *Washington Post* (Style section), November 24, 1996.
4. Sarah Josepha Hale and Lydia Maria Child quoted in Ryan, *Empire of the Mother.*
5. Henry Blackwell quoted in Matthews, *"Just a Housewife."*
6. Elizabeth Cady Stanton quoted in Griffith, *In Her Own Right.*
7. Material on Charlotte Perkins Gilman from Matthews, *"Just a Housewife."*
8. Pearl Buck quoted in Matthews, *"Just a Housewife."*
9. Survey cited in Michaud and Torg, *Total Health for Women.*
10. Beth Brophy, "Fax Me a Bedtime Story," *U.S. News & World Report,* December 2, 1996.
11. Yankelovich poll cited in Alecia Swasy, "Are Their Kids Better Off?" *Wall Street Journal,* July 23, 1993.
12. Poll conducted for Philip Morris by Roper Worldwide.
13. Susan B. Anthony, cited in Barry, *Susan B. Anthony.*
14. Quotations from Lystra, *Searching the Heart.*

Chapter 17: "Soul Food"

1. Roger K. Lewis, "Let's Put Real Dining Rooms Back on the Table," *Washington Post,* October 19, 1996.
2. Nancy Gibbs and Michael Duffy, "Desperately Seeking Lori," *Time,* October 14, 1996.
3. Fannie Farmer quoted in Matthews, *"Just a Housewife."*
4. Karen Hess quoted in Judith Weinraub, "Our Consuming Passion for Cookbooks," *Washington Post,* December 11, 1996.
5. Weinraub, "Our Consuming Passion for Cookbooks."

Chapter 18: "The Art of Living"

1. Editorial criticizing the revised book, *New York Times,* February 4, 1995.
2. Ann Landers's column, August 16, 1995.
3. George Will, column in *Washington Post,* January 28, 1996.

Chapter 19: "Art and Soul

1. Howat, *Hudson River School.*
2. Ken Ringle, "To PC or Not PC," *Washington Post,* December 26, 1993.

BIBLIOGRAPHY

Sources that are listed in the Bibliography are cited by author's last name and short title of work.

Everyday Bible: New Century Version. Ft. Worth, Texas: Worthy Publishing, 1988.

An American Gentleman. *Good Behavior for Young Gentlemen.* 1848; reprint.

"The Censor." *Don't, or Directions for Avoiding Improprieties in Conduct and Common Errors of Speech*. 1891; reprint, Chapel Hill, N.C.: Algonquin Books, 1984.

Acton, William, M.D. *The Functions and Disorders of Reproductive Organs in Childhood, Youth, Adult Age and Advanced Life Considered in their Physiological, Social and Moral Relations*. 1865? or 1875; reprint.

———. *Prostitution*. 1857; reprint, New York: Praeger, 1969.

Alcott, William. *The Young Wife; or, Duties of Women in the Marriage Relation*. New York. 1837; reprint, New York: Arno Press, 1972.

Allen, Frederick Lewis. *Only Yesterday: An Informal History of the 1920s*. New York: Harper & Brothers, 1931.

Anderson, Elijah. *Streetwise: Race, Class, and Change in an Urban Community*. Chicago: University of Chicago Press, 1990.

Arendt, Hannah. *On Revolution*. New York: Viking Press, 1963.

Ashton, James, M.D. *The Book of Nature*. 1865; University of Nevada.

Auchincloss, Louis. *Persons of Consequence: Queen Victoria and Her Circle*. New York: Random House, 1979.

Bailey, Beth. *From Front Porch to Back Seat: Courtship in Twentieth-Century America*. Baltimore: Johns Hopkins Press, 1988.

Baker, Paul R. *Stanny: The Gilded Life of Stanford White*. New York: Free Press, 1989.

Barry, Kathleen. *Susan B. Anthony: A Biography of a Singular Feminist*. New York: New York University Press, 1988.

Beecher, Catharine Esther. *Letters to the People on Health and Happiness*. New York: Harper & Brothers, 1855.

Beecher, Catharine, and Harriet Beecher Stowe. *The American Woman's Home; or, Principles of Domestic Science, Being a Guide to the Formation and Maintenance of Economical, Healthful, Beautiful, and Christian Homes.* Boston: Brown & Co., 1869. Although Harriet Beecher Stowe is listed as the coauthor of this book, historians generally agree that Catharine Beecher wrote the book and Harriet's name was added to help sales.

Beeton, Isabella. *Mrs. Beeton's Victorian Cookbook.* Topsfield, Mass.: Salem House Publishers, 1988.

Blackwell, Elizabeth. *The Laws of Life: With Special Reference to the Physical Education of Girls.* New York: G. P. Putnam's Sons, 1852; reprint, New York: Garland Publications, 1986.

———. *Essays in Medical Sociology.* 1902; reprint, New York: Arno Press, 1972.

Bode, Carl, ed., with Malcolm Cowley. *The Portable Emerson.* 1946; reprint, New York: Viking Press, 1981.

Breathnach, Sarah Ben. *Mrs. Sharp's Traditions: Nostalgic Suggestions for Recreating the Family Celebrations and Seasonal Pastimes of the Victorian Home.* New York: Simon & Schuster, 1990.

Brookhiser, Richard. *The Way of the WASP: How It Made America, and How It Can Save It, So to Speak.* New York: Free Press, 1991.

Bulwer-Lytton, Edward. *The Caxtons.* 1849; reprint, St. Clair Shores, Mich.: Scholarly Press, 1971.

Carter, Rosalyn. *Random Acts of Kindness.* Conari Press, 1993.

Child, Lydia Maria. *The American Frugal Housewife.* 1833; reprint, ed. Alice M. Geffen, New York: Harper & Row, 1972.

Cook, Clarence. *The House Beautiful: Essays on Beds and Tables, Stools and Candlesticks.* 1881; reprint, Croton-on-Hudson, N.Y.: North River Press, 1980.

Cooke, Nicholas Francis, M.D. *Satan in Society.* 1870; reprint, New York: Arno Press,,1974.

Coontz, Stephanie. *The Way We Never Were.* New York: Basic Books, 1993.

Cox, Taylor, Jr. *Cultural Diversity in Organizations: Theory, Research, and Practice.* San Francisco: Berrett-Koehler, 1993.

D'Emilio, John, and Estelle B. Freedman. *Intimate Matters: A History of Sexuality in America.* New York: Harper & Row, 1988.

Day, Clarence. *Life with Father.* 1935; reprint, Boston: G. K. Hall, 1984.

de Tocqueville, Alexis. *Democracy in America;* reprint, trans. George Lawrence, ed. J. P. Mayer and Max Lerner, New York: Harper & Row, 1966.

Degler, Carl. *The Other South: Southern Dissenters in the Nineteenth Cen-*

tury. New York: Harper & Row, 1974.

———. *The Democratic Experience: A Short American History.* Glenview: Scott, Foresman, 1974.

———. *At Odds: Women and the Family in America from the Revolution to the Present.* New York: Oxford University Press, 1980.

Dickens, Charles. *American Notes.* 1842; reprint, Gloucester, Mass.: P. Smith, 1968.

Douglas, Anne. *The Feminization of American Culture.* New York: Knopf, 1977.

Duffey, Eliza. *What Women Should Know.* 1873; reprint, New York: Arno Press, 1974.

———. *The Relations of the Sexes.* 1876; reprint, New York: Arno Press, 1974.

———. *Ladies' and Gentlemen's Complete Etiquette.* 1877; reprint,

Ehrenreich, Barbara. *The Hearts of Men: American Dreams and the Flight from Commitment.* Garden City, N.Y.: Anchor Press/Doubleday, 1983.

Eliot, Charles W. "Democracy and Manners," *Century Magazine* 83 (1911–12).

Ellinwood, T. J., ed. *Henry Ward Beecher: Autobiographical Reminiscences.* 1898; reprint, New York: Frederick A. Stokes Company, c. 1898.

Faludi, Susan. *Backlash: The Undeclared War Against American Women.* New York: Crown, 1991.

Fass, Paula. *The Damned and the Beautiful: American Youth in the 1920s.* New York: Oxford University Press, 1977.

Finley, Ruth E. *The Lady of Godey's: Sara Josepha Hale.* 1931; reprint, New York: Arno Press, 1974.

Fleming, Ann Taylor. *Motherhood Deferred: A Woman's Journey.* New York: G. P. Putnam's Sons, 1994.

Ford, Ford Madox. *The Good Soldier.* 1915; reprint, New York: Octagon Books, 1981.

Foy, Jessica H., and Thomas J. Schlereth, eds. *American Home Life 1880–1930: A Social History of Spaces and Services.* Knoxville, Tenn.: University of Tennessee Press, 1992.

Friedan, Betty. *The Second Stage.* New York: Dell Publishing, 1991.

———. *The Feminine Mystique.* New York: Norton, 1963.

Gay, Peter. *The Bourgeois Experience, Victoria to Freud.* Vol. 1, *Education of the Senses.* New York: Oxford University Press, 1984.

———. *The Bourgeois Experience, Victoria to Freud.* Vol. 2, *The Tender Passion.* New York: Oxford University Press, 1986.

Geist, Bill. *Monster Trucks and Hair in a Can: Who Says America Doesn't Make Anything Anymore?* New York: G. P. Putnam's Sons, 1994.

Gentile, Mary C. *Differences That Work: Organized Excellence Through Diversity.* Boston: Harvard Business School Publications, 1994.

Gernsheim, Alison. *Victorian and Edwardian Fashion: A Photographic Survey.* New York: Dover Publications, 1981.

Goleman, Daniel. *Emotional Intelligence: Why It Can Matter More Than IQ for Character, Health and Lifelong Achievement.* New York: Bantam Doubleday Dell, 1995.

Gordon, Linda. *Woman's Body, Woman's Right: A Social History of Birth.* New York: Viking Penguin, 1977.

———. *Control.* New York: Grossman, 1976.

Gordon, Suzanne. *Prisoner of Men's Dreams: Striking Out for a New Feminine Future.* Boston: Little, Brown, 1991.

Gray, John. *Mars and Venus in the Bedroom: A Guide to Lasting Romance and Passion.* New York: HarperCollins, 1995.

Griffith, Elisabeth. *In Her Own Right: The Life of Elizabeth Cady Stanton.* New York: Oxford University Press. 1984.

Hale, Sarah Josepha. *Manners; or Happy Homes and Good Society All the Year Round.* 1868; reprint, New York: Arno Press, 1972.

Hall, Florence Howe. *Julia Ward Howe and the Woman Suffrage Movement.* 1913; reprint, New York: Arno Press, 1969.

Haller, John S., and Robin M. *The Physician and Sexuality in Victorian America.* Urbana, Ill.: University of Illinois Press, 1974.

Hapgood, Hutchins. *A Victorian in the Modern World.* 1939; reprint, Seattle: University of Washington Press, 1967.

Hartley, Florence. *The Ladies' Book of Etiquette and Manual of Politeness.* 1880.

Hartman, Mary S., and Lois W. Banner, eds. *Clio's Consciousness Raised: New Perspectives on the History of Women.* New York: Octagon Books, 1974.

Haweis, Mary Elizabeth. *The Art of Beauty.* New York: Harper. 1878.

Hilts, Elizabeth. *Getting in Touch with Your Inner Bitch.* Bridgeport, Conn.: Hysteria Publications, 1994.

Howat, John K. *The Hudson River School and Its Painters.* New York: Viking Press, 1972.

Howe, Joseph, M.D. *Excessive Venery: Masturbation and Continence: The Etiology, Pathology and Treatment of the Diseases Resulting from Venereal Excesses, Masturbation and Continence.* Bermingham & Co., 1883.

Howe, Julia Ward. *Modern Society.* Boston: Roberts Brothers, 1881.

———. *Is Polite Society Polite? And Other Essays.* 1895; reprint, Upper Saddle River, N.J.: Literature House, 1970.

Howells, William Dean. *The Rise of Silas Lapham.* 1885; reprint, Bloomington, Ind.: University of Indiana Press, 1971.

Humphry, Mrs. *Manners for Men*. London, England: James Bowden Publishers, 1897.

James, Henry. *Washington Square*. 1880; reprint, ed. Gerald Willem, New York: Crowell, 1970,

Johnson, Emily Cooper. *Jane Addams: A Centennial Reader*.

Johnston, Johanna. *Mrs. Satan: The Incredible Saga of Victoria C. Woodhull*. New York: Popular Library, 1967.

Jacobi, Jolande, ed. *Psychological Reflections: An Anthology of the Writings of C. J. Jung*. New York: Pantheon Books, 1953.

Kasson, John. *Rudeness and Civility: Manners in Nineteenth-Century Urban America*. New York: Hill & Wang, 1990.

Kellogg, Susan, and Steven Mintz. *Domestic Revolutions: A Social History of American Family Life*. New York: Free Press, 1988.

Knowlton, Charles, M.D. *Fruits of Philosophy*. 1878; reprint, Austin, Texas: American Atheist Press, 1980.

Kramer, Peter. *Listening to Prozac*. New York: Viking Press, 1993.

Kunstler, James Howard. *The Geography of Nowhere: The Rise and Decline of America's Man-Made Landscape*. New York: Simon & Schuster, 1993.

LaHaye, Tim, and Beverly LaHaye. *The Act of Marriage: The Beauty of Sexual Love*. Grand Rapids, Mich.: Zondervan Publishing House, 1976.

Lasch, Christopher. *Haven in a Heartless World: The Family Besieged*. New York: Basic Books, 1977.

Leeman, Richard W. *"Do Everything" Reform: The Oratory of Frances E. Willard*. New York: Greenwood Press, 1992.

Leith, Elan, and Susan Leith. *The Secret Life of Victorian Houses*. Washington, D.C.: Elliot & Clark Publishers, 1993.

Leopold, Allison Kyle. *Allison Kyle Leopold's Victorian Keepsakes: Select Expressions of Affectionate Regard from the Romantic Nineteenth Century*. New York: Doubleday, 1991.

Leslie, Eliza. *Miss Leslie's Behaviour Book: A Guide and Manual for Ladies*. 1859; reprint, New York: Arno Press, 1972.

Lewis, Denslow, M.D. *The Gynecologic Consideration of the Sexual Act*. 1900. Weston, Mass.: M & S Press, 1970. Reprint.

Lewis, Howard R., and Martha E. Lewis. *The Parents' Guide to Teenage Sex and Pregnancy*. New York: St. Martin's Press, 1980.

Livermore, Mary Ashton Rice. *The Story of My Life*. 1899; reprint, New York: Arno Press, 1974.

Loden, Marilyn, and Judy B. Rosener. *Workforce America! Managing Employee Diversity as a Vital Resource*. Homewood, Ill.: Business One Irwin, 1991.

Longsworth, Polly. *Austin and Mabel: The Amherst Affair and Love Letters of Austin Dickinson and Mabel Loomis Todd*. New York: Farrar Straus & Giroux, 1984.

Lynd, Robert S., and Helen M. Lynd. *Middletown: A Study in Contemporary American Culture*. New York: Harcourt Brace, 1929.

Lystra, Karen. *Searching the Heart: Women, Men, and Romantic Love in Nineteenth-Century America*. New York: Oxford University Press, 1989.

MacFadden, Bernarr. *Womanhood and Marriage*. New York: MacFadden Publishers, 1918.

Martine, Arthur. *Martine's Hand-book of Etiquette and Guide to True Politeness*. New York: Dick & Fitzgerald, 1866; reprint, Bedford, Mass.: Applewood Books, 1996.

Matthews, Glenna. *"Just a Housewife": The Rise and Fall of Domesticity*. New York: Oxford University Press, 1987.

Michaud, Ellen, and Elizabeth Torg. *Total Health for Women: From Allergies and Back Pain to Overweight and PMS, the Best Preventative and Curative Advice for More Than 100 Women's Health Problems*. Emmaus, Pa.: Rodale Press, 1995.

Miller, Russell. *Bunny: The Real Story of Playboy*. New York: New American Library, 1984.

Moir, Ann. *Brain Sex: The Real Difference Between Men and Women*. New York: Carol Publishing Group, 1991.

Morris, Edmund. *The Rise of Theodore Roosevelt*. New York: Coward, McCann & Geoghegan, 1979.

Ogden, Gina. *Women Who Love Sex*. New York: Pocket Books, 1994.

Page, Thomas Nelson. "On the Decay of Manners," *Century Magazine* 83, (1911-12).

Paglia, Camille. *Sex, Art, and American Culture: Essays*. New York: Vintage Books, 1992.

Pearsall, Ronald. *The Worm in the Bud: The World of Victorian Sexuality*. New York: Macmillan. 1969.

Pike, Martha V., and Janice Gray Armstrong. *A Time to Mourn: Expressions of Grief in Nineteenth-Century America*. New York: The Museums of Stonybrook, 1980.

Pivar, David, Jr. *Purity Crusade: Sex, Morality, and Social Control 1868–1900*. Westport, Conn.: Greenwood Press, 1973.

Post, Emily. *Personality of a House*. New York and London: Funk & Wagnalls Company, 1930.

Reed, James. *From Private Vice to Public Virtue: The Birth Control Movement and American Society Since 1830*. New York: Basic Books, 1978.

Root, R. K., ed. *Lord Chesterfield: Letters to His Son*. 1969.

Rothman, Ellen K. *Hands and Hearts: A History of Courtship in America.* New York: Basic Books, 1984.

Ruddock, E. H., M.D. *Vitology: An Encyclopedia of Health and Home.* Chicago: Halsey Bros., 1885.

Rugoff, Milton Allan. *Prudery and Passion.* New York: G. P. Putnam's Sons, 1971.

Ryan, Mary P. *The Empire of the Mother.* New York: Copublished by the Institute for Research in History and The Haworth Press, 1982.

Sanger, Margaret. *Happiness in Marriage.* 1926; reprint, Old Saybrook, Conn.: Applewood Books, 1993.

Schlesinger, Arthur Meier. *Learning How to Behave: A Historical Study of American Etiquette Books.* 1946. reprint, New York: Cooper Square Publications, 1968.

Sears, Hal D. *The Sex Radicals: Free Love in High Victorian America.* Lawrence, Kans.: Regents Press of Kansas, 1977.

Seidman, Steven. *Romantic Longings: Love in America 1830–1980.* New York: Routledge Press, 1991.

Shiveley, Charles, ed. *Love, Marriage, Divorce, and the Sovereignty of the Individual: A Discussion Between Henry James, Horace Greeley, and Stephen Pearl Andrews.* Weston, Mass.: M & S Press, 1975.

Sommers, Christina Hoff. *Who Stole Feminism? How Women Have Betrayed Women.* New York: Simon & Schuster, 1994.

Stall, Sylvanus. *What a Young Husband Should Know.* Philadelphia: Vir Publishing Co., 1897.

Stanton, Elizabeth Cady. *Eighty Years and More: Reminiscences.* New York: Source Book Press, 1970.

Stein, Leon, and Annette K. Baxter. *Grace Dodge: Her Life and Work.* New York, Arno Press, 1974.

Steinem, Gloria. *Moving Beyond Words.* New York: Simon & Schuster, 1994.
———. *Revolution from Within: A Book of Self-Esteem.* Boston: Little, Brown, 1992.

Stowe, Catharine Beecher. *Treatise on Domestic Economy, American Family Home.* Boston: Marsh, Capen, Lyon, and Webb, 1841; reprint, New York: Source Book Press, 1970.

Susman, Warren I. *Culture as History: The Transformaton of American Society in the Twentieth Century.* New York: Pantheon, 1984.

Trall, R. T., M.D. *Sexual Physiology.* New York: M. L. Holbrook. 1881; reprint, New York: Arno Press, 1974.

Vanderbilt, Consuelo. *The Glitter and the Gold.* 1953.

Vaux, Calvert. *Villas and Cottages: A Series of Designs Prepared for Execution in the United States.* 1864; reprint, New York: Dover Publications, 1970.

Wade, Wyn Craig. *The Titanic: End of a Dream.* New York: Atheneum. 1979.

Wechter, Dixon, ed. *The Love Letters of Mark Twain.* New York: Harper, 1949.

———. *The Saga of American Society: A Record of Social Aspiration 1607–1937.* 1949; reprint, New York: Scribner, 1970.

Wharton, Edith. *A Backward Glance.* New York: D. Appleton-Century Co., 1933.

Wheeler, Leslie, ed. *Loving Warriors: Selected Letters of Lucy Stone and Henry B. Blackwell, 1853–1893.* New York: Dial Press, 1981.

Willard, Frances. *Glimpses of Fifty Years.* 1889. New York: Source Book Press, 1970.

Williams, Redford. *The Trusting Heart: Great News About Type A Behavior.* New York: Times Books, 1989.

Williams, Resa. *Mark and Livy: A Biography of Mark Twain and the Woman Who Almost Tamed Him.* New York: Maxwell Macmillan International, 1992.

Wilson, James Q., and Richard J. Herrnstein. *Crime and Human Nature: The Definitive Study of the Causes of Crime.* New York: Simon & Schuster, 1985.

Wolf, Naomi. *Fire with Fire: The New Female Power and How It Will Change the 21st Century.* New York: Random House, 1993.

Wright, Henry C. *Marriage and Parentage.* 1855. Reprint, New York: Arno Press, 1974.

Wyman, Mary Alice, ed. *Selections from the Autobiography of Elizabeth Oakes Smith.* Lewiston, Maine: Lewiston Journal Co. 1924; reprint, New York: Arno Press, 1924.